KEYS TO THE APOCALYPSE:

Connecting

the

Dots...

F.T. Chisholm

xulon
PRESS

CONTENTS

Preface

<u>SECTION I: Introduction to the Keys:</u>

(A MESSAGE TO THE HEART)

SECTION II: Conflict of Spirits . . . from the Heavens:

(A MESSAGE TO THE CHURCHES)

= = = ================== = = =

I saw when the Lamb opened one of the seals; and I heard one of the four living creatures saying with a voice like thunder, "Come and see."

Revelation 6:1

When the Berlin Wall fell, in 1989, it sounded like friendly thunder in our souls. It seemed that we had entered a brave new world. We had the Cold War behind us with international freedom, democracy, and cooperation appearing on the horizon. When Saddam Hussein dared to resist what obviously seemed like a progressive movement, the international community—led by the American juggernaut, opened its bag of tricks to startle the world with military wonders.

Ditto, after 9/11, when the Green Genie emerged from its bottle, to challenge and terrorize the modern world. We practically walked over the nation of Iraq, and removed a troublesome troublemaker. We were establishing (we thought) a measured degree of peace and civility in the region.

Then, everything seemed to backfire. Suddenly, the term "Vietnam" is being tossed about as an *approximation* of the debacle now facing us. Others, daring to dust off their Bibles, have noticed that what seemed like thunder in our souls, may not have been a blessing after all. In fact, some have noticed that not only is the world's attention now focused in the very area where Scripture forecasts Jesus Christ will return . . . but that this is now the second time we are engaged with the very country that largely contains the Euphrates River—from which, the Bible forecasts, the pale-green horse will ride, ultimately killing *one-third of the human race.*

Nor is this an idle concern. The President of Iran, next door, is making statements that can only be compared to those of another distressed individual who started a war in the last century, spanning several continents (his first name was Adolf . . .).

Something has happened to trip up the American juggernaut, and it seems destined to abort the American Dream, as well. For, although our world is obviously approaching a boiling point, many appear ready to "pack it in" for the night. Is this a good idea? Should we go back to sleep? Or, maybe we should go back to the Book, and dust it off.

And yet . . .

Venturing to actually *read* our Bibles: dare we? Is it true, as some would have us believe, that our biggest problems emerge from persons with convictions too closely held, and believed in? Or with those who actually believe the Bible can speak to us— even before being "left behind"? Can it be that current events have already been forecast in the Bible, and that this is a prophetic call to stop playing politics with our faith, to humble our hearts, open our Bibles—and to get down on our knees, to come to terms with this awesome God, before it is too late?

Come and see . . . .

Section I:

Introduction to

The Keys

It is the glory of God to conceal a matter, but the honor of kings is to search out a matter.

Proverbs 25:2

With the keys to the Apocalypse,

we need not worry

about being left behind:

We are here

Already

Terms to ponder in this section:

- The "Kettle" (or boiling pot) – Society, in general, oblivious to where our world is headed.

- Onion skins – Overlapping prophecies, including the "3 ½ clocks," whose timing relationships are often overlooked.

- Paradigm – a world view, or way of looking at life, that affects what we are *able* to believe.

- Sons of Oil – candidates for the special "two witnesses" of John's Revelation, chapter eleven (11).

- Trinity – That mysterious term, referring to the God of the Bible.

- Saints – the biblical term for men, and women, who fellowship with God.

- Communism – as it relates to the Kingdom of God.

NOT A GENIUS
a personal invitation

Because the foolishness of God is wiser than men, and the weakness of God is stronger than men.

I Corinthians 1:25

There is an urgency of soul, as I daily read the newspaper, and am aware of events taking place *right now* clearly forecast by Scriptures that many "experts" choose to ignore. I have watched these events have transpired over a period of decades, in spite of repeated denials by well meaning theologians. Yet Jesus warned that just before His returning, the church at large would go to sleep. The apostle Paul seconds this observation, noting that this same activity allows . . .the Antichrist to arise. Using this key, plus our "3½ clocks" to line up our sights, we start to connect the dots, and come to an amazing conclusion:

God is speaking to us.

Hi! The book you are about to read was certainly not written by a genius, or even a Ph.D. I am a US citizen, birthed on these American shores. —I would also say Afro-American, yet we live in a diverse culture, and my make up is determined by many factors, with colorful Caribbean and West Indian stock. My father was a technician, and had the privilege of working on the Apollo moon mission. He was very proud of his endeavors, and of our country.

When attempting to follow in his footsteps, I did not find electronics the easiest topic to master. I studied it in the military, and took out a correspondence course. I attended college, and took engineering courses. Calculus also, did not come easily. I took it over, several times. Finally, in 2000, I graduated after reenrolling and taking an accelerated course of study in human development. I was listed as graduating with honors, but largely due to the inclusion of poor grades from earlier years, actually missed the cut by several tenths of a point.

Yet, it is not the geniuses that God calls out, necessarily, when looking to unveil secrets, is it? As Jesus once prayed to the Father,

"I thank You, Father, Lord of heaven and earth, that You have hidden these things from the wise and prudent and have revealed them to babes.

"Even so, Father, for so it seemed good in Your sight."
Matthew 11:25,26

It would seem, therefore, that the Lord purposely reserves some of His choicest gems for the simple at heart (see also I Corinthians 1:27-31). This book is for us.

As well as for the most noble.

When President Ronald Reagan shared his dream of the US being a "city on a hill" such was an idea birthed from history, and demonstrated from within prophecy. It was actually much more than a dream. He was expressing the fulfillment of a destiny: more, it is of prophetic significance, expressing a way of life that has lead to the enlightenment of many by spreading distinctly

Christian values around the globe. Victory then came to a world that seemed hopelessly embroiled in conflicts between political poles of right and wrong, expressing diverging beliefs from the West and, on the other end, from within the Communist world.

Today, the noble ideas that brought down the Berlin Wall are being replaced by gray shades of compromise, both political and religious, as we attempt to transplant the American dream into the Muslim world. Only now, after many lives and much treasure has been lost, is this nightmare of a counterfeit dream becoming evident, and yet . . .

→ This is a book on Bible prophecy.

Bible prophecy actually has two sides: one of kindness and redemption . . . and the other of judgment and final (eternal) penalties. Any honest study of prophecy must come to terms with both of these realities. Exposing ourselves to "partisan politics" while engaging in the study of Bible truths, therefore, must finally meet up with disappointment, in the end. Having said all of this, however, it must be acknowledged that God really *did* have a plan for the world's one, remaining, super power—and for her increasingly unpopular friend, the nation of Israel. God has a love for these special entities, and those whom He loves, He most certainly chastens/corrects (i.e. "spanks") . . . .

I am an evangelical Christian. An Evangelical: not an American, or a world citizen, or Afro-American, first. No, for I am a created being, made in the image of an awesome, and holy, God: Jehovah, the Great "I Am" of Scripture, whose Son Jesus Christ, came to this little spec of galactic dust, to walk around and show us the way to a glory far beyond our wildest dreams. We will meet Him more formally, as we dig deeper into our study.

Evangelicals believe that it is a very big deal for God to send His Son to earth to die for us, when He did not have to. We want to tell everyone, who will listen, about this good news ("the gospel").

Ask any Evangelical about what the most significant event of the last century was, and they will answer (correctly)

"The return of the nation of Israel!" –to her homeland.

He, or she, may not know *why* this is so important, but they sense that this is the case—even if not certain of how Scripture supports the claim. Why is this?

→Because it is a key element, in setting the backdrop for the literal return of Jesus Christ, to this troubled planet.

When Jesus "lifted off" from earth in the first century (the theological term is "ascended") He went back to heaven, and two angels stood by to inform disciples of how He will return.

"Men of Galilee, why do you stand gazing up into heaven?
This same Jesus, who was taken up from you into heaven,
will so come in like manner as you saw Him go into heaven."

Acts 1:11

Why is this statement so significant? It just happens to coincide with an Old Testament prophecy, found in the writings of the prophet Zechariah. Christian Scripture is divided into two main sections: the Old Testament (written before Jesus came) and the

14

New Testament (starting with Christ's birth). The only Bible available to those watching Jesus ascend into the sky, was the Old Testament. So prophecies relating to Christ's returning had to be found there.

What is most interesting, is that when we go back to the text the angels were hinting at, we come to what is now known as the fourteenth chapter of Zechariah's prophecy (there were no chapter divisions, in the original scrolls). By simply noting its context, and the situation surrounding Christ's departure from outside of Jerusalem, at the Mt. of Olives —we are able to discover exactly why, and how, Christ will return to the earth, in the near future.

Let's first look at the fulfillment, and then consider the context (situation surrounding His returning):

The reference made by the prophet of old, reads:

> And in that day His feet will stand on the Mount of Olives,
> Which faces Jerusalem on the east. And the Mount of Olives
> shall be split in two, From east to west, . . .
>
> Zechariah 14:4a

—This is like seeing Jesus' "lift off," in reverse (except for the mountain splitting!). . .

But, *why* does He return in this manner? Backing up a few verses, we see why. Backing up, to verse two, we read:

> For I will gather all the nations to battle against Jerusalem;
> The city shall be taken, The houses rifled, And the women
> ravished. Half of the city shall go into captivity, But the rem-
> nant of the people shall not be cut off from the city.

Then the LORD will go forth And fight against those nations, As He fights in the day of battle.

Verses 2 & 3

What is most interesting, is that until 1948 there wasn't even
an "Israel" for the nations of the world *to confront*, much less to
contend with, for Jerusalem! By the way, the next time you have a
chance, do a little research on the middle east and take note of exactly what the hottest trouble spot is, in the world, today.

Israel? Yes, but where, exactly?

Jerusalem: It is the only city on earth that is being truly "in-
ternationalized." Everyone wants a piece of it: Christians, Jews,
Muslims. Many are even incensed that Israel would dare to claim it
as her own capital. Interesting . . . .

Bible prophecy outlines an entire program of events set to take
place between where we are, right now, and the day of that final
confrontation, just outside of Jerusalem. The most destructive
events will take place sometime (prophetically speaking) "past
midnight."

There are some who imagine that we may simply "turn back
the clock" because we take a fancy to doing so. That we have approached 11:59 PM, have entered Iraq, and now realize that we
have made a mistake. It would be nice to back out, to the good old
days, would it not? —Not so fast, for we are headed for the cry at
midnight (Midnight Cry) "when the clock strikes 12:00." Yes, it
is *past* midnight, that the Lord returns. . . .

Watchers on the wall have already discerned the significance
of these, and other, events, Some would love to reverse the legisla-

16

tive bulldozer already being unleashed in our direction. Some are actively working to repeal legislation already designed to give us a national ID (which we will later discuss). Yet, what we will learn within our study is that this "bulldozer" has not just come out of the parking lot, on its own. It is part of a whole fleet of bulls, designed (forgive the pun) to roll over those who are dozing.

As may be imagined, the "keys" we will expose as the main ingredients, to unlocking Bible prophecy, revolve around the unfolding of historical events that are not always pleasant to consider. Some biases may have to be personally addressed, by the reader. Some repentance enjoined, upon each of us. Yet whatever our attitude towards Israel and the Jews, or towards the world's lone remaining super power, there is one other principle player that we must all come to grips with: the Church of Jesus Christ. Specifically, we must pay particular attention to the place of the Gentile Church, within the plan of prophecy. The Gentile Church is actually made up of those born outside of natural Jewish heritage —who have "bought in" to the Jewish Messiah (Jesus Christ). Thus, we have:

- The nation of Israel
- The Gentile Church
- The last super power (The US)

These are the underlying concepts sitting at the core of the "keys" to John's Apocalypse. Daring to understand them requires an unwavering commitment to seeing the truth as it is, and not as pundits (or politicians) would have us believe.

Those who see the future as the Bible portrays it are not surprised by the "9/11"s of history. Further, the more we take the time to read the Bible, the more we are struck by its bold and fearless approach to handling matters of faith. Such has always been the case, down through the centuries.

When, for example, the king of ancient Babylon insisted that everyone bow to a golden image he had spent much time and money setting up—how would three Hebrew boys have felt, had I informed them that they need not challenge the king's word by refusing to bow? How would I have "enriched" their experience with God, by telling them they need not stand up?[1]

Or, that they could easily "escape" such fiery trial?

For they could not discover that God had made them "fire proof" until *after* having been thrown into the king's oven. Yet, who was the richer for the experience, the spectators . . . or those coming through the fire?

Fortunately, Bible teachers are now emerging who freely acknowledge that the *historical* Christian position (beyond 200 years ago) has usually been to anticipate the triumph of the Church going *through* tribulation. "In this world you *shall* have tribulation," Jesus said, "but be of good courage, I have overcome the world" (John 16:33 –emphasis added).

And this is the victory that has overcome the world; our faith.

I John 5:4

Therefore, although this is not a reference book, in the normal sense of the word, it *is* a work of faith. Faith is always enriched in the crucible of life. This is where the beauty of the Christian experience is hammered out, in every day living. This book focuses on the *keys* to prophetic fulfillment, which relate to every day living. Without them, many questions remain unanswered.

Yet with them, the layers of the prophetic flower unfurl like a rose.

The color of the rose, I must leave to the reader's discretion.

Now, to begin our path to discovery:

Place this key in your "pocket"

One of the most significant keys relates to a comparison of Christ's comment to the disciples in Luke twenty-one—freely accepted by evangelicals as a link between the fall of Jerusalem, in 70 AD, and His returning. Remember, a key requirement for Christ's returning, is the *return* of the Jews to their land. This means that they had to first leave, in what is generally referred to as the "diaspora" (dispersion) of the Jews throughout the whole earth. The connection, which we will now make, opens up one of our prophetic "clocks" referring to the Gentile control of the Church during this time, along with the implication that the fullness (or completion) of Gentile Church history comes to a head (*not an end*),

when Israel returns to her land.

What Christ was saying, in other words, is that at the end of her scattering, Israel would again be re-gathered, and the final countdown would then begin.

The timing of this event begins the close-out of a largely *Gentile* church age. Specifically, the projection/prophecy by Christ reads, in part:

> "And they will fall by the edge of the sword, and be led away captive into all nations. And Jerusalem will be trampled by Gentiles until the times of the Gentiles are fulfilled."
>
> Luke 21:24

This prophecy, given by Jesus in approximately 33AD, refers to Jews who would later be living in Jerusalem, until 70 AD (see verses 21-23). Notice, if you will, that expression, "And Jerusalem will be trampled by Gentiles until the times . . . be fulfilled."

What is most interesting, is that right in the middle of John's Apocalypse[†] (there are twenty-two chapters, this event takes place in its eleventh) there is a symbolic projection of the Jewish Holy Land being *trampled . . . by Gentiles*, prior to (two) witnesses being given special assignment. Its first reference, to forty-two months, is part of a key concept that we will be exploring within this book— the concept of the "3½ clocks." It yields numerical time capsules that enclose the entire church age, in three broad strokes; including Gentile worship, the age of restoration,[2] and of Great Tribulation. Since our first obvious point of interest is that of the Gentile church, it is significant that the angel points to God's temple "and those who worship there" (vs. 1).

[†] We will often refer to John's Revelation of Jesus Christ (the last book of the Bible) by its alternate title "John's Apocalypse" or simply, "the Apocalypse"— to maintain our focus on the awesome judgments foreshadowed, within this prophecy.

...And the angel stood, saying, "Rise and measure the temple of God, the altar, <u>and those who worship there</u>.

"But leave out the court which is outside the temple, and do not measure it, for it has been given to the Gentiles. <u>And they will tread the holy city underfoot for forty-two months</u>."

Revelation 11:1, 2 [emphasis added]

Please notice that it was not the temple alone, that is measured (vs.1), but also those who worship there. Why *measure people*, when measuring a temple?? We will certainly answer this question, by God's grace.

For now, simply pocket the above verses, with those from Luke's gospel, until we get back to this "book mark" in middle of the Apocalypse.

This will be our first "3½ clock"—the period of the Gentiles. It is one of our two, principle, keys. (The second being Israel's returning. We will return to the lone super power, towards the end . . . .). Before we leave this preliminary investigation of the 3½ clocks, please notice the mention of the temple/holy community being *trodden down*. This marks the emphasis of the first clock: diffused worship (or what is commonly called the "dispora" of the Jews). The second begins with Israel's returning, and the final, third "clock" will be marked by Antichrist's short reign. Thus, the three clocks cover three principle areas:

- Diffused worship/disapora
- Spiritual empowerment/restoration
- Final Tribulation

As we advance in our study, the shock of how these simple attributes have played out in human history—and line up for our future, may cause the reader to grieve at how we have come so far without noticing what has been taking place, right under our noses. In answer to this obvious concern and desire to know more, our search is facilitated by John's Apocalypse. † As may be imagined, much more of human history is contained within this short prophecy, than is at first thought possible.

Yet, the very word "apocalypse" is a term that sends shivers of distress, up and down our spines. Its very mention signals the end of the world as we know it(!). What we begin to appreciate while unfurling the layers of this revelation, however, is that God not only has a plan for the distant future—but for our present world, as well. Indeed, some will be truly surprised (others relieved) to find that much of the "American Dream" was intended to go well beyond mere material pursuits of wealth, or "happiness." There is greatness here, as well, within the Scriptures, that we were/are intended to grasp, and make use of. In this sense, this work not only deals with revelation of Jesus Christ, Himself, but also . . .of what He has intended for His people in general: not only within the US, but around the world, as well.

* * *

One standard argument, that the reader may find a useful omission, is the lack of time spent defending the question of whether or not we really are *in* the end time. Such seems immate-

---

† "Apocalypse" (capitalized) will designate John's Revelation. While "apocalypse" will be used to denote end time events, in general.

rial in a world where one hardly sees a week pass without some discussion of pending destruction, either in the matter of global warming, cosmic possibilities (as comets, . . . asteroids), or of some rogue nation acquiring (or testing) weapons of mass destruction. Some may yet prefer plugging their heads into the sand, but it is assumed that such persons will not pick up a book like this to read, ponder, and pray over.

Yet there is the valid question of timing, well worth our consideration. For Christ did say to believers of the first century that it wasn't for them to know the times or seasons of His return.[*]

Within the military we would call such access

"a *need* to know."

When information is classified by the government, its contents are not given to *anyone* unless it falls within the purview of their responsibility. In such a case they are required "to know" and understand what they are handling. Privileged information must not be played with. The prophet Daniel was likewise informed that further unveiling of future events is reserved for the terminal generation (Daniel 12:9). I offer to the reader, therefore, three serious reasons for believing that we are, indeed, within that "terminal generation." There are others, of course (as with more frequent wars, climatic changes, and general unrest) yet these general signs are more often related to "the beginning of sorrows" (Matt. 24:8, (Lk. 21:25,26)).

---

[*] Acts 1:6,7

The third evidence given will relate to our consideration of the "cry at midnight," another key element around which this book most certainly revolves. Please note that these examples are from the Bible, itself.

Just one note of caution, before proceeding down this avenue: you will notice that this book often covers areas that many have *professed* to have an interest in understanding, but few venture into. There is good reason for this: for gaining access to the truth does come at a price. We need not fear paying such a price for knowing the truth, however, for it will set us free (knowing about 9/11 in advance would have freed us to more adequately prepare, for example) —but acquiring such a treasure does sometimes require a measure of courage.

Three Evidences:

1. **Christ specifically stated that the Gentile church age would dominate until after Israel has completed her dispersion.**

   Pointed out earlier (and placed in your "pocket"): this amazing prophecy spans the time frame reaching from the first century, up to our present generation. Christ said, more specifically:

   "And they [the Jews] will fall by the edge of the sword, and be led away captive into all nations. And Jerusalem will be trampled by Gentiles until the times of the Gentiles are fulfilled.

   "And there will be signs in the sun, in the moon, and in the stars; and on the earth distress of nations, with perplexity, the sea and the waves roaring; men's hearts failing them from fear and the expectation of those things which are coming on the earth, for the powers of heaven will be shaken.

"<u>Then</u> they will see the Son of Man coming in a cloud with power and great glory."

Luke 21:24-27 [emphasis added]

The verses preceding the ones quoted above, relate specifically to the fall of Jerusalem in AD 70 (see vss. 20-23). If you compare the above quotation with the verses that follow them, you will notice that Christ speaks of the budding of the fig tree (the nation of Israel - vs. 29) and of all the trees (symbolizing the rise of the third world, to be highlighted, later in our discussion - vs. 30).

In other words, Christ projected that after the Jewish dispersion/diaspora was completed, the world would change radically, in preparation for His reappearing.

Notice, however, one other feature, as well: Jesus did say specifically, that *then* ". . .shall they *see* the Son of Man coming . . ." — nowhere within Scripture is there mention made of a "secret rapture."[3] In every instance, Christ's coming is described as visible, audible, and quite notable. In fact, the world will not only be *able* to see Christ's returning, they will be *forced* to take notice. Christ will return with a *shout,* and at the last *trumpet* (I Thes. 4:16, I Cor. 15:52, Rev. 1:7).[4]

There is one other event related to Christ's appearing, which I have heard very few discuss (I wonder why). Scripture links it directly to the Jewish return from dispersion. In fact, this will actually be the *second time* this particular prophecy has been fulfilled in relation to Christ's coming.

Buckle your seat belts. What you are about to read is *very* politically incorrect.

2. **Scripture projects a . . . "coming out" of homosexuality within our world, prior to Christ's arrival.**

Ezekiel, in pronouncing a judgment upon Israel, and in order to shame her into seriously seeking her God, said that this exposure would take place to shake Israel from her supposed self-righteousness. Some might argue the same, for the Church, today.

Its application was made in regard to the spiritual nature of Sodom's sin. However, obvious fulfillment of the following prophecy must also be realized in the actual practice of Sodom's activity—within the civilizations of both Greece and Rome . . . just prior to Christ's *first* coming. Speaking to Israel, the prophecy reads, briefly:

> "When your sisters, Sodom and her daughters, return to their former state, . . ., then you and your daughters will return to your former state."
>
> Ezekiel 16:55

For those desiring a more direct reference, Christ makes the same observation in chapter 17, verses 28-30 of Luke's gospel . . . .

There is something, here, that we all have to pray about. For, the *context* of the sin of homosexuality (Sodom's sin) is clearly linked to human pride—reflected, as well, in Ezekiel's earlier vss. 49 & 50. Still, it cannot be denied that when the greater darkness of this "coming out" occurs, it triggers the clear precedent for the Lord once more setting foot upon this planet.

Thus, as the society degenerates into this darkness, the Lord Himself prepares to return to set things in order, once again (Malachi 4:6).

I know, you weren't really expecting that one!

2. **Finally, the third evidence: the lowly computer chip, and specifically, VSLI (very large scale integration of electronic hardware, and nanotechnology –resulting in micro chipping capabilities).** This ubiquitous world wide technology now makes it possible to withdraw money deposited in a local bank on Mayberry Street, Small Town, USA—on the main thoroughfares of Shanghai, The People's Republic of China: making fulfillment of John's projected rise of a world-wide cashless society not only a possibility, but now

only a matter of time.

With very little adjustment, it is quite conceivable that at the present rate of progress, we will soon be asked, not only to submit to human "chipping" via electronic inserts, but also to pledge some oath of allegiance to world wide government, or "democratic" system, under the auspices of the UN or other international authority.

For anyone with their head just a above ground level (above the sands of time) this last observation must seem rather obvious, and ominous.

No matter *what* you believe about the timing of the return of Jesus Christ, therefore, a straightforward reading of John's prophecy obviously portends serious, and painful, choices in the near future. All one needs to do, in such instances—is go with the flow.

The "catch," of course, regards those who end up agreeing with Big Brother . . .

* * *

On a lighter note, experienced prophecy students, already familiar with the place of the US within prophecy, may wish to take a speed-read approach to this book. It is arranged in three sections:

- Introduction to the Keys
- Conflict of Spirits: On Earth & From the Heavens
- Connecting the Dots.

The first section focuses of being *able* to unlock prophetic truths: its dangers, and pitfalls, as well as a real appreciation of Who God is.

The final section builds on earlier foundations: showing conclusively the place of the US in Bible prophecy, the nation of Israel, as well as an unusual perspective towards revival.

The middle section fills in the cracks. Speed readers may wish to jump over this section on the first read. It deals with things largely overlooked in the study of Bible prophecy: the concept of democracy, foretold within Scripture, for example, or:

→ A full discussion of the parable of the ten virgins: why does the apostle Paul seem to contradict Christ's statement, concerning these believers???

→ The church age, as laid out in the letters to the seven churches. How is it that we no longer hear this point of view, so widely accepted, last century? You may find it surprising, or alarming . . . and, in a related corollary:

28

➔What is the place of the Charismatic church within prophecy? What part does it (or should it) play? What dangers await, or what powers have been abandoned/aborted?

Now, please, don't *skip to* the second section! My only purpose here, is to show that there is a great deal to be covered, and much to be pondered and prayed over within these pages.

However, the unraveling of such mysteries is not always the most important issue raised, within a book such as this. More important is the realization that when studying Bible prophecy, Christ warns us not to allow anyone to deceive us—not because of a complex plot or conspiracy being unleashed upon our world. — Oh yes, there *are* those who conspire, and even scheme to become the Antichrist: of this there can be no doubt. Yet this is not our greatest danger.

The greatest danger is within.

Even within our churches.

It is the danger of making mistakes, and not being able to admit them.

The danger of having an imperfect understanding of prophecy, while being unwilling to correct it.[†]

It is our pride, and being unable to admit when we are wrong.

This does *not* mean that the truth cannot be known. It *does* mean that we are truly dependent upon the God who is willing to reveal His truth to us. —And that we must be persistent in our pur-

---

[†] I Cor. 13:9,10

suit. For truth and wisdom, like excellence, are not arrived at by mere chance. It must be pursued, and embraced like the true gold that it is, when discovered.

> My son, if you receive my words, And treasure my commands within you, So that you incline your ear to wisdom, And apply your heart to understanding;
>
> Yes, if you cry out for discernment, And lift up your voice for understanding, If you seek her as silver, And search for her as for hidden treasures; Then you will understand the fear of the LORD, And find the knowledge of God.
>
> For the LORD gives wisdom; From His mouth come knowledge and understanding; He stores up sound wisdom for the upright; He is a shield to those who walk uprightly;
>
> He guards the paths of justice, And preserves the way of His saints.
>
> Proverbs 2:1-8

Jesus Christ, the Son of God, came into the world to turn common and ordinary people into saints. He is the Light of the world. He is the Bread of Life, and He is the Water that satisfies my thirsty soul. We will explore His Light in ways that you may have never considered (from the Bible). Our hope is to escape the boiling pot, light a candle in a dark world, and to arrive peacefully with others around His throne, in Eternity.

For now, however:

Welcome to the Kettle:

Please, sit back, take a deep breath, . . . and buckle your seat belt.

Chapter 2:

WELCOME TO THE KETTLE
of signs, wonders –and "end signs"

"And as it was in the days of Noah, so it will be also in the days of the Son of Man:

"They ate, they drank, they married wives, they were given in marriage, until the day that Noah entered the ark, and the flood came and destroyed them all.

"Likewise as it was also in the days of Lot: They ate, they drank, they bought, they sold, they planted, they built;

"but on the day that Lot went out of Sodom it rained fire and brimstone from heaven and destroyed them all.

"Even so will it be in the day when the Son of Man is revealed.

Luke 17:26-30

Welcome to the Kettle:

Welcome to the kettle.

In here, we'll test your mettle

And if you are truly wise enough

You'll find a way to escape the pot

before the whole world trembles.

When Jesus spoke of the end of the age, He couched His description in simple and ordinary terms: of buying and selling, of marrying and giving away the bride. The deception He speaks of, therefore, is one that is almost imperceptible—like that of a frog coming to a slow boil in a big kettle.

The little frog sits in his water, because it is comfortable. He has the power to leap from the pot, and to escape, but does not. Perhaps it is really cold in the room, and initially the waters feel cozy. Slowly, the water is heated. Yet the frog does not notice the rise in temperature, for his senses are designed to detect changes that are logarithmic. That is, we normally detect changes that seem *significant*. If looking at a large bill board from the bleachers of a large baseball stadium, for example, we'd never notice its canvas being stretched by only an inch. It would have to be stretched approximately 25% (several yards) before really taking notice. If listening to music, the change would have to be one decibel.

For this same reason, we are not normally aware of the aging process. With each passing day, month, or year —our time reference stretches. Yesterday (years ago) when only two years old, the next Christmas seemed an eternity away. Now, I may have to anticipate seasonal changes, to prepare for the purchase of gifts. Thus, with each passing year, the aging process seems to speed yearly events up as the years themselves seem to become shorter: And why is this? Because my personal time reference has changed. One day is now referenced to more than fifty years, and life continues to change—although many my age don't seem to notice. Most prefer to sleep, even before closing the box. It's easier to continue in the rat race for retirement . . . .

We are all aging. Similarly, we all tend to be like that frog slowly coming to a boil in the pot. All we have to do, for our "goose" to cook—is to continue as we always have. Delusion is then guaranteed, for when the Lord warns against strong delusion at the end of the age, this is no reference to a man in a long black cape, with an obvious scowl over his face, declaring, "I am Antichrist!" No, nothing could be further from the truth. When he scowls (or laughs at us) it will be in private.

When God does anything, my friend, He does it well! When He forecast that Pharaoh would harden his heart, not once did His word fail. Pharaoh was deceived, 100%.[†] Yet, if you will accept it, the Lord also knows our weaknesses and, at times, makes allowances for them—even within prophecy.

And even within prophetic fulfillment.

Consider how the Lord did this, when speaking of signs and wonders. Why did He throw them a curve ball, when asked to offer that first (New Testament) generation a sign?

> Then some of the scribes and Pharisees answered, saying, "Teacher, we want to see a sign from You."
> But He answered and said to them, "An evil and adulterous generation seeks after a sign, and no sign will be given to it except the sign of the prophet Jonah."
>
> Matthew 12:38

[†] The children of Israel were delivered from Egyptian slavery in approximately 1400 BC after Pharoah repeatedly refused to come to terms with the LORD. This story, so full of the God's grace (delivering His people), and of power (over the super power, of the day: Egypt) has captured the imagination of Hollywood (Cecil B. Demille's Ten Commandments, for example) and is wonderfully recorded in the second book of the Bible, called "Exodus."

—But if you check the context, you may notice something strange. They had just brought a man to Jesus who was so seriously demonized that he could neither speak, hear, or see. Our institutions are full of people in similar situations, today. Very often the most modern medicine may offer is a drug to alleviate the symptoms: an antidepressant, perhaps, or even psychotropic medication. Yet here, Jesus simply discerns the spiritual source, takes authority over it, and heals the man by banishing the demons. So amazing is the man's deliverance that when the crowd sees the man both speak, hear, and see—they can not help but ask if Jesus is the Messiah (vs. 23)!

So I ask you, was this healing not a "sign" of Christ's power and authority?

What of Jesus raising Lazarus from the dead (John 11). Was this not a "sign" of His power?

So what was Jesus getting at, when saying that "no sign" would be given to their generation, except the sign of His death and *resurrection* (as Jonah's three day journey in a great fish implies)??

Jesus understood something not readily discerned. He understood the difference between signs, and wonders. Wonders are unusual (supernatural) events that arouse an interest in the short term. Yet, He also saw the long range picture that would be visible, in the centuries to come. By then, those healings would start to get "old." Those who truly believed in Him would no longer point, so much, to the healing wonders, as to the greater miracle of deliverance accomplished on the Cross of Calvary. Mel Gibson's PASSION OF THE CHRIST, is an example of this. For even though doctrinal questions may arise, he did excel in one principle issue: he presented a bulls-eye view of the one sign that Christ left for us,

34

when coming to "fix things up" with the living God. You may have noticed how little opposition there was to a later movie resting on the Narnia fable, written by CS Lewis. There, a clear symbolism exists on the screen as well—yet, the uniqueness of the gospel did not impact lives nearly so powerfully as did the clear display of the Cross.

People love fables, for they demand very little from adults.[5] Yet Christ actually *died* on the Cross, arose, and has left us a sign of His incredible love—by shedding God's own blood, to save those choosing to put their trust in Him.[6]

God knows our weaknesses, hates our sin, and yet loves us so much that He was willing to put on a human body, walk around on this literal planet to feel our pain, experience our agonies, and even fully endure the ultimate curse (DEATH) to save us. This is the gospel. It assures us that God is holy. He is just.

And . . . He loves us so much that, He has made a way for us to "beat the curse" and be saved. Yet we must acknowledge the truth.

Is Truth "Incovenient"?

Remembering our limitations, we begin to realize that when God gives a picture of the future, He is well aware of the limits of our vision, for truth does come at a price. In fact, this generation has formally rejected the whole concept of absolute truth for this very reason.

Students in college are now told that truth does not exist at all: all is relative. Why are we being told this? Perhaps we may discern the reason from a politician's recent portrayal of his belief in global warming. When presenting his position in a movie, he calls it "An Inconvenient Truth." What is the former Vice President getting at?

That if you accept his perception of truth, you will have to change the way you live.

In other words, truth does come at a price. People reject the truth of the gospel for this very simple reason: to accept it, requires that we change the way we live. Wonderful as miracles are, however, they do not necessarily require a change in life patterns. "Signs and wonders" are just that: things to be wondered at. They are conversation pieces that may be discussed at the local barber shop, or around the dinner table, with no real consequence.

Thus, if Jesus had given the religious leaders a bone fide sign, they would have had to follow Him, then and there, as the Messiah—or else (pay the penalty, with their lives). The sign that He chose, of His death on the Cross, insured that His kingdom would now be within the realm of the soul and spirit of man. People would have a choice. For He would not be on earth to personally enforce a physical kingdom—until after His return.

"Miraculous wonders" do not require a life change. Truth does.

Signs of the times:

Although miraculous wonders have a short term return, the *signs of the times* ("end signs") perform an important function in pointing the way to Christ's final returning — whether we actually read them fully, or not. Signs are posted along the side of the road, for example, whether or not an alcoholic takes the time to read them. He may completely disregard the speed limit, and yet the sign is still posted. Why?

To what purpose, or of what use is a posted sign, that gives the speed limit, to a person deluded by alcohol?

We warn that alcoholic, anyway, because it is our duty to do so. Further, we have police officers who just may pull such a person over to the side, apprehend him, and prevent the loaded driver from turning their vehicle into a missile that will get themselves (and others) killed. A friend may also read the sign and attempt to persuade him/her not to drive under the influence.

Such is an "evangelist:" a person setting out to save someone "in spite of themselves."

We are talking about "signs." Prophecy is full of them, and they have a definite purpose.

Sometimes, we may even witness a wordless sign (picture) that has been posted to assist someone not able to read our language. These "picture signs" may be interpreted differently, and yet (hopefully) will get the message across. The same is true of Bible prophecy. So serious is the time of the end, and so serious are its consequences, that Bible signs are posted which are both "signs and wonders," picture images, and formal warnings.

For this reason, when introducing someone to the fact that we are *in the midst* of Biblical fulfillment as outlined in John's Revelation, I often refer the curious seeker to the website of END-

TIME.COM. There, Irwin Baxter has discerned amazing fulfill-ment regarding the "picture images" of John's Revelation. His in-terpretation of America's place in Bible prophecy is very similar to the one presented towards the end of this book. Yet at the End-time.com web site, a person who is open to considering Bible ful-fillment may more easily relate to his interpretation of the seven trumpets, when pointing out that Chernobyl (in the Ukrainian lan-guage) translates into "wormwood" (Rev. 8:11) and that "Saddam" literally means "Destroyer" in the Iraqi mother tongue, and was so intended by Saddam's birth mother (Rev. 9:11). His most amazing interpretation of the leopard of Daniel's seventh chapter represent-ing modern Germany, has allowed him to make the all important connection with Revelation thirteen, while tracking the rise of the (so called) New World Order —in which the Mark of the Beast will be issued. Through this particular interpretation he was able to proclaim for twenty years, before hand, that the Berlin Wall would come down in preparation for final world government.

This book's interpretation of Revelation eight and nine goes deeper into the underlying conflicts that fuel current events. Fur-ther, we will see another key trend (civil rights) in the symbolism of the multi-colored leopard. His presentation of the US within Bi-ble prophecy is also very similar—for he acknowledges the US in prophecy (not very difficult to do, once getting over a few precon-ceptions)—but not as intense, as will be here presented, for we must dig into certain unpleasant images if there is any hope to make *use* of this information for revival.[7]

As for myself, it was not until 1987 that the presence of the US in Bible prophecy first jumped out at me. It was in response to my pastor's projection that the Stock Market would take a dive (which it did, as foretold).[8] That event occurred two years before the wall fell. I cannot help but notice the similarity in timing, between that event, and the one warned about within this book. . . .

These statements are made to intentionally underline the imminent danger implied within Christ's parable of the ten virgins. We will hammer on this issue, throughout this book. Make no mistake about it. There is a danger. There is also a price for discovery.

And there is glory, when knowing that our risen King will soon return!

As a "thief in the night"

The key issue of the parable of the virgins, most often overlooked, and which will most certainly assist in our quest for secrets contained within John's Revelation is this: that the church sleeps while preparations are being made for ultimate judgment. This is the exact meaning of Christ's statement regarding His coming as "a thief in the night".[9] For in New Testament times, the outlaw and "house breaker" did just that: he dug through the wall quietly, as his unsuspecting victims remained asleep. It was not until he had actually penetrated the wall, that his intentions were known.[10]

The fact that our little frog continues to sit in hot water, while ignoring the many signs active even within his own little pot, is similar to the way many believers remain asleep in spite of a rapidly changing world.[11] "You can detect a change in the weather," Jesus asked, "why can't you discern the signs of the times?"[12] Some even continue to insist that the Mark of the Beast is only symbolic, in spite of the fact that our world is obviously moving towards a fully functional cashless society based on "plastic": involving both smart cards and contactless,[13] credit and debit cards.

39

We now have EZ Pass for tracking automotive movement, ATMs, and the World Wide Web, all leading directly to . . . . a sub-dermal computer chip (a computer chip, injected under the skin).

Thus, we really have two dangers:

- First, of slow significant change, which may escape our notice.

- Second, of an unwillingness to see, address, or admit such change.

From Heaven, all of these dangers may be clearly seen (thus, the Lord's admonition to John to, "Come up hither!"[14]). Yet from a purely earthly plain, "inside of the pot," these changes are not so readily discernable, at all. In a word, *it takes faith* to see things the way God does. Further, the world about us is incredibly resistant to Heaven's perspective, for God does not respect its values or its trinkets.

 Think, for example, of the national baseball leagues from the perspective of Eternity. Consider the latest Hollywood offerings (unless they be on a par with the PASSION . . . .).

Our present world all but buries its actors and players with golden crowns (Emmys, Oscars, Hall of Fame. . .). Yet, of what interest are these things to the Lord of heaven and earth? Within a few hours (a week, month, or decade at most) it will hardly matter, even upon earth. Yet, many will forego the maintenance of their undying souls for the sake of a baseball series, or super bowl—and woe to the preacher who dares to say otherwise!

No wonder we have difficulty seeing things God's way.

Such very "natural" and distracting influences are exactly what Christ has in mind, when warning about the "boiling point." Yet, those who are busy sharing the love of the Lord Jesus with others, are less likely to be deluded by such influences.

> "And this gospel of the kingdom will be preached in all the world as a witness to all the nations, and then the end will come.
>
> "Therefore when you see the 'abomination of desolation,' spoken of by Daniel the prophet, standing in the holy place" (whoever reads, let him understand),
>
> → "then let those who are in Judea flee to the mountains".

Matthew 24:14-16 [emphasis added]

This "abomination of desolation," within the passage, is the boiling point. Translating this Old Testament event (which occurred in the time of the Maccabees)[15] into a New Testament context, is an all important "detail" necessary for discerning what Jesus was referring to. Yet, is it only a detail? Jesus clearly warns, "whoever reads, let him understand"! So let us consider another warning over the "boiling point" from our central parable, of ten virgins. This "detail" is the midnight cry (Midnight Cry).

> "But while the bridegroom was delayed, they all slumbered and slept.
>
> "And at midnight a cry was heard: 'Behold, the bridegroom is coming; go out to meet him!' "

Matthew 25:5,6

Without question, the "bridegroom" described here refers to Jesus Christ.[16] The delay involves His second coming, and return to earth. Yet, just at the boiling point, when we least expect it, a cry is issued at midnight. Do you notice the similarity, to our earlier text (by the arrow)? Go out to meet him! What does this mean??

Now, before we go on to another warning about the boiling point, notice just one point more about the above text. —That they all slumbered and slept (vs. 5). This will be discussed in detail, in the next section (the next *chapter* will explore the danger of false paradigms). For now, simply notice how this detail is handled at our next "boiling point" warning, through what appears to be a contradiction. The apostle Paul was writing to the church located at Thessalonica.[†]

> Therefore let us <u>not</u> sleep, as others do, but let us watch and be sober.
> For those who sleep, sleep at night, and those who get drunk are drunk at night.
>
> I Thes. 5:6,7 [emphasis added]

In this passage—given within the same context as the previous parable (of Christ's returning)[17]—Paul takes an approach quite different from the one given to the Church at large. Paul challenges a faithful remnant, "let us not sleep as others do." In other words, Paul actually advises these believers to "get out of the pot"! —To avoid the boiling water, altogether. This is not to avoid the consequences of knowing the truth, or of what is coming. He is not even advising them to "head for the hills," but rather to be prepared for the Midnight Cry, when those in the pot may actually prefer . . . being

---

[†] Thessalonica: A Greek town, well known in New Testament times for its commerce. It was named after the wife of Cassader, a general of Alexander the Great. It forms an excellent sea port on the Thermaic Gulf, near the Aegean Sea.

boiled alive (exactly the point being made by Christ, in Luke 21:36).

Finally, just one more consideration, to those reluctant to heed Paul's advice. For some had actually crept into the church teaching that they had *already passed* the boiling point. Paul explicitly warns: Christ's coming (i.e. "that day") will not take place until after Antichrist arises. The specific quote:

> Now, brethren, concerning the coming of our Lord Jesus Christ <u>and our gathering together to Him</u>, we ask you, not to be soon shaken in mind or troubled, either by spirit or by word or by letter, as if from us, as though the day of Christ had come.
>
> Let no one deceive you by any means; <u>for that Day will not come unless the falling away comes first,</u> and <u>the man of sin is revealed</u>, the son of perdition, who opposes and exalts himself above all that is called God or that is worshiped, so that he sits as God in the temple of God, showing himself that he is God.
>
> II Thessalonians 2:1-4 [emphasis added]

Please notice that Paul, a Jew, is speaking to a Gentile congregation, and referring to "our" being gathered together to meet the Lord in the air (vs. 1). Notice also, that the rapture (Christ's miraculous removal of the church from this world (I Thes. 4:16,17)) *had not yet* occurred. This may seem rather obvious, for it *still* hasn't taken place. Yet now, as we meditate on these lines, we find that we have already reinforced our awareness of the serious dangers outlined earlier, as we enhance our understanding of:

What the boiling point is –and Midnight Cry.

Who will turn the heat up.

What will be required to "get out of the pot."

If any of these points "went over your head" we will return to them, many times over. Do not worry. God is very concerned with our being prepared for the Midnight Cry. Prophecy that is vitally important to the church's future is so critical that the Lord *has* also allowed "word pictures" and "graphic signs" to assist us in understanding what we are viewing, when looking at current events. The Spirit led believer can readily detect when "something is wrong." Here, in this book, we are doing a more detailed study of just what that "something" is. Yet, even when we do not understand *the details* of prophecy, God promises that sincere men and women following him, "though fools," will not err on the road to Heaven (Isaiah 35:8).

Even the foolish virgins, if willing to awaken early and face the truth, may escape the danger that presents itself to us at midnight.

Yet . . . we must also confront the fact that in many instances it is not so difficult for the careless onlooker to be fooled.

We may even confuse monsters, with angels (or visa versa).

For, we really must come to terms with just how big this monster really is, called "the great tribulation." Is there no escape?

Chapter 3:

OF MONSTERS AND ANGELS

The Perils of Paradigms & . . . *Onion Skins*

> . . . behold, a ladder was set up on the earth, and its top reached to heaven; and there the angels of God were ascending and descending on it.
>
> Genesis 28:12

We are headed for some real monsters,

and the only way of escape, is UP. . . .

When Bela Lugosi played the classic blood sucker, Dracula, he acted in a manner so convincing that viewers found it difficult to throw off the impression he had created. No matter if directors later tried to cast him in a comedy role, "Dracula," was no laughing matter.

Nor are the issues being discussed here. The mind is a delicate thing, and the simple power of suggestion may delude it: leading it to wrong conclusions. Yet as we saw earlier, the God of the Bible seeks to assist those who pursue the truth—even when that pursuit may be somewhat flawed. . . .

→When first presented as the God of Abraham, Isaac, and Jacob within a world starting to forget its origins—the God of the Old Testament was largely ignored as they sought to escape His notice, and especially His judgment. The antediluvian world, existing before the flood, was now well behind them. Jacob, the third patriarch mentioned, and from whom we would later get the modern state's name (Israel) had somehow grasped an appreciation of God's blessing, but was not always the most honorable of persons in his pursuit of it. He eventually prevailed and was finally named "Israel," but discovered it a long and difficult journey into that place of victory. He so yearned to be a part of what God was doing on earth, that he even cut a few corners to get there. So . . . as the younger son of the clan, he conceived of a plan to trick his older brother into selling him a place within God's future kingdom

for a bowl of soup.

"Sell me your birthright!"

Now the birthright was the right of inheritance, not only to his father's physical wealth (which, by the way, he forfeited through his mischief) but also to the promises given by God to his grandfather, Abraham.

Esau (also called Edom, whom we must revisit in our discussion . . . of the Green Horse)—cared nothing for it at all, and cast aside the blessing, family covenant, and eternal glory for the whim of a momentary *urge*.

> Esau said, "Look, I am about to die; so what is this birthright to me?"
>
> Genesis 25:32

It really is quite doubtful that Esau was *actually* about to die. He had come in from the field, after a hunt, and was tired and exhausted. It does not seem feasible to assume that he would have actually starved to death while living with his parents, or that he could find nothing to eat within their many tents. (Surely, even Jacob would have recanted, had he seen his brother truly on the verge of death!) The point is that Esau was impulsive: he wanted, what he wanted, *NOW*. He allowed the momentary impression of hunger to cloud his eternal outlook. (Must remember this, when fasting. . .)

What his brother Jacob had failed to consider, however, with all of his wheeling and dealing—is that God is the One who sees everything, and that He balances the scales. What Jacob was sowing, he would most certainly reap. Even for those outside of the promised line, God is yet the God of justice. Poetic justice doesn't just happen.

God plans it all.

So when Jacob found that he had to run from his brother after tricking him one too many times, he ran into someone just like himself: his uncle Laban, who finds a way to trick him out of . . . of all things, his rightful bride. Déjà vu? How was this possible? One answer seems obvious, for his bride wore a veil. The other is not so easily grasped: Jacob wasn't looking to be deceived.

He thought he had it all together.

Jacob loved Laban's younger daughter, Rachael, and might easily have compared Leah's mannerisms with those of the woman he loved: the way she walked, perhaps, or sat (or perhaps chuckled, or not). Yet, Jacob's "antenna" were not up. He did not feel it necessary to be so cautious with this veiled woman presented as his new bride. He took the events going on about him at face value, and accepted the power of suggestion presented by his uncle, as he went in to consummate the relationship.

In the morning light, the deception became obvious. Yet by that time, it was too late.

Thus, we have seen two simple examples of mental misjudgment: both involving preconditioning. In one case, it was a simple environmental issue. It was simply the way an actor presented himself, so that the viewer always associated a certain role with his personality. When we saw Bela Lagossi, we saw the monster.

In the second case, there was intentional deceit, through a mis-representation that was not readily detected. —It's the old magician's slight of hand, trick; keep their eyes focused on one hand, while you manipulate the rabbit in the hat, with the other. In both cases the problem arises from the way a person sees the world in which they live. Even with more subtle errors, this concept of a *paradigm* is involved. Yet to further illustrate this point, consider the next example:

Imagine that you are camping in the woods, at night. The moon is shining, but there is some obstruction: overhead clouds, perhaps. You have been sleeping, and are not certain of whether you are awake or still sleeping when noticing a disturbance outside of your tent. The camp site is considered a safe haven, however, and no bears or wild animals have been known to prowl about. This fear being allayed—you verify that something *is* outside of your tent. There appear to be glowing figures just beyond easy range of sight. They seem to be standing upright, like men(?).

What are they?

Are they:

   - Men in phosphorescent sheets?

   - Angels?

   - Extraterrestrials?

Your answer to the above question reveals your basic mindset, and way of looking at the world in which we live. Prior information that has been absorbed, from news reports perhaps, or through books and magazines that you have been reading, will influence the way you view what you are now looking at. This has helped to form your personal *paradigm:* the way you look at life. Yet, when you have the ultimate paradigm, you "will know the truth, and the truth will set you free" (Jn. 8:32)!

The Ultimate Paradigm:

For many—even within the church today, considering things spiritual, or supernatural (especially, prophetic) seems increasingly difficult to grasp. There are reasons for this, as we have hinted at earlier, not the least of which may be a failure to be truly born again.[18] Rebirth does require a radical departure from the old life, after all. For the baby must leave the womb—however, it is also more than merely *denying* (or repenting of) the past, as important as this is. For there must also be a re-*birth.* That is, new life must be injected from that external Source far more powerful than ourselves—this Source already possesses the life, and thus initiates the life-giving birth. This life has more power than death, itself.

It is the power of the Holy Spirit.

> But if the Spirit of Him who raised Jesus from the dead dwells in you, He who raised Christ from the dead will also give life to your mortal bodies through His Spirit who dwells in you.
>
> . . .
>
> "However, when He, the Spirit of truth, has come, He will guide you into all truth; . . . and He will tell you things to come."

> Romans 8:11, John 16:13

49

The *Deadly* Paradigm:

Many within our world, today, while seeking to be all knowing (or all knowledgeable) think it cool and sophisticated to deny the simple proclamations of the Bible. Without realizing it, they are preferring the death of secularism, to the life of the Spirit. In the process, they would even castrate Bible prophecy of its message and purpose.

→Preterists, for example, believe that the apostle John was simply sending coded messages to brethren in "Babylon" (a code name for the city of Rome, in I Peter 5:13). He did this, they think, to communicate with other brothers being persecuted for their faith in the first century. Since John was imprisoned on an island, they reason, he must have been using this extreme imagery to get his letters past the censors. . . .

However, Christ explicitly told John to write of things "which you have seen, and things which are, and the things *which will take place after this*" (Rev. 1:17 emphasis added). Most interesting, as well, is the fact that this particular comment is made within the direct context of the seven letters being dictated to seven churches (starting at verse eleven). When John turned to see who spoke with him, it was not a man in a white sheet.

It was the Son of the living God, giving instructions to the saints, both near and far, down through time.

We will harvest this gold mine, later.

In the case of Jacob, the fellow we were discussing earlier, a similar instance produced a very definite response as he saw a ladder reaching up into the sky. He recognized the presence of angels ascending and descending. Then, the God of Abraham spoke to him, assuring him that he would indeed inherit the blessing, and that he would be the father of a very important nation of people.

And he was afraid and said, "How awesome is this place! This is none other than the house of God, and this is the gate of heaven!"

Genesis 28:17

In Jacob's case, his imperfections were overruled by his faith. His desire to know and to truly please the Lord, were rewarded by the God he was seeking. These things are important to remember in the pages that will follow. Many attempt to pull the wool over the eyes of others—but we never fool God. People may misrepresent the world in which we live, and seek to portray God as some sort of monster. We may even hear people blaming God for the evils about us, while taking credit for many positive changes happening our way (politicians are famous for this)—yet the greatest loss derived from this last perception, is that it becomes more difficult to hear God, when He would actually whisper to us, and share with us His great love and comfort (Deut. 5:25-29, John 3:16).

Throughout the writings of the prophets we may gain incredible insights into the way our Lord, Himself, looks at our universe. "For the testimony of Jesus is the spirit of prophecy" (Rev. 19:10). For those who love it, here is a veritable spring of life, full of eternal truths that are fit to dive into, like a man taking a plunge in a refreshing river.

—Or, onion skins. For, in many ways, accepting the perspective of the prophets requires a radical restructuring of human thought. It really is like diving into onion skins, for the outer layer seeming easy enough to conquer, but as soon as we plunge in the knife—the results bring tears to our eyes.[*]

Patience is often required, therefore, as we climb out of the pot, layer upon layer.

DOES IT MATTER?

To myself, I cannot help but notice how the Lord seems to be "setting things up" in ways that are amazingly coincidental. Take the present population of our planet, for example. Its population now hovers somewhere around six point six billion (that's "66" with eight zeroes after it!). As we will see, in a moment, there are seven overlaps in John's Revelation, along with seven seals, seven trumpets, and seven vials. Six is the number of man. Seven, of God. Christ returns at the last (seventh) trumpet.[†] At the sixth, there is a projection that a full 1/3 of humankind will be destroyed. Our "66" population number seems particularly suited for the study we are about to engage in, for it is easily divided by three. (One third of sixty-six, equals twenty-two, for example.) Dividing the earth's 6.6 billion souls by *twelve*, furthermore, yields . . . five hundred-fifty million (550,000,000) persons. Please remember this, as we proceed in our study, and especially as we get towards the end of this particular chapter. For, a catastrophe that would

---

[*] Revelation 10:9 –notice that within this text, the sweetness is within the mouth. It first appears that sweetness comes after eating when, in fact, on second glance the bitterness is within the belly. It tasted good going down, but later, you realize what you ate (or read). God's judgments are often like this. We at first rejoice at things being made right—then sorrow over those being judged.

[†] I Corinthians 15:52

envelope a *mere* 1/12 of the earth's population would encompass more persons than now inhabit . . . all of these United States.

I do not believe a disaster of such magnitude would be overlooked in the unveiling of John's Revelation of Jesus Christ— particularly as we examine the increasing detail contained within the latter part of his vision. The key attribute that we have labeled the "onion skins" assures us that this is certainly not the case. There are many secrets to be found beneath the surface

of this onion. We will now look at a few.

THE ONION SKINS

"For precept must be upon precept, precept upon precept, Line upon line, line upon line, Here a little, there a little."

Isaiah 28:10

Where be the boiling pot,

Without an onion in the soup?

Where to discern the serpentine

Evils,

And its judgment roots?

Where to find God's divine jealousy,

and love for His beloved?

Where else to discover the Lover's secrets,

Than deep in these sacred Covers?

Here, between the Sacred Covers of God's Holy Book we have a very large, and mysterious onion, indeed. What we will now discover, is that the layers of prophecy (which we will refer to as "overlaps") –properly understood, do give us the ability to make very special comparisons between different parts of the same prophetic writings. Lining up these overlaps will give us a much clearer insight into its message, as they are lifted from the isle on which John was held a prisoner, and held up to the light day in our present-day environment.

As we take the time to read and reread Bible prophecy, however, it may at times seem tedious and leave the eyes red and tired: puzzling over the manner in which it is written. Prophecy often does have overlapping visions, which do repeat in a manner westerners are not accustomed to encountering within "light reading"— discouraging all but the most determined. It does sometimes seem like an eye watering onion! Some Bible scholars have even proposed that more than one author be responsible for the writings (as with Isaiah, for example: First and Second Isaiah). Yet this tendency to overlap Jewish prophecy is not intended to confuse, but to elaborate—while yielding much fuller detail, as we press beneath the surface for some very serious insights.

When a prophet declared a vision, he shared what he was allowed to foresee. He often did this over and over—and over again. Isaiah, for example, speaks of the planet in its final throws, as we witness the upheaval of divine judgments sending the cosmos reeling from two different points in perspective (chapters 2 & 24).

Ezekiel shares visions of Heaven in both chapters 1, 8 and then of God's Heavenly Kingdom (from its temple) from chapter 40, on. Daniel also had very specific revelation regarding the composition of the final global empire (now known as the so called "New World Order") in chapters 2, 7, and 11. Yet, when we get to John's Revelation of Jesus Christ, it is as though the Lord did a new thing. He actually seems to structure this prophecy for Gentiles!

Indeed, this seems to be a special attribute of this apostle. For if you compare the four gospels, you may notice that John's gospel differs from the other three in two important ways. What ways are these?

Differences: in structure, and focus:

John's Structure:

It is standard fare, and commonly taught in Bible survey courses[1] that Matthew, Mark, and Luke are synoptic gospels. That is, the pattern of their story line, and general historic content *synchronize* with one another. They generally follow the same pattern. The structure of John's gospel is different. It is topical, written later than any of the others, and with an independent theme. This is common knowledge, and generally understood.

John's "focus:"

The other way that John's gospel differs, however, is in its focus and perspective. John, a Jew, seems to almost identify with the Gentiles. Of all the writers relating the story of Christ's life, for example, John uses the term "of the Jews" more often than any other.

A man does not refer to his friend as "one of those Italians" or "one of the Africans" or "one of those Chinese"—if he himself is one of them. "They" are one of "us"! When speaking of one's own people in this way, there is a feeling that you are on the outside, looking in. "Yes, I'm one of those blacks." —So saying, you make yourself conspicuous, and you call attention to your differences. For this reason, Matthew, Mark, and Luke utilize the term no more than five times in each of their gospels, and then, only when referring to the Jewish nation from a Gentile perspective (as on the Cross: Pilate's declaration that Jesus was the "king *of the Jews."*)

When the servant of a Roman Soldier gets sick, Luke records that he sends to the elders "of the Jews" –asking them to intercede with Jesus on his behalf. The Roman soldier, an outsider, wanted an audience with that great teacher "of the Jews." Seldom did the other writers of the gospels utilize this term, but John makes use of it *twenty-one times.* Why? I believe that he was comfortable thinking outside of the box. He somehow identified with Gentile believers. For this reason, I think of John as the other apostle to the Gentiles.

An "onion" for us!

For this reason also, John's prophecy seems particularly well suited to the Gentile reader who is attempting to understand the future, as God reveals it. The Lord goes to great pains to (almost) force us to peel the layers of the onion, and realize that this prophecy is composed of overlapping visions. This is done

56

through the use of seals (chapter 6), trumpets (chapters 8 & 9) and bowls (or vials - chapters 15 & 16). Although their *major* emphasis shifts (from general, to spiritual, to national judgment/wrath) they overlap the same general time frames. In other words, within their greatest fulfillment, they are best understood when applying their symbolism to the last generation (i.e. to the generation that sees the budding of the fig tree—the returning of the nation of Israel to her land: Matt. 24:32-34).

Remember this last point: the outer layers generally point to the terminal generation.

and . . "Allegorical" overlaps:

Although the Lord has given three obvious overlaps, there are four more for the serious Bible student to consider. As may be supposed, these are the most difficult to discern, and often most controversial. Two of them are allegorical: with events taking place at another point in history, while having a deeper meaning when applied to our present time, or setting.

For example of how allegories work, consider Abraham: Abraham had two sons, by two different women (Sarah, and Hagar) but one was conceived by faith while the other, naturally. Isaac, Sarah's son, was by faith—for Sarah womb was sterile. It took a miracle for her to have that son. Hagar, who was rushed in to, while Abraham grew impatient for a son, was born as a son "of the flesh." These were two actual sons, both born to Abraham, the Bible tells us, but with large implications for us, as an allegory. Hagar will forever symbolize, for us, those who try to please God by their own efforts, and the manipulation of circumstances.

Thus, allegories tell a deeper story, than the physical event that actually took place. Two of our remaining (hidden) overlaps are allegorical: one is in the past, the other in the future.

<u>Those "hidden" overlaps:</u>

One distinguishing feature of each of all the "hidden" overlaps, is that *they each span the entire church age*: from the time of Christ's departure, to His return. Yet, outside of the millennium of Revelation chapter 20—the literal event in the future, with allegorical implications for the church in the present[19] these snap shots of the church age will enrich our present study with some very important and useful information. The three remaining hidden overlaps are:

- the letters to the seven churches (the historical allegory)
- the 3½ clocks of Revelation 11-13.

Why did I say that there are *three* remaining overlaps, and give only two? Forgive me, this is because the 3½ clocks are actually doubled. They are first stated by John, and outlined, in Revelation, chapter eleven (vss. 2, 3 & 9) and then used *again*, in much more detail—and from a slightly different perspective—in chapters twelve and thirteen (12:6, 14 & 13:5).

We will explain exactly what these "clocks" are, and how they may be applied later, in our next chapter. Without question, these 3½ clocks unlock some of the most interesting (and important) secrets of this Revelation.

By taking the time to unpeel this onion we have already uncovered some interesting number structures: utilizing the Lord's favorite numbers (3 & 7) –in relation to the earth (represented by the number 4 – Isa. 11:12). Later, when unlocking the "clocks" we will also discover the number 2, which is the minimal number required for a core of true believers – Rev. 11:3-11, Matt. 11:16, 20 . . . who do not sleep.

Thus we already have:

3 outer overlaps (seals, trumpet & vials)
+   **4 inner overlaps, spanning the church age (3 churches, 3½ clocks doubled & millennial)**

----

7 total overlaps

Such an unusual "onion" sits within this very rich soup!

Getting back to unlocking their secrets.

We will often make use of the letters to the seven churches, when referring to trends within the church world. "Philadelphia," for example, may be used to describe the church era most dominant in the evangelical world, just prior to the nation of Israel's returning to her land. Philadelphia is mentioned in Revelation, chapter three (vs. 7). This section of the overlap relates directly to the founding of the United States, as well. We will examine this overlap in the next section, and conclude it in the third, final section. Philadelphia, itself, is quite easy to consider, because there is so little said about it, that is negative. We notice only that she has an open door and little strength (vs. 8).

Here, we may note that the "open door" given to Philadelphia represents the door of freedom within the historical sense . . . . and that it may be because of this very freedom that she now has little strength (it took strength to gain the freedom, that we now take for granted . . .). For it is through pain and strain that we often gain the greatest abilities, even within the kingdom of God. Especially in this situation, His strength is made perfect in weakness.

This last comment is not meant to be derogatory, but encouraging, for freedom is like material wealth. There are dangers, this is true, but we usually try to overcome its dangers, and live with the blessing.

We have now gained a very broad outline of the layers of the onion through which we must peel and dig in order to gain access to the "meat" of this prophecy. We have noted three outer layers (seals, trumpets, and vials) and four inner layers. There is one very important point about the outer layers, seldom emphasized, that we must not miss:

These layers cover the same general time frame. Therefore, increased revelation may be discerned if the layers are held together, and peered through (at times) as a unit. As we have already observed, it is important for those who want to discover greatest secrets in God's Word . . . to repeatedly return to the Bible's most basic concepts. For we have already observed Jesus commenting to the Father, "I thank You Father, that You have held these secrets from the eggheads, and revealed them to babies" (paraphrasing Matthew 11:25)!

John's Revelation of Jesus has a lot to say about God . . . and about humankind, which He loves. Further, people are often insensitive to things spiritual, but quite responsive to physical pain and distress. Therefore, when a section of prophecy notes that people are crying out in agony (even despair) it is fairly reasonable to assume that the incidents being recorded there are *physical events*. Noting the *placement* of these events brings us to the conclusion that these overlaps generally progress from the spiritual to more overtly physical judgments –where the overlap ends (as in Revelation 6:15-17 and 11:13, for example).

Yet, there is also that other attribute that we *must not* ignore, or overlook: God's love for us. His love, which is so enormous and overflowing, was best demonstrated on Calvary when God, wearing flesh as a man, allowed Himself to be disrespected, spit upon, and nailed to a cross like a common criminal—just so that He could take our place and open the door of salvation for our deliverance—forever!

This is the same generosity, and giving nature, that has birthed the Universe, and that we are allowed to bask in, when coming to faith in Jesus Christ, the Son of man. He is the God of the created Universe, and Savior of all—especially of those who believe in Him (I Tim. 4:10). In other words:

God loves us.

God cares about our well being.

He is not a vengeful God, and does not even take pleasure in the death of the wicked.

It seems inconceivable, therefore, that the Lord would pronounce incredible devastation within one overlap (as with the pale/green horse, exterminating ¼ of the human race - Rev. 6:8) and ignore such an event within parallel passages. –As within the trumpet overlap, for example, where is mention is made of the destruction of a full 1/3 of humanity.

The pale-green horse kills ¼.

The sixth trumpet sees 1/3 of humankind killed.

→Where is judgment after Antichrist clearly arises, within the terminal overlap, containing the seven vials (Rev. 13-19)?

We will show conclusively, by book's end, that we now stand at the opening of the thirteenth chapter of John's Apocalypse. Yet this "terminal overlap" gives no "body count" of those destroyed.

It does mention however, with particular emphasis, the destruction of "Babylon" as well as the battle of Armageddon. These are two distinct judgments. Because the battle of Armageddon is a straightforward conflict, it does not seem a stretch to assume that the remaining 1/12 (the difference between the pale-green horse and 6th trumpet) would be destroyed within this confrontation. It is, after all, the final conflict/battle of the age. A "mere" one twelfth of the present world population comes to approximately 550 million souls(! –what a monster, is this Great Tribulation!)

This does seem commensurate with John's description of their blood flowing up to the horse bridles for approximately 180 miles (Rev. 14:19,20). Note that, to date, our most devastating World War (WWII) has "only" claimed approximately 60 million dead!![20]

We are dealing with BIG numbers, here.

Seven Continents:

Where are the other 1½ billion killed in the final overlap? (Please excuse the morbid details, there really is a point to this number counting.) I believe this is "the big deal" mentioned in Revelation 17 & 18. Forgive me, but this simply *must* refer to more than the destruction of the Vatican, and it must be more carefully considered. For we must note that while many Protestants have been killed by this mother of all harlots, there are many more in bed with her, by time Antichrist comes fully into power. So, is "Babylon" the city that sits on seven hills, or seven *mountains* as Revelation 17:9 states?

Rome does sit on seven hills. Yet, the economy described in the terminal overlap (Revelation thirteen through nineteen) is a *global* economy. Is it possible that God's perception of our world may actually transcend the European ego?[21] The Babylon of Revelation seventeen and eighteen, therefore, must sit upon seven mountains *much larger* than those surrounding Rome. For Mystery Babylon sits upon . . . seven continents.

Put another way, the Green Horse will be allowed to wreak its greatest havoc when Mystery Babylon is to be extinguished. For God's wrath, is something to be reckoned with.

> And great Babylon was remembered before God, to give her the cup of the wine of the fierceness of His wrath.
>
> Revelation 16:19

It is stated three times[22] that such destruction will take place within only one hour—originally inconceivable, but now made quite possible, given the full scope of what we now know of weapons of mass destruction (a concept that should truly make our eyes water!!). Scripture states that God will place it within the hearts of the world leaders to trigger this conflagration (Rev. 17:17)—and then, remorse.

> "The kings of the earth who committed fornication and lived luxuriously with her will weep and lament for her, when they see the smoke of her burning,
>
> "standing at a distance for fear of her torment, saying, 'Alas, alas, that great city Babylon, that mighty city! For in one hour your judgment has come.'
>
> "And the merchants of the earth will weep and mourn over her, for no one buys their merchandise anymore:
>
> "merchandise of gold and silver, precious stones and pearls, fine linen and purple, silk and scarlet, every kind of citron wood, every kind of object of ivory, every kind of object of most precious wood, bronze, iron, and marble;

"and cinnamon and incense, fragrant oil and frankincense,
wine and oil, fine flour and wheat, cattle and sheep, horses
and chariots, and bodies and souls of men."

Revelation 18:9-13

Remember these things, the next time you hear of Iranian
President Mahmoud Ahmadinejad's desire to acquire (and use)
WMDs. Remember, also, that there are segments within Islam (of
which Mr. Ahmadinejad participates)—expecting just such a conflagration to initiate the final appearance of an Islamic messiah,
called the 12th Mahdi.[23] Most are familiar with Islamic radicals
referring to Israel as the "little Satan"—which the nations of the
world attempt to destroy in the Battle of Armageddon. That's in
Revelation 19. Do we first see a destruction that includes the
"Great Satan" in Revelation 18?

What could possibly precipitate such an awesome (and awful)
event? This is where the symbolism of Revelation's earlier chapters becomes significant. For if there is anything that Christians
know, it is this: that God does not execute judgment (or allow it to
be executed) simply to see a fireworks display! "I have no pleasure
in the death of the wicked," the Lord of Glory says, "but that the
wicked turn from his way and live."[24]

Where shall we start digging, into this "onion" for truth? Indeed, when one digs deep enough, it starts to get sweet. Time
grows sweeter as we dig into God's chronometers: Sweetened by
the love of God, and the power of His Holy Spirit. It is here that
we must continue our search and journey into John's secrets: into

64

the very heart of God's love for His people. Here, we will find the 3½ clocks in which are manifest some of God's greatest plans for His own.

At the opening of this section, it was mentioned that the overlapping visions assure us that the destruction of a *mere* 500 million souls (1/12 of the world's population) is not overlooked by John's Revelation. Actually, at issue is much more than that number—for, if there were no overlaps, there would be no limiting of human destruction to 1/3 of the world's population. For, to honestly interpret Bible prophecy, we would then have to *add* the 1/4 of humankind destroyed in Revelation six, to the 1/3 found in Revelation nine.

This would result in *over one-half* of the earth's population being devastated by world-wide disaster! I know that we are accustomed to the idea of widespread destruction, when thinking "Apocalypse," but the God of the Bible has great interest in limiting devastation—even in a time of great judgment and wrath. For, consider this: If *over one half* of the planet's inhabitants die from nuclear holocaust and disease . . . how will the *other half* survive (Matt. 24:22)? It seems unreasonable, therefore, to make use of such careless math, by disregarding the presence of Revelation's overlaps.

Yet . . .if you are like most persons of sanity and reason, there is just the possibility you may be saying to yourself. "Is there no hope of averting such horror?"

"Why must we go through so much devastation?"

"What is it, that the Lord is getting at? Why is it that we have been able to enjoy such peace and affluence, up until now, only to have it all threatened by 9/11—and worst, in the coming years?"

→First, it *is* being "threatened" and more.

Secondly, let it be stated clearly that the events in the Middle East are not going to "Go away" simply because we wish for them to vanish. Members of congress have accused the President of living in a dream world, in reference to fighting a War on Terror. Let us set the record straight: those who believe that we can simply bat our eyes, pull out our troops, and go back to the "old days" that existed just after the Berlin Wall fell are truly sleeping in La-la land. If the US bails out of Iraq, such *will not* appease the "Green Horse."[25] If you get nothing else out of this book, get this: the prospect of judgment is real. Our world *is* rushing to an appointment with destiny, whether you and I hide our heads in the sand, or not.

Earlier, it was stated that it is because of freedom that there is some weakness within our social framework. In another sense, the response of our young men and women in uniform has been most admirable in the way they have risen to the challenge presented by 9/11—their willingness to go to Iraq, for example, to drive a stake in the ground—is quite noble. They were only too willing to attempt to give to the Iraqis, what we have enjoyed for so long, within the West.

Yet, it must again be emphasized that what we have enjoyed is not something that can be transplanted at the point of a gun, as Islamic Sharia law may be, through sectarian violence. Islam may "advance" in this manner, Christian freedoms may not. The American Revolution, as we shall see, was not simply a revolt, or uprising. It was an experiment engaging a much higher principle, of "freedom." Such freedom is, in itself, only found within the Christian gospel (John 8:36).

We will *never* succeed in transplanting what we have in the US by military efforts alone, especially within the domain of the Green Horse. Success in Japan, at the end of WWII came at a high price, with the detonation of a nuclear device. Japan was then devastated, not only militarily, but morally (and, to some degree, religiously) by its failure to dominate the Pacific Ocean. Further, there was the extraordinary "Korean experiment" wherein extensive ministry was lavished on Korean, Christian, orphanages—which is paying extensive dividends, today. Such is not the case in Iraq, where Muslims perceive themselves to be morally superior to a degenerate, Western world, and consider it a sign of dishonor to surrender to our way of life and system of government. Thus what we are engaged in, is as much a moral conflict, as a military one.

→It is this moral aspect, that the modern western world has displayed little stomach for. Nor are the Iraqis as open, to overt Christian missionary activities (as in Korea). Such a door could only be opened, I am certain, by extensive prayer and fasting.

I say again, there is no solving or escaping these issues, except through prayer.

As we shall all soon see, there is Another whom we will have to give answer to, who ultimately controls the Green Horse. He also takes a dim view of Western depravity. Thus, if the Lord does not save us, how may we expect to win such a war, or to avert the pending judgments upon our land???

Please secure these matters firmly in your heart and mind, as we now continue our discovery into one of the most amazing keys to Bible prophecy: its prophetic "clocks." Yet no matter how intriguing these issues may become, we must always keep our perspective in balance from Heaven's grandstands—as well from the earth's boiling pot.

Welcome, to the 3½ clocks.

Chapter 4:

WHAT (3½) CLOCKS ARE THESE?

And I further answered and said to him, "What are these **two olive branches** that drip into the receptacles of the <u>two gold pipes from which the golden oil drains</u>?" . . . .

So he said, "These are the two [sons of oil][26], who stand beside the Lord of the whole earth."

Zechariah 4:12,14 [emphasis added]

"And I will give power to my two witnesses, and they will prophesy <u>one thousand two hundred and sixty days</u>, <u>clothed in sackcloth</u>."

These are the **two olive trees** . . . standing before the God of the earth.

Revelation 11:3,4 [emphasis added]

What an interesting contrast, between *golden oil* and sackcloth! Before, they were branches, now they are trees! They are obviously not the ten virgins, for they do not sleep, they *stand*.

Nor are they apathetic. They actively seek God's Presence!

Yet, what a contrast. Whatever does it mean? It forces the mind to consider the mix between a church that is rich, in her own mind, and those truly poor in spirit, and empowered. —Almost like the difference between fool's gold, and real gold: or between foolish virgins, and virgins so wise, that they never fall asleep at the wheel. . . .

To this point we have embarked on considering the churning of human events relating to those ten virgins who fall asleep while awaiting the Lord's return past midnight. We have not yet examined this parable in detail. We will do so (you guessed it) in the next section. Yet, we have already come to realize that in the darkness of that hour, an event transpires that places half of them at risk. It is not a physical devastation, as outlined in our last chapter, but an eternal danger, relating to the human soul. Yes, as difficult as it may be to fathom, there are actually issues more intense than those of "saving the planet!" Yet the same Scriptures that forecast the coming apocalypse also promise a rejuvenation of our troubled world, after Christ appears in the skies.

For when Jesus Christ descends to begin reigning, His kingdom *will* then be "of this world!"

Yet how may ours be a pleasant journey, while peering through onion peels (and overlaps) to detect the future of the US—as we now suspect it? It's enough to keep us awake in the night! (Perhaps, even on our knees . . .)

A bit later, we must peek into Heaven's prayer chamber, to see the outflow of spiritual judgments directed out *towards* our world. As they at first occur almost without notice, we observe them progress steadily towards the fifth, and then next to last, trumpet. As we continue to stand by, we realize that Heaven is not impotent, at all—its just that earth's hapless inhabitants do not, at first, realize what we are losing, as our foundations continue to be destroyed. Eventually, however, we begin to notice events heating up to such a fevered degree that even the most feckless among us starts to sit up and take notice.

Within the next section we will also witness similar trends evident through projections served upon seven churches. We will observe the stated mission of the four horsemen of the Apocalypse, as well.

We will deal with the Pale-Green Horse, separately.

For now, we will be content with a serious examination of the 3½ clocks—those time capsules that will be remembered throughout Eternity as the Church Age in which the Lord of glory first came to redeem His people—before returning to rescue us from the perils of a blaspheming and unrepentant world, running madly after a mad man, commonly called

the Antichrist.

Through most of this, the world about us will remain sound asleep; determined not to awaken to the fact that it is God (not Mother Nature) who is displeased with us. Then, mid point between the third phase, the virgins do finally awaken. While others continue to sleep, therefore, let us continue digging into the Book—to discover that these "3½ clocks" are actually part of a much older prophecy.

They are part of a group of sevens, projected from the Old Testament. It will help to notice that 3½ fits very neatly into the number seven (7), two times . . . .

When He came the First Time:

When Christ came the first time, the prophets stated His coming would avert a world wide tragedy emerging from moral collapse. You might say that God's people were "asleep" at the wheel in that time, as well. This moral breakdown, it was prophesied, would have forced the Lord to pronounce a decimating curse upon the earth (Malachi 4:6). Yet that curse was never issued. In fact, so definite was the arrival of the Messiah to be, that an earlier prophet had already given a coded numerical projection of exactly when the Messiah would arrive. Known as the "seventy weeks" prophecy, this projection outlined seventy *sevens* (most often translated "weeks" because a week has seven days)—the last of which includes the rise of the Antichrist . . . and then the return of Christ.

The prophet, Daniel, living in Babylon during the time of Israel's first captivity (during a sort of Old Testament diaspora) is the one responsible for conveying this projection. This amazing prophecy, given to him by the angel Gabriel, provided a prediction of future events that rounds out the entire program of God for Israel, while also completing the plan for redeeming *all* of His people. The relevant text relating to Christ's *first* coming reads:

"Know therefore and understand, That from the going forth of the command To restore and build Jerusalem Until Messiah the Prince, There shall be seven [7] weeks and sixty-two [62] weeks; The street shall be built again, and the wall, Even in troublesome times."

Daniel 9:25 [emphasis added]

The capstone (the seventieth "week") would follow later, in verse 27. [27] This last floating "week," as we shall see, "lands" in our final generation. The point here, is that the above sixty-nine weeks (7 + 62 weeks) were fulfilled *to the letter* when calculating from the time of the decree (in Nehemiah 2:6) to Christ's triumphal entry into Jerusalem on Palm Sunday (483 years of 360 day years). [28]

However, in the Lord's *second* coming, we have no such time arrow, pointing through the centuries. Contrariwise, Christ specifically warned against trying to calculate the exact day or hour of His returning (Matthew 24:36). Instead, we have that "floating week" and . . . the 3½ clocks. —Two of which, fit into that final "seven" (2 x 3½ = 7) of Daniel's prophecy.

These "3½ clocks" are described, with startling detail, in John's eleventh chapter of Revelation. As was noted in our last chapter, these "clocks" will also be overlapped and further amplified within John's twelfth chapter.

A Special Overlap:

Continuing to turn our attention towards John's Apocalypse therefore, we dive back into the "onion skins" to discover spiritual keys that are useful for unlocking the more literal, or physical, part of John's Revelation. Yes, we really are about to dig into those 3½ clocks! Yet, so close is this overlap to the surface that the apostle makes the very unusual move of issuing a caveat to readers to warn that this particular passage *must* be applied in a spiritual manner. Thus, in the eighth verse of this amazing section, the apostle affirms that the main characters within this part of the vision (accomplished by two witnesses) will suffer martyrdom in such a manner that:

> . . . their dead bodies will lie in the street of the great city which spiritually is called Sodom and Egypt, where also our Lord was crucified.
>
> Vs. 8 [emphasis added]

This really is an unusual notation for John to make, is it not (in a prophecy *filled* with symbols)? Why mention that its name is a spiritual name, at all? Just how unusual this is, may be better appreciated when later considering the concept of a world church that will actually be *supporting* the Antichrist. There, the apostate church is code named: "MYSTERY, BABYLON THE GREAT, THE MOTHER OF HARLOTS AND OF THE ABOMINATIONS

OF THE EARTH" (Rev. 17:5). Even though this mysterious "Babylon," is obviously intended as a code name for another location on the planet, it is interesting to note that the apostle does not find it necessary to inform the reader that Babylon is a *spiritual* reality. Yet He does take the time to say this, in Revelation's eleventh chapter!

In other words the Lord, knowing the danger of misinterpreting this overlapping vision in a literal and physical manner— makes the unusual step of informing the reader that this chapter is indeed symbolic! I constantly find it necessary to remember this as well, for I have spent many unnecessary hours trying to make physical applications to this chapter, as have others. We must *force* ourselves to remember this warning: this is a spiritual overlap!

You may recall, that we noted last chapter, that the outer "onion skins" focus on the terminal generation. Like a trail of star dust, these outer overlaps come out of the past and into our present, clustering about the terminal generation. Inner overlaps tend to be like marked rulers, ticking off specific eras and epochs from the 1st century up to our own. We will find the letters to the seven churches displaying a picture of the entire history of the church, for example, with a rather detailed message.

We have already stated that the last two, of the seven letters, are addressed to Philadelphia and Laodicea.

- Laodicea (the lukewarm church) sleeps up until the Midnight Cry.

- Philadelphia, with her open door, was predominant until Israel returned to her land.

The issues of the seven church ages (or phases) will be uncovered within the next section on spiritual conflict (our third section, begins the resolution . . .). We must be careful to remind ourselves of the interrelationship of these overlaps: of the outer ones, being like star dust sprinkling out of our past and clustering in our present. Of the inner overlaps acting like rulers, spacing out the epochs: for these inner (less obvious) layers of our "onion" openly span *the entire church age*. Yet, their most colorful overlap, seems to have a mind of its own, neither clustering from the past into the present, nor following a more strict ruler-like rigidity. For the "clocks" follow the flexibility of their "3½"s . . . .

This is the point we opened with, in our first chapter, when first introducing the 3½ clocks. In the span of Christian history, stretching from Christ's first coming, to His second—the first 3½ clock represents:

- The era of the Gentile church.

- The second, covers a time of restoration.

- The final one, of Tribulation.

Now, to consider two questions:

First query:

When considering the Church going through great trial—is it really the Lord's intent for the Church to greet Him in the sky as a limp-wristed, watered down, banal assembly of believers—barely limping into eternity??

Second question:

Since the Lord's intention has obviously been to revive the *physical* nation of Israel, in a physical restoration, is it unreason-

74

able to expect for Him to plan a *spiritual* restoration for spiritual Israel, as well? For he is not a Jew who is one outwardly, only, but one who is circumcised in the heart and spirit.[29] We must be very careful here, not to exclude either one branch, or the other. For, as the apostle to the Gentiles points out, the Gentile church has actually been grafted into the stock of the Jewish tree. Salvation *is* of the Jews.[30] Jesus, after all, did come as the Messiah to the Jewish nation.[31] Therefore, Paul cautions his Gentile audience to be very careful not to disrespect the tree into which we have now become a part!

> do not boast against the branches. But if you do boast, remember that you do not support the root, but the root supports you.
>
> You will say then, "Branches were broken off that I might be grafted in."
>
> Well said. Because of unbelief they were broken off, and you stand by faith. Do not be haughty, but fear.
>
> For if God did not spare the natural branches, He may not spare you either.
>
> Romans 11:18-21

Now, remember my question: Is it not logical for the Lord—even within the context of judgment—to make provision for restoration of the Church, as well, when restoring natural Israel? Please consider this question, as you read the next verse (one of the most remarkable, in this respect) recorded within the very same context as the verses quoted above. Here, the apostle to the Gentiles asks his readers, almost in a dream:

> For if [Israel's] being cast away is the reconciling of the world, what will their acceptance be but life from the dead?
>
> Romans 11:15

Life from the dead! For who? For themselves and the Gentile world!!

A Love Story:

What I propose within this section, therefore, is that the eleventh chapter of John's Revelation is actually a love story. It is a view of the church age, and of the final tribulation, from Heaven's perspective. This is Heaven's cheering section.

> "And I will give power to my two witnesses, and they will prophesy <u>one thousand two hundred and sixty days</u>, clothed in sackcloth."
>
> Revelation 11:3 [emphasis added]

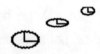

The "3½ clocks"

The 1260 days mentioned above is actually the *second* 3½ clock of this eleventh chapter. It is derived from the fact that dividing 360 into 1260 comes out to 3½ years. The 360 day prophetic year is most easily derived from the Genesis account of the flood, wherein we are told that the flood started on the 17th day of the 2nd month, and that Noah's ark later rested <u>150 days later</u>, on the Mountains of Ararat on the 17th day of the 7th month (the second, subtracted from the seventh= five months).[32] In other words, each of those <u>five months</u> had exactly <u>thirty days</u>. None of the months fluctuated in length, as ours do, within a modern calendar.

A full prophetic year, therefore, lasts for 360 days (12 months x 30 days).

Making use of this prophetic year (of 360 days) allows us to observe some rather amazing patterns in John's eleventh, through thirteenth, chapters. For although we will not actually see another 1260 day "clock" until the twelfth chapter, we are introduced to two other 3½s within this eleventh. In each case (within this over-lap, and within the one beginning in chapter twelve) *the 3½ clocks appear in groups of three*. Briefly, they are arranged as:

Revelation eleven:

- vs 2 – Forty-two months (3½ years)
- vs. 3 – 1260 days (3½ years)
- vs. 9 – 3½ days

Revelation twelve & thirteen:

- 12:6 – 1260 days (3½ years)
- 12:14 – time, times & half a time (1 + 2 + ½ = 3½)
- 13:5 – forty-two months (3½ years)

I have used the term "3½ clocks" because it is important to remember that these time references are themselves *symbols*. That is, they are God's time pieces, counting down periods of time or-dained by God in which *certain events must take place*. In the sounding of the trumpets, and riding of the four horsemen, we will see prophecy dependent upon external events. Here, we see events dependent upon God's time table, alone.

This is also similar to the way in which we plan the events of our own lives, is it not? For example, you may plan to go to the store to buy only those things that are on sale. (Thus, your plans are contingent upon a sale taking place.) You may also have an appointment to see the dentist, at 11:00 AM. (A fixed time limit for your trip to the Mall.) Therefore, you can only participate in a blue light special that takes place before eleven o'clock! (Both conditions being met: of a time limit, and of a shopping goal that was set.)

In the Lord's case, however, He also controls when that "blue light special" takes place! He also knows the end from the beginning. Further, He controls when the store closes down. . . .

The mystery of the temple:

These clocks also allow us to gain a special insight into the temple where the abomination of desolation (at the midnight cry) will take place. Further, as we look at the way the clocks are named (months, days, time & times) we begin to suspect that even these names have a meaning. For months are longer than days. In the first set of "clocks" therefore, the first 3½ clock is designed to express a prolonged period of time within church history. In it he describes the temple:

> * Then I was given a reed like a measuring rod. And the angel stood, saying, "Rise and measure the temple of God, the altar, and those who worship there."
>
> "But leave out the court which is outside the temple, and do not measure it, for it has been given to the Gentiles. And they will tread the holy city underfoot for <u>forty-two months</u>."
>
> vss. 1, 2 [emphasis added]

As we shall see more clearly, when later examining the second set of clocks (in Rev. 12 & 13) this time frame represents the church age, from the time of Christ, up through the middle ages and Reformation, until the returning of the nation of Israel. The "holy city" (Jerusalem) was completely under Gentile control until Israel reclaimed it during the 1967 war. There is the possibility that we could time the final two clocks, therefore, from the re-claiming of Jerusalem, instead of from the re-founding of the na-tion of Israel—but we shall not, for it is in the *budding* of the fig tree, that the count down begins.[33]

The nation of Israel need not be fully grown.

Some also propose that this eleventh chapter also refers to the rebuilding of the temple, in Israel. There are major problems, with this view, however:

- John was told to measure the temple, in the *present tense*. The physical temple was destroyed in AD 70. This vision was given in approximately 90 AD.

- There is *no mention* of the temple being rebuilt. Since the temple had been destroyed, reference to a *physical* temple would have to first make note of such a rebuilding (as was the case in a parallel prophecy[34]).

- Temple sacrifice had been superceded (abolished) at the Cross, as its veil was ripped from its most holy place (Matt. 27:51). When the apostle Paul sought to make use of it, during his ministry, the Lord *forcibly* aborted his intended offering of animal sacrifice (Acts 21:26-31).[35]

Yet in all fairness, it must be noted that there is very good rea-son for us to be looking for a rebuilding of the temple, prior to Christ's returning. For the same passage that has Paul warning that the falling away must first take place [†]—also states that when the

---

[†] We will cover this issue, of the falling away, within the next section, as well.

Antichrist *does* arrive, he will be a man who, "opposes and exalts himself above all that is called God or that is worshiped, so that he sits as God in the temple of God, showing himself that he is God" (II Thessalonians 2:4).

This will be no small event!

It is, in fact, related to the Midnight Cry.

It is the boiling point.

Returning to basic principles, while remembering that events critical to the salvation of our souls will always be clearly outlined within Scripture, we must now turn to the best commentary on prophecy available to us: the Bible itself. Please note the wording, and context, of the verses quoted earlier (by the star), and that it clearly implies that:

- The temple already existed while John was having his vision, and—

- It had been (or was already in process of being) built in his lifetime.

- There is a command to also measure *those who worship there*

- The outer court was *being trodden down*/was under the control of, the Gentiles.

This last aspect of the vision at first seems rather unusual, given the fact that John has been called up into Heaven to view these events (Rev. 4:1,2). This reference to the temple's outer court being trodden down by non-believing Gentiles, therefore, must refer to the disrespect that men on earth hold, for things regarded as sacred in Heaven (as, for example, when people take the Lord's name in vain).

Another, valid, perspective would hold that the "treading down" of the outer court represents the general disrespect that non-believers hold for . . . the church. This view has weight, because of the fact that the "outer court" was reserved for the un-clean/Gentiles, and it is now through the doorway of *the church* that men and women may enter into *Heaven's temple*, and the true worship of God.

What church is this?

It is the church of the living God, made up of all true believers.

What *temple* is this?

It also is the Church, to which other passages in the New Testament clearly allude. (This is one reason that John is told to measure "those who worship there." If measuring an edifice, why also measure those who walk in and out of its doors? In this case, the answer becomes obvious: It is because the people in the church *are* the temple of the living God (I Cor. 3:16,17). Therefore we may also *measure the people* in order to measure the temple!

These truths are absolutely central to our understanding of the Midnight Cry, and we must explore them more fully after laying a little more groundwork. For now, please note that the two remaining 3½ clocks refer to the activity of two witnesses, also referred to (in the original Hebrew) as the two "sons of oil" in the writings of an Old Testament prophet, named Zechariah.

The Sons of Oil:

You will notice, in our succeeding study, that in contrast to the five wise virgins (with their extra[36] oil in their lamps) there are others, with flowing oil. These sons of oil are *connected to the pipeline.* They are first mentioned in Zechariah's prophecy.

> Then I answered and said to him, "What are these two olive trees; at the right of <u>the lampstand</u> and at its left?"
>
> And I further answered and said to him, "What are these two olive branches that drip into the receptacles of the <u>two gold pipes from which the golden oil drains</u>?"
>
> Then he answered me and said, "Do you not know what these are?" And I said, "No, my lord."
>
> So he said, "These are the two [sons of oil], who stand beside the Lord of the whole earth."
>
> Zechariah 4:12-14 [emphasis added]

You will notice that I've not only underlined the "pipeline" from which the oil drains, but also drawn attention to the *lamp stand.* This is because this passage, which runs parallel to Revelation's eleventh chapter, has something missing:

A second lamp stand.

Now, returning to John's description of the two witnesses (in the New Testament version of the two anointed ones, or "sons of oil")—we notice the inclusion of a *second* lamp stand.

> "And I will give power to my two witnesses, and they will prophesy one thousand two hundred and sixty days, clothed in sackcloth."
>
> These are the two olive trees and the <u>two lampstands</u> standing before the God of the earth.
>
> Revelation 11:3,4 [emphasis added]

The second lamp stand:

The lamp stand (Menorah) through which oil flows to give light, represents a living covenant between God and His people. In the Old Testament, there were "other sheep"[37] who on rare occasions came to know the living God (as with Balaam,[38] for example). These other sheep, however, did not have the covenant promises, that Israel had. Now, in the New Testament, Gentiles may have the same full rights and provisions of a covenant people. This is, in fact, the whole point and purpose of the temple that is displayed within this chapter, as was affirmed by the first church council in Jerusalem.

In other words, the second lamp stand represents God's full covenant provision for Gentiles who come to Him by faith in the Jewish Messiah, Jesus Christ.[39] The menorah was made by hand, at instructions given by God to Moses.[40] In this, there is the demonstration of special communion between God and man, in bringing light into the world. In the Old Testament, it was hidden under a bushel (within the temple). For the covenant was with Israel, alone. Within the New Covenant (New Testament), it is to be shown, and allowed to shine out, into all the world. Salvation is through the Jews, and now also fully offered to the Gentiles.[41] As the Jerusalem council notes about the *rebuilding of the temple*:†

> "And with this the words of the prophets agree, just as it is written:
>
> 'After this I will return And will rebuild the tabernacle of David, which has fallen down; I will rebuild its ruins, And I will set it up;

---

† Some may note that the following passage is inferior to a *temple* in the sense that it is a tent, or temporary structure. My response is that believers' bodies are also tents (II Cor. 5:1) and tabernacles (I Cor. 3:16)—and that Christ, Himself, called His body . . . a temple (John 2:19). So I ask you, Which is more glorious?

So that the rest of mankind may seek the LORD, Even all the Gentiles who are called by My name, Says the LORD who does all these things.'

"Known to God from eternity are all His works."

Acts 15:15-18 [emphasis added]

Checking the context of the above verses verifies that what is being spoken of here is indeed the inclusion of Gentiles into the church of the living God (see also I Pet. 2:5 & I Cor. 3:16).

Please do not forget what we have covered within this very important chapter. We have looked at keys—not all of them, but certainly at key issues that are normally left outside of the range of what is usually considered, when studying Bible prophecy in this closing hour. We might even say that, as John was invited up into Heaven, we have been riding piggy-back to view these matters along with him.

Both of these key topics: of Revelation's overlaps, and of the 3½ clocks, will be revisited as we continue our study. As may already be seen, there is good reason for calling them "keys" to the Apocalypse. For one thing, the two lamp stands in John's eleventh chapter, make the issue of God's dealing with Israel and the Church much clearer. We can see that God is indeed dealing with these two branches of the same olive tree in somewhat different manners.

→With Israel, there are physical aspects yet to be fulfilled (some, coming into full fruition only within the millennium, after Christ's returning) and with the Church, God yet has a plan for restoration, through "the sons of oil." This last point will have to wait a bit, until we uncover it. There are, as one may suspect, a few surprises here, as well.

We have viewed a vast expanse of prophecy: spanning both the entire church age, and our terminal generation. How should we now consider these matters, to apply them to everyday living? How may we appropriate these issues, or understand the purposes for which this clash of titanic powers is being unleashed? Of course, we could do no better, than to turn our attention to the Lord of Creation, Himself, to first adjust our view of Him as we approach the end of the age, as we now know it.

For while other ancient writings tend to become outdated, as we grow more advanced through science and technology, the Bible remains timeless (literally, as we shall see) and is always one step ahead of us. The God of the Bible, Himself so beyond us, and so often the subject of debate—is a truly wise and infinite ruler.

Thus, we humbly turn now, to this incredible triune God, reigning in the Control Room of all Creation.

Welcome, to the Throne Room of the Universe:

Chapter 5:

THRONE ROOM
OF THE UNIVERSE

. . .thus says the High and Lofty One Who inhabits eternity, whose name is Holy: "I dwell in the high and holy place, With him who has a contrite and humble spirit, To revive the spirit of the humble, And to revive the heart of the contrite ones."

Isaiah 57:15

Disclaimer:

Jesus warned believers of the first century that there were some things they could not understand, or receive in their day. Within this context some may be astonished to realize that while there has been an explosion in scientific advance and of general knowledge—the God of the Bible is still well ahead of us, and more than able to perform His Word.[†] However, let us be careful not to allow our imaginations "run away with us," or go "over the edge." Nothing you are about to read is to be taken as an invitation to adopt the view that we may now "understand" God, or that UFOs or other strange phenomena "really explain" what the Bible is all about. To the contrary, UFOs, I am convinced, are intentionally presented as enigmas because of their true source. They continually present themselves in a manner designed to seduce the in-

---

[†] Isaiah 55: 8-11!

tellect and enslave the imagination, while preferring to remain in the Dark . . . as does someone else the Spirit filled Christian is familiar with.[42]

For ourselves, Christians approach, and dwell in the Light where God Himself lives. It is here, in His Light, that we will meet the Triune God, in the Throne Room of the Universe.

Who is this Jesus? Even Who the Bible says He is. He is the image of the invisible God. He is the Son of the Blessed: The Son of God.

Our Creator.

Let us now consider, the Holy Trinity.

First: Who He is.

A responsible consideration of this matter requires that we quote several passages in full, before attempting this question.

"I am the way, the truth, and the life. No one comes to the Father except through Me.

"If you had known Me, you would have known My Father also; and from now on you know Him and have seen Him.".

John 14:6,7

[Jesus] is the image of the invisible God . . . .

Colossians 1:15

[Jesus] being the brightness of His glory and the express image of His person, and upholding all things by the word of

His power, when He had by Himself purged our sins, sat down at the right hand of the Majesty on high,

Hebrews 1:3

"And I will pray the Father, and He will give you another Helper, that He may abide with you forever; the Spirit of truth, whom the world cannot receive, because it neither sees Him nor knows Him; but you know Him, for He dwells with you and will be in you.

"I will not leave you orphans; I will come to you."

John 14:16-18

Above are several, of many, quotes found within Scripture that support the view that God is a Triune God. In the words of Nicodemus, many are asking themselves, "How can these things be?" Yet, as with Jesus speaking to the ruler on that fateful night, there are times when the answer to a paradox may dawn upon us with such clarity that it seems almost embarrassing.

→ An examination of the first and second quotes, above, may lead some readers to the conclusion that Jesus and the Father are the *same person*. Yet Trinitarian belief holds to three persons existing in one God (or Godhead – Col. 2:9). Since we think of a person as an individual, however . . .how can three persons be one?? Jesus *forces* us to consider this question, as He allows us to listen in on Him praying to the Father.

Jesus requests, of the Father, for us (Christians):

"that <u>they all may be one</u>, as <u>You, Father, are in Me, and I in You</u>; that they also may be one in Us, that the world may believe that You sent Me.

John 17:21 (emphasis added)

Above, the pronoun "they" refers to us as believers. The words "as You, Father, are in Me, and I in You"—refers to the Godhead. There is the definite implication that individuals may become fully united as one (even as God is, through the Father, Son, and Holy Spirit). How may this be???

Let us consider a solution so simple that, at first, it seems embarrassing. Consider the moral opposite, for a moment, of someone totally opposed to God—a person "possessed." May there not be many personalities (demons) within that individual? So you have one man walking down the street, having many personalities within the same body.

The difference with demon possession,[43] however, is that these personalities are both confused and divided (the clear implication of Mk. 3:26, I Cor. 14:33). They are not united, and are certainly not at peace—either within the body, or among themselves.[44]

Yet, it *is* one man walking down the street.

One man, having many personalities. We cannot deny this.

We need not "fuzz our brains" to understand this truth. It is simply the way we are made: after the image, and in the likeness, of the God of Heaven (Genesis 1:26).

However, we must be careful about thinking that we fully "understand" God. We must ever approach Him with complete humility. Our Lord, Christ, when speaking about his own power and greatness, had a tendency of demonstrating this same quality (we may call it modesty). Do you remember His statement about us being able to do greater things than He (Jn. 14:12)? How many persons have you met who have walked on water, lately? How about those who have calmed seas, or stopped hurricanes at will? You see what I mean.

89

We must be careful of how we speak about Jesus, or even think about Him. His "modesty" can sometimes be disarming. We must force ourselves to remember just who He is.

And the scope of His power.

Reflections of His power:

In astrophysics, a "light year" refers not to a period of time, but to a distance covered in stellar space. This is the distance required for light to travel within a vacuum for one year: approximately six trillion miles (or ~ 9 ½ trillion kilometers). As an appreciation of the distances spanned by such an experience: our sun is a mere 93 million miles from earth, requiring less than 8 ½ minutes for light to traverse the distance. . . .

As one may expect, everything about outer space tends to be "large:" even its concepts regarding power and destruction. When stars go "bang" within the universe, the explosion is *very* big: especially when stars die. Stars give us light, but when they fail/collapse the result is a super nova and black hole: first giving incredible light, and then incredible darkness—both accompanied by great destruction. When **very** large stars die (or twin stars collapse) they experience what is called a "gamma ray burst"—an explosion of power so awesome that its power would utterly wipe out our planet and all of life upon it should such an event occur anywhere in the neighborhood of our *galaxy* at a distance closer than *1500* light years away—if aimed in our direction. Yet these events have been observed to take place at a fairly regular intervals—mostly on the other side of the universe.[45] Even from outer space, therefore, the God of Creation is incredibly gracious.

There are uncounted trillions of stars in the universe, and trillions of cells within the human body. The God of Creation has demonstrated His ability to make things incredibly big, small, and complex. Every human being is a micro-universe—and yet God, Himself, spans the full universe of creation, while living in a "place" called eternity. It is this last point, that we will now explore: how God rules.

God's governance, and rule, over the universe:

For the rest of our discussion, we will simply "connect some dots" while endeavoring to explain how the three Persons of the Triune Godhead: Father, Son, and Holy Spirit—work together in perfect harmony to run a universe more vast and all encompassing than most of us even imagine. Let us now consider the existence of God reigning within three distinct dimensions, as three distinct personalities.

What follows now, is an expansion of a tract on this subject, posted on the ministry web-site.[46]

ONLY THE TRINITY MAY EXPLAIN THIS . . .

There are certain things that only the Trinity can explain, and certain tasks that only the Triune God may accomplish. Consider, for example, a question that Jesus asked the most learned religious leaders in Israel: "How is it possible for David to say of Christ, 'The Lord said unto my Lord, sit on my right hand, until I make your enemies your footstool?' " Focusing on one problem within the text, He then asks, "If David then calls Him 'Lord,' how is He his Son?" (Matthew 22:44,45).

They could understand Christ being the son of David (David's descendant -Isaiah 55:3) but how could David's descendant also be his "Lord"?? Worst (what they really didn't want to think about) was the question, "How could David's Lord . . . have a Lord?"

That's like saying, "God said to my God..."

How can God speak to God?? Does not Scripture say, "Hear, O Israel: The Lord our God is one Lord" (Deut. 6:4??) and— what of wise, King Solomon's, description of God:

> ... Behold, the heaven and the heaven of heavens cannot contain thee;
>
> . . .
>
> . . . Do not I fill heaven and earth? says the Lord.
>
> II Chron. 6:16, Jeremiah 23:24

and John, in his glorious gospel declares,

> No one has seen God at any time. The only begotten Son, who is in the bosom of the Father, He has declared Him.
>
> John 1:18

Ah, so that's it!

But, can it be? Can it? Can it be that all we know of God, is through the Son? Then, it was He whom Moses saw in the mount, when seeing God's back (Exodus 33:23, 34:5-7). It was He, whom Abraham spoke to, while pleading for the lives of those in Sodom (Genesis 18:20-25) and it was He, whom the king saw in the fire with the three Hebrew boys (Daniel 3:25)!

Then, it really is true, what the Old Testament prophet recorded of Him, in his writings:

> "Come near to <u>Me</u>, hear this: I have not spoken in secret from the beginning; From the time that it was, I was there. And now the <u>Lord GOD and His Spirit Have sent Me</u>."
>
> Isaiah 48:16 [emphasis added]

Incredible! The LORD God (the Father) and his Spirit (the Holy Spirit), have[47] sent our Lord (Christ) into the world to deliver us –and that's Old Testament!

> For unto us a child is born, unto us a son is given: and the
> government shall be upon his shoulder: and his name shall
> be called Wonderful,
> Counselor,
> The mighty God,
> The everlasting Father,
> The Prince of Peace
>
> Isaiah 9:6

So then, Jesus really is God?

Yes! -and before you ask another question, consider this. If God were only like a man, sitting on a throne in the sky —how could He ever answer your prayer? If He took time to solve your problem, and something went awry in a galaxy at the other end of the universe . . . would it simply have to go hay wire, while He stopped to answer you?

How could He answer your prayer, and your neighbor's at the same time? How may He keep tabs on the developing DNA in your mother's womb (Psalm 139:16) . . . while at the same time be filling heaven and earth? In fact, Scripture says that God is so high that He actually has to humble Himself to behold events taking place in Heaven (Psalm 113:6)! How is all of this possible?

Of course, we cannot answer all such questions, here. God is quite beyond us (Isaiah 55:8,9). Yet, it is helpful to realize that the God of the Bible lives in a universe much larger than most of us conceive of.

God's universe, you see, also includes a "place" called "eternity."

> For thus says the high and lofty One who inhabits eternity,
> whose name is Holy; I dwell in the high and holy place, with
> him also who is of a contrite and humble spirit,...

> Isaiah 57:15

This "place," made by Jesus (John 1:3) is what we would generally call another dimension. It is a "place" which transcends time and space. In this "place," "That which hath been is now; and that which is to be hath already been; and God requireth that which is past." (Ecclesiastes 3:15 AV). In other words, the past, present, and the future—are all accessible in this one "place. "

The fourth dimension: time itself

When I hold my hand in front of my face, I see three dimensions: length, width, and depth/height. Yet within this "fourth dimension," I can see across one other domain as well: time itself. That's what wise king Solomon discerned: that the place where God dwells *transcends* time and space. God can *see across* time, and yet "seals" the past (requires that the events, that have already taken place, be accounted for in judgment). Again, in that "place" the past, present, and future are all accessible at once!

—But wait, how can this be? Solid people (in three dimensional time and space) cannot inhabit eternity! When I move my hand in front of my face, one second it is here, then there, and then still further away —for my hand cannot be in all places the same instant . . . unless I were ... a spirit.

> God is a Spirit: and they that worship him must worship him
> in spirit and in truth.

> John 4:24

As Eternity transcends time and space, the Father who dwells there, literally fills heaven and earth. Yet (if your mind hasn't been blown yet!) —how can such a God now communicate with us?? Perhaps, he can thunder at us, from the heavens (John 12:28,29).[48] Or, . . . he may also allow the luxury of having another expression of Himself within our dimension of time and space, via the Son, "Who is the image of the invisible God . . . ." (Colossians 1:15).

Yes, the Son really has declared him. Yet, there is more.

And . . . the Mind:

For God, who sets His own limits, and literally inhabits both time and space within Eternity, also inhabits . . . the dimension of the mind, so that He not only transcends time and space (in Eternity) and can walk among us (through the Son) —but He may also inhabit the hearts and minds of men and women everywhere, through the Holy Spirit (Romans 8:5-9).

> Therefore, as the Holy Spirit says, "Today, if you will hear his voice, do not harden your hearts, as in the rebellion, ..."
>
> Hebrews 3:7,8

An awesome God!!

Where, in time or space, may we ever hide from Him?!!

What problem can we think of, that He cannot solve?

What sin is there, too great for such a God, to overcome?

Surely, there is only one —a refusal to turn from our rebellion and sin, to accept His gift of forgiveness, with open arms!

Why is all of this possible?

Because the only thing greater than God's power and majesty is His love.

"For God so loved the world that He gave His only begotten Son, that whoever believes in Him should not perish but have everlasting life."

John 3:16

A thoughtful consideration of these matters, must yield a singular conclusion—that there is one God. When the faithful get to Heaven we will see only One—The Lord Jesus Christ, Who is the image of the invisible God (Col. 1:15).

This does not mean that the Father cannot assume a visible body (as in Dan. 7:9-14) but that as we are the temple of the Holy Spirit (I Cor. 3:16) so too, Christ is the tabernacle of the Father (Rev. 21:3). There is, if you will, humility within the Godhead. It has pleased the Father that in Christ all fullness dwell (Col 1:19).

Such is the nature of true love.

God is love (I John 4:16).

An awesome God!

Now, with our heads still spinning, where else may we turn, but back to the beginning to consider, and take a closer look . . . at ourselves.

Chapter 6:

BE NAKED, OR SAINTS

And they were both naked, the man and his wife, and were not ashamed.

Genesis 2:25

"You are worthy, O Lord, To receive glory and honor and power; For You created all things, And by Your will they exist and were created."

Revelation 4:11

As we leave the Control Room of the Universe (where God dwells) and return to earth, we start to clear our heads and ask, "Where do we fit into all of this?" The answer may be found in the Garden, where it all started. Here we may gain a perspective on just why we have come here—and where we are going. We were derived from innocence, and are destined for sainthood. In innocence we felt no responsibility, and in sainthood would find a new glory. Yet when we open our Bibles and seek to understand exactly what has happened when man fell and was kicked out of the Garden, we begin to sense that something was actually missing at Creation: something very dear, and that only the man could supply, willingly.

There was something that could only originate in the heart of man; that would truly turn the Garden, into a Paradise, if you will.

If you open a copy of the Authorized King James Version, you will note that it translates our second opening quote, with the angelic hosts declaring, "and for thy pleasure [all things] are and were created." For God's *pleasure?* Yes, God identifies with His Creation. —More, as woman was made for man, humankind was made for God. Further, the prophet Zephaniah describes the Lord's heart and purpose regarding His people—showing that God actually desires to *rejoice* over the saints, and enjoys our fellowship. Says Zephaniah:

> "The LORD your God in your midst,
>
> The Mighty One, will save;
>
> He will rejoice over you with gladness,
>
> He will quiet you with His love,
>
> He will rejoice over you with singing."
>
> Zeph. 3:17

And that's Old Testament! The whole concept of God actually taking pleasure in His people is totally foreign to anyone driven by the Green Horse, or green money, for that matter. To think, the God of the Universe actually *loves me!*

Forgive the emotional outburst. After all, we are students of Bible prophecy. (*Maranatha!* Behold, He is coming!)

Again, where were we? Ah, yes. Our goal, at this point, is to retrace our steps and to remember man's purpose in creation. It was to produce saints. For, until we come to grips with why God initiated movement in the cosmos of time and space to begin with, it will be impossible to appreciate the way in which He will wrap it all up. Scripture shows that man was created so that God might delight in us, as we worship Him forever.

The Westminster Catechism assumes that the reverse is also true (that we may enjoy God, forever[49]) but Scripture states explicitly that we were created by God for His pleasure. When we strip the key issues down to their bare bones, the issue comes down to one point:

That God is boss, and because He made us, He has the right to call the shots.

Yet we *were* made in God's image—not as robots, or as androids, or as some inferior thing. No, as incredible as it may seem, we were made as loving copies (in many respects) of the living God. We were made for fellowship, and are incredibly complex.

Again, in terms of our present discussion, there are three attributes that come prominently into play, within our purpose and make-up. They are:

- Our capacity for companionship and fellowship with God, and

- Our capacity to express both love, and personal worship (with worship being an extension of our love).

Finally:

- This love must also include an aspect of . . . faith: for love *believes.* [50]

In simple, and concrete, terms the above attributes become evident as we engage in simple obedience, as we are confronted with the decisions of life—reacting in an either positive, or negative, manner. When we love Him, we obey Him.[51] Shortly after Adam and Eve were created, God came for a stroll in the Garden in the cool of the day. They were both innocent, and naked as new born babies. "Allow the little children to come," Jesus said, "for of such is God's Kingdom." Thus, in a pristine and fuller way, the first man and woman enjoyed free access and fellowship with the God of creation.

Human *praise* and *adoration*, however, would require a more radical restructuring of the spiritual universe. For such praise must come from deep within, of one's own volition, as we truly understand *our need* for God, within ourselves. "Self esteem" is rapidly becoming the humanist's first commandment: the elevation of *my* personal wants and desires. Heaven's first command centers around *His esteem*: the worship of the One true God.

Loving my neighbor, then becomes an extension of my love for God (Mk. 12:29-31, I Jn. 4:20,21).

When Jesus, the second Adam, came to earth He expressly informed us that all fulfillment flows outwards from this initial fountainhead: of knowing and pleasing God, above all else: Seek first the Kingdom of God, He said, and everything else will follow (Matt. 6:33). Adam and Eve's initial mistake, then, was to seek their own glory, and to throw Paradise out the window . . . .

You may notice that in John's Revelation the believers are always called "saints"[52] this is because, from Heaven's perspective, this is what a "virgin" (believer unspotted by the world) is. A "saint" is a holy one, made holy by the atonement of Christ's blood.[53] However, it must be understood that to be "holy" involves much more than merely being innocent. Adam and Eve were created without sin. They were totally innocent, when created. To be *holy* however, requires the ability to be good.

Yet being truly good, demands that one be able to resist evil.

Put another way: to be a virgin living within a sealed convent, or monastery, means nothing. To be a virgin studying on a modern university campus, means a lot. In the first case, there may simply never have been exposure to sexual trial and temptation. In the second, resistance must be offered every day! God's purpose in creation was directed towards the final goal of making us into saints. Such requires that we be able to resist evil.[54] This was the reason they were commanded *not to eat* of the tree of the knowledge of good and evil. The point was not the knowledge, it was the simple obedience.

All the knowledge they could ever want or dream of, was readily available through proper channels: through their all knowing Teacher: God, Himself. But they rebelled.

Now, there would be trouble in Paradise.

Trouble in Paradise:

Already, there had been rebellion in Heaven, and this new creation (man) would have to be fully engaged in a special plan to prepare him for the experience of God's ultimate communion with humankind. God knew that Adam would sin, for Scripture states the Father had already prepared a means of redemption before Creation had even started. Jesus Christ is the "Lamb slain from the foundation of the world" (Revelation 13:8).

We were created similar to angels, but are different in the exercise of one key attribute: we have the right to exercise free will. When we take the time to meditate on the way the universe was framed, we recognize a purpose and method in His planning—for by allowing humans to inhabit an environment separate from Heaven, itself, freedom of choice may here be freely exercised, without disrupting God's domain and rule.

—And if you will accept, it: here the Lord may court his bride.

Some men propose with an expensive ring. God did so . . . with the blood of his Son. As Scripture would one day admonish husbands:

> Husbands, love your wives, even as Christ also loved the church, and gave himself for it; that he might sanctify and cleanse it with the washing of water by the word,
>
> That he might present it to himself a glorious church, not having spot, or wrinkle, or any such thing; but that it should be holy and without blemish.
>
> Ephesians 5:25-27

So that while the angels can worship, in measure, and speak to God.

The human creation, may do so . . . freely, and appreciate that this great God of Creation has *demonstrated* His love, with the Ultimate Gift: Himself.

In all of the created universe simple obedience, birthed from a trust and simple confidence in God, is the highest and purest expression of personal worship demonstrated by created beings. Lucifer, a created angel, was beautiful and brilliant in both body and spirit—but then violated the trust God had placed in him, as he led a rebellion against God in Heaven.

> "You were the anointed cherub who covers; I established you; You were on the holy mountain of God; You walked back and forth in the midst of fiery stones.
>
> You were perfect in your ways from the day you were created, Till iniquity was found in you."
>
> Ezekiel 28:14,15

Cherubim and Seraphim are created beings whose purpose is to worship God and minister to the saints (Hebrews 1:13,14). Angels, having been granted direct contact with God in Heaven, had maintained their privileged position only so long as they maintained their purity. Otherwise they met with God as Judge, were required to state their case, and leave (as with Satan's encounter requesting permission to attack the saintly man, Job[55]). The "war in heaven" mentioned in John's twelfth chapter, was actually a prayer war, as will be later explained.[56] Again, anyone engaged in rebellion against God, through willful disobedience, will feel hopelessly uncomfortable within His Presence. Such an encounter will either force us to display (and repent of) the evil within, as we are exposed to the Light—or be excluded from Glory. Because there was no atonement provided in Heaven, only the second option was left open to Lucifer. For there are no "penitentiaries" in Heaven, and no police. There is only the Judge at the Door, clean living, and simple godliness.

> LORD, who may abide in Your tabernacle? Who may dwell in Your holy hill?
>
> He who walks uprightly, And works righteousness, And speaks the truth in his heart;
>
> Psalm 15:1,2

Any who violate God's holiness, are exposed by His Light. This was also true as Jesus walked the earth.

> " . . .everyone practicing evil hates the light and does not come to the light, lest his deeds should be exposed.
>
> "But he who does the truth comes to the light, that his deeds may be clearly seen, that they have been done in God."
>
> John 3:20,21

Exposure by this Light produces a nakedness in the mind that becomes unbearable in God's presence. This is what happened when Adam and Eve sinned, willfully choosing not to obey God. – They violated their right to commune with Him.

Forfeiting their right to live in God's Light,

　　They chose the Darkness, over doing the Right,

　　And trembled.

Exposing their nakedness, to sweat and endeavor

They lived on in sin,

　　And continual terror.

For no longer did Jehovah "have their back."

No longer did He "have them covered."

Nor did humankind have the right

To commune with the Divine Lover

　　and their soul's own,

　　　　sole Creator.

No longer were they saved from themselves, or the consequence of inadvertent error, ignorance, or simple weakness as when created in innocence. They had "blown it," and were now accountable for every single, detail, and misdeed,

and so were now banished from the beautiful Garden.

Thus, when we finally examine the actual conditions existing within Eden's Garden, we come to realize that there was really only one Law within that domain. Only one: trust God.

> And the LORD God commanded the man, saying, "Of every tree of the garden you may freely eat;
>
> "but of the tree of the knowledge of good and evil you shall not eat, for in the day that you eat of it you shall surely die."
>
> Genesis 2:16,17

Why call it the tree "of the knowledge of good and evil"?? Why, of course we now know. For it symbolized all of the decisions we must now make, when *knowing the difference* between right and wrong . . . and being held accountable for those decisions, as well. Indeed, they were like new born babes, in full grown bodies, yet remaining perfectly innocent, before the Fall.

Now, however, they were "adult" purveyors of secret sins. No wonder Jesus told us that those who come to him must approach like little children (Matthew 18:3)!

By taking matters into their own hands (literally) they had become accountable for every moral decision. Staying under God's authority (via obedience) would have kept them under God's covering. After all, weren't they naked, and unashamed?

It's just that their nakedness, like that of others in creation, had been freed from the weight of moral law. It simply did not matter that they were (physically) naked.

Cats and kittens do not "feel" naked.

Nor do fish who swim in the seas.

In fact, even now, a woman's long hair, the Scriptures tell us, is given to her as a spiritual covering—if she knows how to use it (I Corinthians 11:15). For as man was made for God, and men and

106

women for each other—rebellion against who and what we are, exposes our nakedness to His displeasure.

"I heard Your voice in the garden, and I was afraid because I was naked; and I hid myself."

And He said, "Who told you that you were naked? Have you eaten from the tree of which I commanded you that you should not eat?". . .

[Therefore] cursed is the ground for your sake; . . .

Genesis 3:10,11,17

As we examine the ingredients of the Garden mix, and of man's initial state, we again realize just what that "missing ingredient" was. For, when commanded not to eat of that tree, there was no way for them to *know* what "death" really was, having never seen it demonstrated in their presence. They simply had to take God at His word.

And that was exactly the way the Lord would have it.

As His word had created the Universe—the faithful must now hang our lives upon that very Word.

Faith is what marked the old Patriarchs, of the Old Testament. It is what motivated Noah, when building his ark of safety, even before seeing it rain. It also motivated Abraham, when believing against the odds, for the son of promise through his barren wife, Sarah. For, with those having faith in Him, God will move Heaven and earth to find a way to us get back into the Garden.

This is why Jesus, the Second Adam, came to the earth: to supply what Adam and Eve let slip through their fingers. Adam had only to miss the mark, and let go of immortality and fall to death. He then passed that mortal flaw down, to the rest of the human race. Jesus, however, had to enter a planet already polluted by sin, and redeem an entire race, by His perfect and incorruptible blood: the blood of God (Acts 20:28). Thus, Christ paid the price for our wayward disobedience—allowing us to escape the cycle of death as we came leaping from the cradle and heading for the casket—by voluntarily dying, Himself, and conquering Death, and then by rising again. The Judge barred out way back to Paradise, but His Son has ransomed us from the grave.

> For He made Him who knew no sin to be sin for us, that we might become the righteousness of God in Him.
>
> II Corinthians 5:21

Please pay close attention to what is being said, here. It has everything to do with the Midnight Cry. Sin is missing the mark of God's holiness—not merely because we are not good enough, but because we refuse to come back to Him, through the doorway of deliverance now provided. The angels did not have such a Doorway. Yet the Door now stands fully open, with unlimited access, for us.

Like a simple lamb, offered on the altar of sacrifice, the Lamb of God exchanged His life for ours on the Cross to be able to escort us back into Paradise, at His returning.

Then He rose, again. At His coming the cycle of deliverance will be made complete. Faith, united with His love, will then bring His bride Home.

We need be naked, no more.

What a lot of ground we have covered in our "introduction" to the keys! Yet, now we have a better appreciation of just what is at stake at midnight, and of what the "horsemen of the Apocalypse," are really after.

→ Of this we may be certain, they are *not* concerned with a "warming trend" (which the saints may also discount –Matt. 6:25-34).[57] No, for in the world in which we now live, men's hearts are truly growing cold. This will not be the case, however, past the Midnight Cry—for some . . . .

Chapter 7:

A FEW HORSEMEN

And they cried with a loud voice, saying, "How long, O Lord, holy and true, until You judge and avenge our blood on those who dwell on the earth?"

Then a white robe was given to each of them; and it was said to them that they should rest a little while longer, until both the number of their fellow servants and their brethren, who would be killed as they were, was completed.

Revelation 6:10,11

In contrast to the modern world's openly secular mindset, church fathers had a distinct advantage over us. With an eye on the Heavens that had received Christ back into Glory, they were willing to give all—including their very lives, for the privilege of *sharing* the good news. For they could easily see, and identify with the apocalyptic horsemen who seemed to ride the airwaves all around them, even as they shared the wonderful gospel to a trampled generation. Though at times a seemingly thankless task—whether reviled by the pull of family, friends, or the simple power of brute persecution—theirs was nevertheless a world that most often held the religious, and the supernatural, in high esteem.

—Sometimes confusing it with superstition, and the occult.[58]

Into this hot bed of boiling emotions the Christians arose with their message of love, hope, and of the resurrection unto eternal life. Life after death could be much more than mere philosophy, they contended. Jesus Christ had actually *arisen from the dead!* It was a message truly worth dying for.

And die, they did.

Their strength of conviction did not make their dying much less painful, or the hatred of their adversaries any less real—nor the coming judgments of God, any less certain. For Rome would some day fall, as will all kingdoms of merely human origin—as the kingdom of Christ's love finally triumphs that will "break in pieces and consume all these kingdoms, . . . shall stand forever" (Dan. 2:44).

That will be the day when Christ returns the second time.

It will also be the day when Christ's Kingdom *will* be of this world. Yet, in the interim, we have the biblical roadmap into our future: laid out by the prophets, and most beautifully described by John's Apocalypse.

So, what kind of a Book *is* this?

Those special elastic "Horsemen:"

What kind of prophecy, is John's Revelation of Jesus Christ? It is a book that is largely typified by its "horsemen." For it is within this mysterious symbolism that we quickly become aware of its cardinal virtues that are both elastic *and* definite. It must be able to stretch out, and adapt over the centuries. . . and then spring back into "shape" to regroup with a specific message in the terminal generation. Yet at first glance its message seems enigmatic and very puzzling, indeed. Only after peeling through the multiple "onion skins" may our eyes begin to peer into its special design and purpose, and start to observe its secrets. For the church had need of both specific instruction in the short run, as well as purposeful discernment and insights within the terminal generation as Israel has finally returned to her land.

This "elastic mission" is accomplished with the remarkable flexibility in John's Revelation of Jesus Christ. Its symbols have given the church both the comfort and general understanding needed down through the ages, while holding close to its bosom specific secrets needed for the closing hour. Those "horses" really did seem to go in great circles, but have finally exited the merry-go-round, in the terminal generation.

In other words, John's Apocalypse fulfilled its mission by yielding:

- specific instruction to the first generation of Christians

- a general world view of spiritual events, needed down through the centuries, and finally,

- specific warnings and instruction, within the terminal generation.

An example of the above guidelines' fulfillment may be seen in the way Christians in all ages, and at all times, could identify with the general message given through the first two horsemen of the Apocalypse: the white horse, with Christianity advancing—always followed by the red, of persecution, conflict, and martyrdom. Round and round the symbolism went . . . until the terminal generation.

However, as we advance through Revelation chapters 9 & 10, we begin to get the distinct impression that we are either getting into secrets reserved for a privileged people—and/or that a special key is needed to unlock its secrets in the closing hour. This is particularly true, as we pass by John's vision of a mighty angel declaring that "there should be delay no longer" (10:6).

but in the days of the sounding of the seventh angel, when
he is about to sound, the mystery of God would be finished,
as He declared to His servants the prophets.

Revelation 10:7

Remember, the seventh angel sounds at *the last trump*. This trumpet is sounded at Christ's returning.

That "mighty angel," therefore, is actually telling us of a time when prophecy must advance without further delay. He is informing the final generation that "the cycles are ending." The symbols of this prophecy will now yield their ultimate secrets to us.

A brash, new global culture, now emerges, as it attempts to harness the forces and the powers that we have already begun studying earlier. Essentially, these emerging influences will come from three main fronts. These will be the "front men" for the two *real* combatants: of Light and Darkness (or God and Satan). The line up of these combatants may be seen in a careful line-up of the closing verses of twelfth chapter leading into the New World Order. Since that chapter both describes events already behind us, both within the church and in human history,

While bridging into our future (chapter thirteen).

Because these visions overlap, we may gain greater insight by taking a peek at the way the geopolitical forces are lined up within its chapter summary (we will study these two chapters, in much greater detail, in the next two sections . . .). We will then go back to the horsemen of the apocalypse, and apply this insight, to gain greater insight into how these forces are actually aligned, with the horsemen of the Apocalypse.

Let us look at these, more carefully, shall we?

The Forces backing the Horsemen of the Apocalypse:

It is important, as we prepare to examine the horsemen in greater detail, to consider the focus of the opposing forces being assembled in the terminal generation: Both religious and political, private and public—which stand on the one hand, behind the Dragon, and on the other, behind the woman/nation that gave birth to the Christ (Rev. 12:4&5).

For the whole world does stand, either behind the Dragon, or the woman:

> And the dragon was enraged with the woman, and he went to make war with the rest of her offspring, who keep the commandments of God and have the testimony of Jesus Christ.
>
> Revelation 12:17

As we shall see later in our study, the woman spoken of here, is none other than the nation of Israel: the nation with twelve stars, representing her twelve tribes. We know that this is Israel, because the verses following describe Israel's diaspora, where she goes into the wilderness. Yet, even there, within the time of her scattering, God protected the little nation, and everywhere her feet landed (even with painful steps) her place is "prepared by God" (vs. 6). In the aftermath, the powers of the world are found aligning themselves into three main power blocks of influence:

114

Judeo/Christian

Secular

Religious

These correspond to the White, Red, and Pale Green horse. There will be no other "fourth" alternative (although there is a fourth (Black) horseman which, as we shall see, is a result of the previous Red. . . .). Before separating them out, we must first remind ourselves that there is always an intermingling of forces, even within the purest of political empires. Even within the Western world, for example, there is some vestige of socialism: within our welfare system, if nothing else. . . .

→ When speaking of the secular forces, we refer principally to the Humanist outlook on the world: believing that man is the measure of all things.[59] From this point of view it is but one short step into convincing ourselves that we (men and women) are really the only God there is(!) through the wonders we are able to accomplish: in science, technology, and in the healing arts.

We may be certain that many who end up worshipping the Antichrist, will often feel that they are really worshipping . . .themselves.

Within the most aggressive wing of humanism and socialism we also find those who hold to the Communist persuasion: wedding the concept of social engineering to wealth redistribution—by making use of an oppressive central government that imposes its will upon the population.

Those embracing this last mindset see no authority above themselves, but often engage in what is sometimes called "conflict theory"[60]—seeing all of right and wrong as issues ultimately fought between weak and strong people. Although there is often an assumption that those in the right will ultimately become strong (as, for example, when the down-trodden arise to overthrow their oppressors) in the final analysis, mere rebellion will do little more than expose a new form of corruption within the ranks of these secular "saviors." Soon the rationale seizes upon its children that "might makes right" or that "he who has the might, makes the right." For these, there is no higher moral law than . . . what you can get away with. This will also be backed by the religion of the Antichrist (Daniel 11:38 AV).

→ When speaking of "religion" as a major factor in the Antichrist system, I refer to both true and false in collusion: Islam and other religions, as well as apostate Christianity, becoming driving forces within world government.

COMMUNISM, Satan's Baby:

One myth that we must quickly dispel, before going further, is the belief that Communism, and its principle agents, died as a major force in the world, with the collapse of the Berlin Wall. Nothing could be further from the truth. The Communist ideal has its roots within the human soul.

The greatest appeal of Communism is to draw upon the roots of human rebellion found within the lower nature of both men and women: not to work harder, nor to take the personal risks needed to build a better world for themselves (as with the Christian ethic, and constructive capitalism, for example)—but to forcefully take away the material goods of those who have already gained them wrongfully (they think) from undue advantage.

In other words, the driving force between this form of wealth management is . . . covetousness: seeing the greener grass growing on the other side, and kicking your neighbors off their land, to acquire it. This does not mean that all people within such a state are, necessarily, lazy. It does mean that *covetousness* is the engine that lifts this form of government into power.

> 'You shall not commit adultery.
>
> 'You shall not steal.
>
> 'You shall not bear false witness against your neighbor.
>
> 'You shall not covet your neighbor's wife; and you shall not desire your neighbor's house, his field, his male servant, his female servant, his ox, his donkey, or anything that is your neighbor's.'

Deuteronomy 5:18-21

Please notice how the final command in the Bible quote above—not to covet —seems to encapsulate all of the previous evils into one final command, on what is forbidden. Covetousness is bad news (literally): it forms the hotbed for the most vile of human governments.

Nor may Capitalism claim freedom from this vice at all times. Much of what drives our consumer oriented society (through advertising, for example) is based upon the lust of the eye, and pride of life.[61] The distinction that separates all of secular economics from a truly Christian based system of money management is . . . faith. Through faith, for example, the government may free its people from oppressive taxation—only to find that the resulting freedom so stimulates the economy, that it creates a surplus of tax revenue.

<u>Constructive Capitalism</u>:

What we may now call, "constructive capitalism," requires simple faith. The business man, or woman, must believe that what they have conceived of, is worth their investment of time and money and will, in fact, be rewarded (with a profit). In this, capitalism has a healthy ingredient of the unknown which does place somewhat of a strain upon the character of those individuals willing to venture into this arena. Communism and socialism, by government fiat, seek to erase this need for economic venture/faith. Socialism seeks to replace faith in God, with a faith in the State. The fall of the Berlin wall, however, has demonstrated that such "faith" is not well founded.

Faith in God is a sure thing (Romans 10:11).

Yet the life of faith is not as "easy" as some may seek to portray it to the congregation on Sunday morning. There is a price tag to having and holding faith, as the oldest writings in the Bible attest, through the lives of Job and of Abraham.[62] The man or woman who simply believes in God must do so, through both thick and thin. What we have sought to get the reader to consider, here, is how this principle drives constructive capitalism. It is personal *character*, and *strength of the heart and soul*, that propels any society towards excellence. People of faith will naturally venture forth into areas of the unknown when trusting in God, once this has become a way of life for them, individually. This is symbolized by the white horse (White Horse) of Revelation six. We will cover this later, when preparing to introduce the place that the Scriptures hold for the world's one remaining super power . . . .

The Other Horses. . . destroy:

Communism's twin sister, aggressive socialism, will one day bring the world to the brink of utter distress through its massive wealth redistribution schemes, just before the Green Horse rides in earnest. Oh, forgive me, we have been discussing the next two Horsemen: the Red horse, and now the Black.

So notice with me, if you will, the Black Horseman's description.

> When He opened the third seal, I heard the third living creature say, "Come and see." So I looked, and behold, a black horse, and he who sat on it had a pair of scales in his hand.
>
> And I heard a voice in the midst of the four living creatures saying, "<u>A quart of wheat for a denarius, and three quarts of barley for a denarius</u>; **and do not harm the oil and the wine**."

Revelation 6:5,6 [emphasis added]

The precious AV translation (which I love and treasure) translates this verse as "A measure of wheat for a penny, and three measures of barley for a penny;"—but a "penny" makes our next observation somewhat difficult to discern.

It is true that the coin in question was the lowly Roman denarius, but it is also true that within those less cosmopolitan communities, where money was used less aggressively than today—especially among farmers—the denarius represented a full day's wage.[63] In other words, what we see projected in this Black Horse is a collapse of the world's economic systems, so that **a loaf of bread costs the laboring man <u>a full day's wage</u>**.

Why should this happen?

It has to do with the humanist vision of Heaven on earth.

The Next Best Thing: Money

The larger issue of this phenomenon is something just now coming into view through the Kyoto Protocol.[64] For, by proposing to have the wealthier nations pay the less developed states "air credits" as a sort of penance for having developed faster (and polluted the air earlier) than the rest of the world—it hides its real purpose: To have an excuse for the less developed nations to raid the coffers of the industrialized West. If such a scheme is on the books, today, we may be certain that another (or the same agreement, with more muscle) will be instituted by the Antichrist after rising to power. The "liberal" mind-set instinctively leans towards wealth redistribution (and the welfare economy) as a cure-all for human ailments. "If only we were to give the poorer nations more money," the reasoning goes, "there would be less suffering."

Just so long as that abundance of money comes from someone else's pocket (or everyone else's, through taxation)—we will eventually be able to create a Humanist Paradise.

The same principle is increasingly held concerning our Public Schools, Health Care, and any other social malady that causes discomfort within our world today. If there is a problem, throw money at it (this is not funny. I am not even smiling. It is the truth.) For within a world that does not believe in God, the next best thing is . . . money.

Yet when the Black Horse rides over the whole earth —and there is no longer any Capitalist State holding out, to fall back upon, as during the Cold War— the economies of the world will collapse. Then the grand secular experiment, designed to produce a Paradise upon earth via the mere force of human will, will itself fail. So much for the Humanist Paradise.

So much for Utopia.[65]

There is nothing intrinsically wrong with working for a living. It is commendable. There is nothing wrong with encouraging people to pursue excellence; it is the fountainhead of blessing. Yet there *is* something wrong with making a virtue out of laziness.

> For you yourselves know how you ought to follow us, for we were not disorderly among you; nor did we eat anyone's bread free of charge, but worked with labor and toil night and day, that we might not be a burden to any of you,
>
> not because we do not have authority, but to make ourselves an example of how you should follow us.
>
> For even when we were with you, we commanded you this: If anyone will not work, neither shall he eat.

II Thessalonians 8:7-10 [66]

Thus, when seeking to "stay awake" in the midnight hour, we must resist the temptation to be lazy. For the night is coming, when no one can work.

But wait! Why does the angel say not to hurt "the oil and the wine"? Did you notice something? Are we being reminded that the Lord's power is made perfect in weakness? What does the oil, and wine, represent? What of the oil in the lamps of those wise virgins?

That is the power to live the Christian life.

What of the wine? Do not both oil *and* wine represent the Holy Spirit? Yes, but the wine represents . . .the *joy.* For those with flowing oil, this will continue to be a time to "be strong, and do exploits" for the Lord.[†]

Thus, the mystery of the Kingdom (the gospel) *will* continue to go out into all the world.[67]

[†] Daniel 11:32

And do not be drunk with wine, in which is dissipation; but be filled with the Spirit, speaking to one another in psalms and hymns and spiritual songs, singing and making melody in your heart to the Lord . . .

Ephesians 5:18, 19

I further answered and said to him, "What are these two olive branches that drip into the receptacles of the two gold pipes from which the golden oil drains?"

Then he answered me and said, "Do you not know what these are?" And I said, "No, my lord."

So he said, "These are the two anointed ones, who stand beside the Lord of the whole earth."

Zechariah 4:12-14

These are the *sons of oil*. As we have noted, they have an intimate relationship to the 3½ clocks. These saints are the antithesis of the ten virgins, who must ration their oil.

Ten virgins, who must awaken at midnight to a sudden jolt, and awareness, within the boiling pot . . .

Section II:

Conflict Of Spirits:

On Earth &

From the Heavens

"You stiff-necked and uncircumcised in heart and ears! You always resist the Holy Spirit; as your fathers did, so do you."

Acts 7:51

Yet we would not follow those who draw back,

to their own destruction, but join with those who believe,

and are saved unto Life

Eternal.

Terms to ponder in section II:

- The ten virgins – true believers who awaken to find their most valuable possession (their souls) imperiled.

- The Midnight Cry – another name, for the abomination of desolation, that Christ clearly warned about.

- Dispensation – a framework in which God's people can worship Him in spirit and truth—in a particular era.

- Materialism – (What is the difference between materialism . . .and success?)

- Moral slippage – If the heavens withdraw their shining, what can the righteous do?

- Israel's destiny – what place does this little nation have in the heart of God?

- The Green Horse – will the West sell its soul to this bandit?

Chapter 8:

STARTING TO BOIL

(a love despised . . .)

1 "Then the kingdom of heaven shall be likened to ten virgins who took their lamps and went out to meet the bridegroom.

2 "Now five of them were wise, and five were foolish.

3 "Those who were foolish took their lamps and took no oil with them,

4 "but the wise took oil in their vessels with their lamps.

5 "But while the bridegroom was delayed, they all slumbered and slept.

6 "And at midnight a cry was heard: 'Behold, the bridegroom is coming; go out to meet him!'

7 "Then all those virgins arose and trimmed their lamps.

8 "And the foolish said to the wise,

'Give us some of your oil, for our lamps are going out.'

9 "But the wise answered, saying, 'No, lest there should not be enough for us and you; but go rather to those who sell, and buy for yourselves.'

10 "And while they went to buy, the bridegroom came, and those who were ready went in with him to the wedding; and the door was shut.

11 "Afterward the other virgins came also, saying, 'Lord, Lord, open to us!'

12 "But he answered and said, 'Assuredly, I say to you, I do not know you.'

13 "Watch therefore, for you know neither the day nor the hour in which the Son of Man is coming."

Matthew 25:1-13

Waiting for a loved one, or one betrothed, can seem like an "eternity." Think of the many wives and mothers, waiting for Johnny to come home from the war. Our present mid-east conflict, and the public disgust now evident in its plodding advance, illustrate the difficulty of staying focused in the night. This is a battle that requires much more than carrying a football over the scrimmage and into the end zone. A simple "home run" will not win this game, nor will the "game" itself be over after only nine innings. In the midst of these battles, the goal grows dim in relation to the sweat and toil required to achieve the prize. In such a time it helps to lay hold of why failure is *unacceptable,* in order to keep our eyes focused, and the conflict (and prize) in a clear focus.

For the Christian, this involves reaching for the promises of God, lying out there, beyond the point we now refer to as the "Midnight Cry." For, it is past midnight that all of the warnings of this study become ever more precious than mere academics: It will be life and breath (literally) as we remember that very soon, the world will look up into the sky one more time, to see:

> " the sign of the Son of Man will appear in heaven, and then all the tribes of the earth will mourn, and they will see the Son of Man coming on the clouds of heaven with power and great glory.
>
> "And He will send His angels with a great sound of a trumpet, and they will gather together His elect from the four winds, from one end of heaven to the other.
>
> Mattehw 24:30,31

Such is the promise that men and women, for millennia, have clutched closely to their bosoms: earnestly looking forward to righteousness being restored, and God's Paradise being regained. As with the first man transferred into Heaven ("translated!") in the Old Testament—Enoch proclaimed:

> Behold, the Lord cometh with [myriads] of his saints,
>
> To execute judgment upon all, and to convince all that are ungodly among them of all their ungodly deeds which they have ungodly committed, and of all their hard speeches which ungodly sinners have spoken against him.
>
> Jude 14,15 AV

"The judgments of the LORD are true and righteous altogether. More to be desired are they than gold,..." wrote the psalmist, "by them Your servant is warned, And in keeping them there is great reward" (Ps. 19:9-11). The judgments of God, therefore, are designed to carry us up to, *and past,* the final decision at midnight.

At this point it is imperative to uncover secrets held in the parable of those lying fast asleep until that hour of danger. It is truly a story of a love despised, within a world largely taking the love of God for granted; indifferent to His claim upon the church— while forgetting the price that He has paid, Himself.

Jesus spoke this story as a mystery unknown: as a parable given to listeners who thought they understood, but did not. Its secrets were hidden over the centuries as it passed over men (and women's) heads, waiting to be fulfilled in this closing hour. For

He was really speaking to us, in the terminal generation: enjoining us to escape the pot before reaching the crisis at midnight. For in that hour, the spirit of this world will come into final conflict with the Spirit of the living God.

A similar warning is later sounded in John's Revelation, chapter eighteen, where we also hear "another voice from heaven" saying, "Come out of her, my people, lest you share in her sins, and lest you receive of her plagues" (Rev. 18:4). Although this last warning is issued to those still within Babylon (the apostate organization, which we must shun like the plague) it is obvious that in both instances the warnings are given to *God's people.*

An uncomfortable (but obvious) truth:

Notice, however, this uncomfortable truth: that if they had died before midnight, all of the virgins would have been spared.

Note also that, as Jesus relates it, there is no reproof for those who sleep. This seems quite appropriate, given the fact that the term "virgins" refers exclusively to true believers within the New Testament. "I have betrothed you . . . as a chaste virgin to Christ," wrote Paul.[68]   –A truth made even more evident, within Heaven itself, as John is informed that those redeemed are virgins.[69] What strikes the reader, therefore, is the uncomfortable awareness that the virgins were all safe and secure . . . until midnight. As Jesus informs the church in Philadelphia,[70] "Because you have kept My command to persevere, I also will keep you from the hour of trial which shall come upon the whole world, to test those who dwell on the earth." (Rev. 3:10). To which Isaiah adds agreement:

> The righteous perisheth, and no man layeth to heart: and
> merciful men are taken away, none considering that the
> righteous is taken away from the evil to come.
>
> Isaiah 57:1 AV

At some point, however, their taking God's love for granted, turns to indifference, as hearts turn cold towards the Savior. So that at the start of the age, Christ warns, "I have this against you, that you have left your first love," –while at the closing, He answers in disgust, "So then, because you are lukewarm, and neither cold nor hot, I will vomit you out of My mouth" (Rev. 2:4, 3:16). Yet even in all of this, there is a remnant, remaining true, whom we may discern within the second 3 ½ clock . . .

As we prepare to connect the dots, therefore, the message given above is clear: that if the virgins pass on to Glory before the Midnight Cry sounds . . . they are spared the test of the final generation. It would no longer matter that the water in the pot was coming to a slow boil (although the discerning are held accountable).[71] Also evident, is the fact that the church to whom the promise of escaping *is* addressed in Revelation 3:10 (Philadelphia) —obviously symbolizes the dominant evangelical structure *just prior* to the generation hearing the alarm being sounded.

Cutting to the chase: the *Philadelphian church age* existed up until the return of the nation of Israel to her land. Our present generation (that is, the generation existing since Israel's return) shall not pass away before Christ returns.[72] We return, repeatedly, to this concept of Philadelphia and of the terminal generation (Laodicea), for they represent the dominant evangelical church structures just prior to, and then after, the re-founding of the nation

130

of Israel. I realize this may seem a major hurdle for some, but must ask that you hold your options open until we can more fully broach this subject in the chapters following.

It is true that this is merely an introductory discussion of Bible prophecy. Yet the sheer breadth of what has already been fulfilled is so encompassing that its scope may simply seem to startle the reader. We are launching from 0- 60 (mph) in a few short pages, for we must quickly recoup these concepts, and capture the big picture of what God is planning for our world today. At "midnight" we will have no such luxury.

Remember the foolish virgins. They simply will not be able to deal with what they see within the world about them, when they do awaken.

Yet there is, as we have noted, another option open for Christian believers beyond sleeping with the ten virgins within a predominant, sleepy, church age. As we have noted previously, there is the possibility of remaining awake, with a faithful remnant who refuse to sleep. "Therefore let us not sleep, as others do" (I Thes. 5:6).

Now that we really are beginning to sense being part of the terminal generation, we again eagerly reread the opening text, with a renewed interest. Once more, its urgency pushes in upon us, to consider its key points with a focused mind while observing that:

- This parable is all about believers (virgins, as already pointed out)

- There is a sudden awareness that Christ is indeed returning: "Behold, the Bridegroom is coming, go out to meet Him!" (Go out? To where? It is time to escape the pot: to cast off apathy and indifference.)

- The wise have extra oil (symbolic of the Holy Spirit) *within their vessels* (remember this, for such oil is contained within a vessel—we will meet others, with *flowing oil,* who need not sleep.)

- There is apparent terror, at the prospect of being unprepared: The foolish request from the wise, "Give us some of your oil"!

- Yet it soon becomes evident that such requests will require a personal encounter with the living God. "Go rather to those who sell, . . ." —Reminiscent of our Lord's command to terminal, and lukewarm, Laodicea: "I counsel you to buy of Me gold, tried in the fire, that you may be rich . . ." (Rev. 3:18).

—This is definitely not a message well received in the current western world! Yet it is within the *fire* of personal trial and hardship that we often encounter what is most precious in the eyes of the Lord (I Peter 1:7).

In conclusion:

- It is quite obvious that these believers are not "battle ready" (II Tim. 2:2ff, II Cor. 10:3-6).

- When the Lord returns, and the foolish believers miss out.

The obvious question must now be asked, and answered: What is the midnight cry (Midnight Cry)? We know that it is not the rapture. It cannot be so. For we know that the rapture takes place in an instant (in an atom of time). Notice again how eerily the following text conveys this truth within a framework of sleeping (or not).

> Behold, I tell you a mystery: We shall not all sleep, but we shall all be changed;
>
> in a moment, in the twinkling of an eye, at the last trumpet. For the trumpet will sound, and the dead will be raised incorruptible, and we shall be changed.
>
> I Corinthians 15:51,52

This event describes what is commonly referred to as the "rapture" —Yet those sleepy heads in Christ's parable are able to awaken, stand about, and even discuss the issue at hand. Such cannot be the rapture, therefore, for those in this parable have time to engage in the issues of this life. However,

It soon dawns upon the virgins that their crisis will require a full court press: demanding all that one can muster, to "go out" and remain faithful. The foolish have trouble merely handling the decision, much less warning their unbelieving neighbors of the impending danger to their souls. I say again, this is *not* the rapture. It is an event, a test, that confronts the church in such a way that:

- It reminds us of the Lord's returning, in no uncertain terms, and

- Demands a response requiring an all out commitment (all of the oil/ personal reserves at our disposal).

Before going one line further, let me once again remind the reader (as in the previous chapters) that any issue demanding a definite response, for the salvation of our souls, will be clearly, and definitely, be stated within Scripture. Even one slow of understanding will be able to discern the obvious demands of our Lord. You may not acknowledge it, and you may turn a blind eye, but the issues will be clearly spelled out within those pages of Holy Writ.

We may debate and argue, for example, about whether or not it is necessary to be born again, but Jesus clearly states that unless a man *is* born again, he can't even *see* the Kingdom of God (John 3:3)! In the text that we will eventually quote, regarding the test to confront us at the Midnight Cry, these issues will be stated in even clearer terms.

In fact, the text describing the test at the Midnight Cry warns that anyone engaging in this particular action will be tormented in the presence of God and of the holy angels—with fire and brimstone, forever!

No "if"s, "and"s, or "but"s!

→   There was a day when Christians would go to the stake (to be burned) before violating their conscience on such "technical" issues as eating the wafer at the Roman Catholic Mass. Foxes Book of Martyrs, for example, records that, "A native of Malda was burnt by a slow fire, for saying that Mass was a plain denial of the death and passion of Christ." While "James Cobard, a schoolmaster in the city of St. Michael, was burnt, AD 1545, for saying 'That Mass was useless and absurd'."[73]

The Bible clearly agrees with these brethren. When remembering Christ's death on Calvary, through the eating of the wafer and drinking the blood of the grape—this is not to *re-sacrifice* Christ, but to remember what He did for us on the Cross. The book of Hebrews states clearly that Christ died *once for all*. (See Heb. 9:26-28, 10:10).

134

The general discounting of the seriousness of such obviously clear biblical doctrines—by "Protestants" today, is a clear example of the "slow boil" we have been addressing, and the breach of faith that we will be considering more clearly when studying certain parts of John's Revelation. For now, consider only that we need to be wary of slowly losing our salt and light (our distinctiveness as Christians). Believe me, within a "tolerant society" this is no easy task!

What does all of this mean to us? How does this relate to our everyday living? It does *not* mean that God does not love Roman Catholics. In fact (surprise!) there is reason, as we shall see, to believe that Heaven views some of these brethren more favorably than certain main line Protestant denominations. Yet, when a doctrine is in error, it *is* in error. We must not gloss over corrupted belief systems.

We must remember that God does not change. For while our world has been going tolerant to the extreme, Heaven has not been shifting its position at all. God does not change, although entire societies and *the world* may shift, with ever increasing degradation. Yet, when the Lord does allow such a "slow boil" to exist, it is because He has other plans, even more awesome and terrible(!), scheduled for the future. As the Psalmist wrote, millennia ago:

> When the wicked spring up like grass, And when all the workers of iniquity flourish, It is that they may be destroyed forever.

> But You, LORD, are on high forevermore.

> Psalm 92:7,8

This is a key to John's Revelation of Jesus Christ. God is *never* inactive in the Heavens; never wringing His hands and wondering what to do next. No, quite the opposite is true! Always!

In fact, He is purposely allowing things to appear to get out of control so that He may bring all of evil to a definite head, and judge the entire ball of wax: secular, historical, and religious—in one crushing blow.[74] This is a key element within the concept of Mystery Babylon and of the beastly ruler described within John's Apocalypse, chapters 13-19. They bring the nations of the world to Armageddon for judgment.[†]

It truly does matter how we live today: whether we prove faithful, or not, whether pursuing new souls for the kingdom of God, or not. Whether we lift up His name, and live for Him, or not. For all of our actions will certainly be rewarded or judged, as this whole unraveling of the Apocalypse is played out. It is better to have extra oil, than to be a mediocre Christian.

More so, it is better not to "sleep" at all!

For there will be no middle ground, at the Midnight Cry.

Dabbling in Babylon will only breed confusion. Compromise, only endangers your soul. The safest place to be is in the will of God, *outside* of the corridors of the politically correct. This is what Scripture means when it says that we should "go forth to Him, outside the camp, bearing His reproach.

[†] Mystery Babylon is judged slightly before the rest of the world, in the eighteenth chapter of the Apocalypse.

136

For here we have no continuing city, but we seek the one to
come."

Hebrews 13:13,14

So now we know: the first application of "going out to meet
Him" –is in being willing to become *marginalized* by the society in
which we live. We bear His reproach, and the ostracism of those
who look down their noses on "those ignorant people"—who just
happen have the inside track of where this world is heading, and
know just where our deliverance is coming from—and from
Whom(!). For it is only as we let down the standard, that Antichrist may arise fully.

Now, this last statement highlights a more specific danger, and
we must take a short detour to a passage quoted in chapter two regarding the approach of the boiling point. There was an issue
mentioned there, that is *absolutely critical* when confronting the
decision required at that boiling point. Remember our earlier premise: that **critical issues will be clearly defined within Scripture**.
If we need to jump through hoops to find what is required of us at
midnight, we do not have the truth. Let us again lay bare an open
quote regarding this issue, now.

Let no one deceive you by any means; for that Day will not
come unless the falling away comes first, and the man of sin
is revealed, the son of perdition,

who opposes and exalts himself above all that is called God
or that is worshiped, so that he sits as God in the temple of
God, showing himself that he is God.

II Thes. 2:3,4

This is the "falling away" that precedes the cry at midnight. This is what people are doing, while "asleep" in the night—they are letting down the standard, and receding from the point of true spiritual victory. The translators of the (New) King James Version did us a great service in so translating this passage. We must consider this in following chapters, when examining the eighth and ninth chapters of John's Revelation (specifically, the eighth). For now, notice that Paul clearly insists that **Christ will not return unless the church first apostatizes and Antichrist rises to power, standing in the temple of God.**

Did you understand what you just read? If not, read and re-read it, until it sinks in. Antichrist cannot arise until the church has gone to sleep.

WHERE IS THE TEMPLE???

Now, it is important to thoroughly understand how all of these matters will come to a boil—not just what the cry at midnight is. Yes, the Midnight Cry is found clearly stated in Revelation thirteen and fourteen, this is true. Yet, we must understand where this temple is, that Paul has mentioned, for none is described within that very intense, and rather detailed, thirteenth chapter of John's Apocalypse. It is there (in the thirteenth) that this fearful creature arises having seven heads and ten horns.[75] Yet, where is the temple?? How is it that Antichrist arises, issues the Mark, and no temple is discussed within those most intense & detailed chapters of John's Revelation?

We simply *must* answer this question. Paul tells us that Antichrist will stand in the temple declaring himself to be God, and yet the most detailed account of the Antichrist's rise displays no earthly temple whatever, anywhere in sight. Have they hidden it under a rock?

Even if the Dome of the Rock (in Israel) were cleared away, tomorrow, and a Jewish temple built in its place, the Christian community would still have to answer this question: why is no temple mentioned in Revelation thirteen, as Antichrist arises???

Consider this possibility: that the church sometimes misses the crossover between the spiritual and physical worlds. How important, for example, is prayer in the eyes of those in Heaven? Do you know? This we will also explore in succeeding chapters. Just because we are studying prophecy in no way means that we must forget (or forsake) the basics of the Christian faith!! For now, remember that Jesus stated emphatically that His kingdom *is not of this world,* period. —And He made this statement "with a gun to His head" (John 18:36)! In other words, even at peril of His life, Christ refused to revert to the physical to save his own flesh, when a larger issue was clearly at hand.

Someday (soon!!) Christ's Kingdom *will* reign on earth. Yet in the interim, how important are spiritual things, to us? Should we ignore, for example, the biblical statements that state clearly that the Church is the body of Christ, and that *we* are the temple of God (I Cor. 3:16, I Pet. 2:4-7)? What about the clear statement, made by the first church counsel, that informs us that God is *already building* this temple (Acts 15:15-17)? No wonder John was told to measure the temple *"and those who worship there"* (Rev. 11:1)!!

(Hallelujah!)

Calm down, Frank. Calm down! We went over those points, before, and we still have a lot more to cover.

Yes, I know, but it is good to review. . . .

The answers to more questions will be unfolded in the overlapping visions of John's Revelation of Jesus Christ, as we dutifully apply the keys to unlock them.

Having placed our cards on the table, we are now more able to address one of the most interesting, and controversial, aspects of John's amazing prophecy: the letters to the seven churches.

So controversial is this point, in fact, that it will take us two full chapters to get into. First, we will have to address a dangerous paradigm, seeking to rob us of one of our most effective weapons, in spiritual warfare. Of course, such never does limit Heaven . . . .

Chapter 9:

IS THAT A FACT?
—do we need a cleansing?

For we dare not class ourselves or compare ourselves with those who commend themselves. But they, measuring themselves by themselves, and comparing themselves among themselves, are not wise.

II Corinthians 10:12

As our opening quote implies, those who subject themselves to group think, often refuse to "come clean" when confronted with the truth. . . .

An interesting controversy arose after the restoration of the Sistine Chapel in Rome began, in 1981. The famous ceiling of the papal chapel may now be viewed in all its original colors—as painted more than four centuries earlier. "Some conservationists complained about the loss of a brown patina that had developed over centuries, composed of candle smoke, soot, and repeated applications of poor quality varnish."[76] Yet, as it now displays its original colors, the ceiling actually reveals Michelangelo's original portrayals, giving the viewer the full effect of biblical themes in bright and lively colors, easily viewed from the floor below. Some resist this enlightenment, however, preferring the antique effect brought on by years of soot and aging. In other words, the world had grown so accustomed to this masterwork being covered by the deteriorating effects of time and abuse, that they now *object* to the removal of the fresco's corrupted layers!

The same may be true of corrupted viewers . . .

Members San Francisco's Tenderloin (AKA "red light") district have now objected to recent attempts made by a local contractor and her husband to clean up the community by launching a program to remove trash and debris, as well as by instituting a program to plant 400 new trees within the neighborhood. She launched this latter campaign by enlisting homeless youth for $6 a day, to plant the trees. The program is still in process (only 26 young palm trees have been planted thus far) but it has already drawn quite a bit of fire from local residents.

> . . . the tree campaign struck a sour note at Gay Shame. The youths were hired "to do grunt work, and what they should be learning is computer skills or learning how to be an architect, not planting palm trees," fumes Mr. Sycamore. "It's exploitation."[77]

Mr. Sycamore, who resists the tree planting, is a transgender associate of Daisy Anarchy (real names) working together to disrupt neighborhood meetings organized by the local contractor (Ms. Abst). When community meetings are held they seek to counter her message with their loud outbursts and general distractions. In addition, both Ms. Anarchy and Mr. Sycamore appear to be instrumental in having posted "Wanted" posters featuring Ms. Abst's smiling face. The posters requested that residents call a local phone number, when spotting her on the street. The posters were a "prank" Mr. Sycamore contends—but did succeed in frightening (without stopping) Ms. Abst, while focusing a lot of attention on her clean up efforts.

142

So, is cleaning up our act, a bad thing?

The answer, in the case of the second story seems obvious. In the first, however, lives and reputations may be at stake as well, as respected professors and an entire collegiate culture revolving around the worship of defaced frescoes on a chapel ceiling, come tumbling down.

Are we willing to forsake our traditions . . . for the truth?

After venturing back into our culture's hallowed halls of learning, a professor very dutifully assigned me a well known writing reference. Its title reads: FACT, VALUE, POLICY: Reading and Writing Arguments (by A. Harris Fairbanks, McGraw Hill publisher: 1994). It is an excellent reference manual, designed to introduce students on modern researching techniques. Basically, there are three main premises:

1. Facts: those ideas approaching "truth" —through incidents actually observed, or,

2. That have been agreed upon by others within the academic/scientific community.

3. Values –even moral values—structured upon those "facts" thus established, by "research."

4. Policy—both private and public (as within government) based upon said research.

All of this is very well and good, of course—except for where the situation exists highlighted by our opening (and observed in our chapter on monstrous paradigms): What of generational errors?

What of "Group Think"?

What happens when things universally agreed upon, are also universally false—as when western civilization once believed the earth was flat, or that the sun revolved around the earth(?) What happens when erroneous "authorities" become alternate reference points to simply feed more error? As I once told a professor: "You have your opinion, and I mine—but only what God says, really matters."!

Of course, when making such a comment—even within many Christian colleges today, some look your way as if you have three heads(!!). How dare you presume to know what God thinks!

Yet, this is exactly what those who have encountered the God Who is there—have actually discovered in the Holy Bible. This is, in fact, the revealed word of Almighty God. It is the truth. Having had its generational accounts born out through history (in archeological digs, for example) it will also be exonerated in the future, through fulfilled prophecy. The Bible yet stands in spite of all the "soot and varnish" seeking to cover its original message.

Yet, even within a world going flat, there are a few authorities willing to "think outside of the box" and to see the world as it is. Columbus did this, and discovered the New World. Respected authorities were willing to give him the benefit of the doubt, in order to test his theory. We will, therefore, yet quote from a few points of reference generally considered valid within the Christian community, to jump-start our next discussion. Because of the nature of the material we are about to explore, such support may prove helpful. In the end, we will eventually display two alternate views of the United States, as well, as we continue with more keys. These

144

divergent views from prophecy, however, reflect the same United States, undergoing a change. . .

Many such views, rounding out our perspectives, will stir controversy within heated waters, I am certain. Yet it may at least form a framework for the restructuring our individual, and personal paradigms.

And prepare us for the Midnight Cry.

"Of course," you say, "—but what of your subtitle mentioning a clean up (of the church)? Yes, and here we must be especially careful to examine more than at first meets the eye. For if nations are important in the outline of Bible prophecy, the everlasting *kingdom of God*, is more so.

Will there be denominations in Heaven? Put another way: it seems obvious that the varied denominations and factions within the Christian church have come from *somewhere*. There must be some historical (and even eternal) reference point for all of these differences.

→Is there one—even within prophecy? (I know, how dare we presume such a thing, this side of Heaven? Such may not be known . . . or can it?) Further, when we consider that the Lord is so intimately involved with His people, may we not also expect that He has left some pattern, or blueprint, of the advance of His church down through the ages?

He has, and does have a plan. In fact, this is the best way I know to give an explanation for the varied denominations and affiliations within the body of Christ, today. Even before finishing the sentence, however, I feel like one on a battlefield who must duck behind a Rock—dodging the eggs and tomatoes being hurled in my direction. For this reason I urge sincere believers to consider how the churches of the first century must have felt when the Lord first placed the "finger" upon *their* particular assembly. Would they pout, or prevail?

That is your (and my) personal decision to make, today.

Are we really willing to do "house cleaning"?

With the above challenge to our status quo, I present an alternate reference for consideration. Its statements come from one of the best known and respected Bible teachers of the last century; Cyrus I. Scofield, editor and commentator of the famous Scofield Reference Bible, originally released in 1909, and remembered most fondly for his 1917 edition. I remember an old worn copy my parents had, in a red hardcover edition. For younger readers not familiar with this landmark work; Brother Scofield opened a new day in Bible study by making it popular to have Bibles with the commentary printed upon the same pages as the sacred text. In addition, he made free use of the now popular "chain reference" system, whereby Bible verses may be cross linked through-out the Book—a technique, by the way, no other text in the world should make ready use of, for it makes it so much easier for the reader to validate—or to contradict, various teachings throughout the written document.

Brother Scofield (1843-1921) was an able preacher in his own right and well distinguished among Christians who believe in the fundamentals of the faith. He is widely known for his views on prophecy, based upon the "dispensational" model: believing that there are seven distinct periods of historical involvement within the history of man, relating to human experience and worshipful com-

146

munion. Within each of these dispensations, men and women may relate to God in a specific manner: each "step" bringing us closer and closer to the original harmony found in Paradise.

For example, when Adam and Eve sinned at the Fall of humankind (covered earlier) they could no longer abide within God's presence, and enjoy communion with Him as they had previously. This was because they had lost their right to reenter Paradise.

Paradise, within this context, is where God dwells in harmony *and favor* with His people.

When driven out of Paradise they sought some means of sacrifice, as an opening back into God's favor. This is what their two sons, Cain and Abel, were attempting to do when Abel found that his offering was acceptable, but Cain's was not (Genesis 4:3-7). In this Old Testament example, Abel demonstrated the need for a blood sacrifice, to atone for humankind's sin. It was by offering of an animal's blood, that he acknowledged that sin is a life-and-death matter. "For the life of the flesh is in the blood" (Lev. 17:11). Thus, instinctively, Abel had come to terms with the "dispensational change" that occurred because of his parents' sin in the Garden—and was well on the way to finding the solution (completed by Christ, on the Cross).

Utilizing Scofield's view of Christian history, we are already within the sixth dispensation (of grace) and awaiting the final dispensation, at the return of Christ. At that point, not only will the Christians' sins have been forgiven, and souls redeemed—but our bodies will be glorified, as well, as we become immortal. Scofield also taught, however, that Christ would first return to earth in an (essentially) secret appearance after which a period of great trial and sorrow would take place upon the earth. This painful era, that

147

births Christ's second coming, is commonly referred to as the "great tribulation" (as mentioned in Matthew 24:21-22). The key problem with this view, and reason this book is thus structured around the parable of the ten virgins—is that the events outlined in Scripture, and scheduled to take place within the great tribulation . . . are evident at the Midnight Cry . . . and are right now beginning to *stare us in the face.*

In other words, if you will accept it, the thing that most shocks the foolish virgins within the parable of ten virgins is exactly this: that they had expected to avoid what they will see facing them, with their very eyes. They had believed that because of what Christ has done for us on the Cross, they had found such favor with God . . . that they might also expect *favoritism* and freedom from great trial.

Or, to put it more simply:

They in no way expected to witness the rise, and unveiling, of the Antichrist, as was discussed, earlier. They thought they were privileged and deserving of forever escaping serious persecution and trial, within their free societies (that's why they have "little strength") . . ..

In all fairness to Scofield, however:

- It must be remembered that his work took place before the return of the nation of Israel, into her land (an event he anticipated through Ezekiel's writings: chapters 36 & 37).

- He did acknowledge that an understanding of end time prophecy would be further clarified, as we approached the end of the age. Specifically, his commentary from the 1917 edition reads:

> Interpreters of the Revelation should bear in mind two important passages: 1 Peter 1:12; 2 Peter 1:20,21. Doubtless much which is designedly obscure to us will be clear to those for whom it was written as the time approaches.[78]

From this last quote we begin to appreciate Scofield's long and enduring ministry, for he was not only learned, but also humble enough to admit his own personal limitations: something all of us may consider, today. For he clearly states that special insight may expected within the terminal generation (reread the above quote). My greatest concern for those teaching a pre-tribulation rapture[†] is that they will be too embarrassed to change their position at the Midnight Cry. Will they mourn the loss of the soot, and outdated varnishing that covers an incorrect view of prophecy?

In that event, holding to an erroneous point of view may send many multitudes into the lake of torment, simply because men (and women) are seeking to save face! If you wish to throw eggs and tomatoes in my direction, to relieve your frustrations, have at it.

→It is obvious that many lay persons will persist in this false belief, because their pastors tell them not to worry about these matters. Therefore, . . .

[†] A "pre-tribulation rapture" –believing that the rapture foretold in I Thes. 5:14-17, will take place *before* the Antichrist arises . . . a teaching we have already exposed earlier, as totally erroneous, from Paul's second letter to this very same church at Thessalonica (II Thes. 2:1-3).

Why bother?

One of my chief reasons for releasing this book, is to allow Christian leaders time to reconsider, and to reposition themselves, before the Midnight Cry *does* break. A wise minister of the gospel may never mention that he even heard of this book. Fine. Please, please, *please* however, do research and prayerfully consider the issues presented here. The main issue is that of eternal souls: both ours, and of those we may influence forever.

When we take the time to read the Scripture references highlighted by Bro. Scofield above, we come to two very important issues within prophecy. The second (from II Pet. 1:20) we have already breached: that prophecy is given on a "need to know" basis. His first reference text, quoted below, speaks not only of prophecy, but of prophecy's *purpose* in the salvation of human souls.

The "end game" is all about eternal life, and the salvation of individual believers!

It is not about faith only, or about "spirituality" but about connecting with the God who is there, *through* our faith and believing. Faith, for the Christian, is about uniting with the eternal God, through the Holy Spirit. This is so that you may:

[receive] the end of your faith; the salvation of your souls.

Of this salvation the prophets have inquired and searched carefully, who prophesied of the grace that would come to you,

. . . .

150

To them it was revealed that, not to themselves, but to us they were ministering the things which now have been reported to you through those who have preached the gospel to you by the Holy Spirit sent from heaven; things which angels desire to look into.

I Peter 1:9,10,12

Please notice how easily and with what comfort, the apostle Peter converses about the prophets, the Holy Spirit, and of angels. This is the world of the Spirit in which these brethren lived. It was part and parcel, not only of their paradigm, but of their actual experience, and may be of ours, as well (Gal. 5:24,25, Rom. 8:11-14). The apostle Paul also addressed these matters within his letters, speaking of the Christian's family in heaven and on earth (Eph. 3:15). It should not surprise us, therefore, when we find John being invited up into Heaven to view the things revealed in his Apocalypse.

Returning to Scofield's point; the prophets were performing a service—not only to the generation in which they lived (assuring them that the Lord will win, in the end) but also to the terminal generation actually experiencing the fulfillment of those prophecies.

Having now introduced the reader to Bro. Scofield, we are ready to now take a look at what he said regarding the letters to the seven churches. Please note how he outlines the multi-layered nature of John's Revelation of Jesus Christ: a concept repeatedly greeting us within this study. There is one error/misperception that I would like to point out beforehand, however. For he states that the church is not mentioned beyond the third chapter of John's vision. This is a common misconception. Therefore, it must be remembered exactly:

- What the church is, and,

- Where most of John's vision, in the Apocalypse, takes place.

What the church is:

The Greek word for "church" is *ekklesia.* Composed of the first syllable (pronounced "eck") and *klesis,* "a calling" from *kaleo,* "to call" and was thus:

> Used among Greeks of a body of citizens "gath-
> ered" to discuss the affairs of state, Acts 19:39.
> In the Sept.[†] it is used to designate the "gather-
> ing" of Israel, summoned for any definite pur-
> pose, or a "gathering" regarded as representative
> of the whole nation.[79]

In other words, this term "church" refers to God's "called out ones." Now, while we live upon earth, it seems quite appropriate to utilize such a term, for we are indeed "called out." Christ says that we are "in the world, but not of the world" (Jn. 17:16). However, in Heaven, will the saints be the "called out ones" –or the ones on the *inside?* Further, upon earth, members of churches are identi-fied by location: the church at Antioch (Acts 13:1) –or the church at Cenchrea (Rom. 16:1), the church at Corinth (I Cor. 1:2) . . . . So, would it be appropriate to speak of the church at Heaven? No,

---

[†] The Septuagint, a Greek translation of the Old Testament completed approxi-mately 500 years before Christ.

in Heaven the church is no longer "called out"—we have come Home. We are one body. We are simply, "the saints."

Where most of John's vision takes place:

Much is made of the statement, recorded in Revelation 4:1 "Come up hither" (AV). −As though this were an invitation for Christians to bodily arise with the apostle into the throne room of God, at this point. (Has the rapture taken place, at this point? — Remember the warning, about jumping the gun over the rapture (II Thes. 2:1-3)!)

Remember our discussion on monsters and angels, as well. Of paramount importance is John's *perspective*. For John to see the future, he had to be brought up to where God sees things. This is what the angel's call seeks to accomplish. There is no mention, whatever, of John permanently escaping this world (he returned to us on earth, to deliver the message, after all)—or of any others being invited, from his associates, into heaven to view these things along with him.

The specific quote reads:

> After these things I looked, and behold, a door standing open in heaven. And the first voice which I heard was like a trumpet speaking with me, saying, "Come up here, and I will show you things which must take place after this."
> Immediately I was in the Spirit; and behold, a throne set in heaven, and One sat on the throne.

> Revelation 4:1,2

Notice, John is "in the Spirit" −not experiencing a bodily transfer. From this point on, John's view of things regarding the

153

future, is uncluttered by the world around us. His mind is given an untarnished ("cleaned up") view of the future. Therefore, all references to those in the church, while in Heaven, will be made in regard to their Heavenly identity, *as saints*. Again:

This is a heavenly view of God's people, at home; not yet eternally empowered. When Christ actually returns, in the skies overhead, He will call His Bride (the earthly Church) to His side, as glorified flesh unites with living spirits, "and so shall we ever be with the Lord" (I Thes. 4:17 AV, II Cor. 5:1-3, 8). Thus the triune nature of man: body, soul, and spirit,[80] interrupted at death, will once more be complete.

 Then, as Christ continues to descend with His Bride by His side, it will be "payday" for all who have, to that point, blasphemed and resisted this Holy God.

"Behold, the Lord comes with ten thousands of His saints,

"to execute judgment on all, to convict all who are ungodly among them of all their ungodly deeds which they have committed in an ungodly way, and of all the harsh things which ungodly sinners have spoken against Him."

Jude 14,15

It is this ultimate reality, of Christ's final return with His Bride by His side, that we must ever be mindful of while considering the "Apocalypse" that so terrorizes most, within our world. Christian brothers and sisters, we are on the winning side!! But, for now, getting back down to earth . . .

Remember those seven churches!

Now, to summarize from Bro. Scofield's comments regarding those *letters to the seven churches*. He states that there are essentially four applications. Some are a little technical, but well worth our trouble when unlocking their insights.

He notes that the letters to seven churches are:

- local: to the actual seven churches then upon the earth (in the first century)

- "admonitory," admonitions/teachings to all churches in all time as tests by which they may discern their true spiritual state in the sight of God;

- personal, in the exhortations to him *'that hath an ear,'* and in the promises *'to him that overcometh';* —assisting us in our quest to make a difference, with how we live our lives.

- →prophetic, as disclosing seven phases of the *spiritual* history of the church from, say A.D. 96 to the end.

Then he adds two further, very insightful, comments regarding this section of prophecy. Says Scofield:

> It is incredible that in a prophecy covering the church period there should be no such fore-view.[*] These messages must contain that fore-view if it is in the book at all, for no church is mentioned after Chap. 3.22. Again, these messages by their very terms go beyond the local as-

semblies mentioned. <u>Most conclusively of all, these messages *do* present an exact foreview of the spiritual history of the Church, and in this precise order</u>. [underlining added][81]

* A telescoping view: looking out over a broad landscape of the church's future.

Aside from his comments regarding churches not being present past chapt. 3.22 (which we explained, before making the quote) I have only one reaction:

Wow! Would to God more would stand up and speak so plainly today, within this overly-permissive and lukewarm era (Oops! We haven't fully exposed that one, yet . . .).

What we have covered within this chapter lays the groundwork for looking at the prophetic "foreview" of this section of the Apocalypse. By "foreview" of course, we refer to John's foretelling of future events, related to the church as it has passed down through different eras and phases. In other words, he acknowledged that the seven churches . . . represent seven general phases in church history: from the time of Christ, up until His final returning in the sky.

Notice also, the very bold statement, that has been underlined, which states that the arrangement these seven letters display the history of the church from John's day to the end of the age, "in this precise order." In other words, the exact order in which the weaknesses and strengths within the seven letters was presented—was with divine purpose: to foreshadow the exact order in which the

156

succeeding generations would encounter those specific spiritual maladies and judgments, down through the ages.

As the reader considers exactly what has just been stated, I can easily imagine their reaction being similar to my own: first

"Wow! What a gold mine!" and then,

"Whoa! Where are *we* in all of this?"

Which reminds me of the statement made by the angel, in the tenth chapter, inviting John to eat the "little book" (the Bible).

> So I went to the angel and said to him, "Give me the little book." And he said to me, "Take and eat it; and it will make your stomach bitter, but it will be as sweet as honey in your mouth."
>
> Then I took the little book out of the angel's hand and ate it, and it was as sweet as honey in my mouth. But when I had eaten it, my stomach became bitter.
>
> Revelation 10:9, 10

Bittersweet, or not, we dare not halt our quest for the truth now. For it is only the truth that will set us free, and truly prepare us for the Midnight Cry. Turn with me, now, to the seven churches. Perhaps, we will find ourselves in the line-up here, as well.

Chapter 10:

THE BEREAN CALL

"I know your works, that you are neither cold nor hot. I could wish you were cold or hot.

"So then, because you are lukewarm, and neither cold nor hot, I will vomit you out of My mouth..."

Revelation 3:15,16

Then the brethren immediately sent Paul and Silas away by night to Berea. . . . .

These were more fair-minded than those in Thessalonica, in that they received the word with all readiness, and searched the Scriptures daily to find out whether these things were so.

Acts 17:10a,11

These Bereans, they were a people searching the Scriptures for themselves, and it saved them a lot of heartache. Unfortunately, this seems to be a vanishing breed within today's technocratic age of Instant Cathedrals. . . .

We are all familiar, I am certain, with the phenomena of the "cussing saint." You arrive at work, one morning—perhaps on a new job—and are introduced to a guy or gal who seems amicable enough, except for their tongue. It's all very civil, mind you (by modern and post-modern standards) . . . it's just that it's what used to called "filthy." Then the shocker, on another day like Monday morning, when it just happens to "slip" that you've attended church yesterday—they insist that they are very religious, as well. Or (heaven forbid) you may ask the all important question:

"Do you know what it is to be born again?"

They answer in the affirmative, "Oh, yea. I've been there, done that. I've been saved for _____ years!"

"'taught Sunday school, yesterday!"

Or, the woman whom you meet at the office, who is ever so effervescent and free wheeling about her Christian faith: inviting fellow co-workers to her church and functions, who just happens to think that "all men are stinkers," has been married several times, and is in love with listening to New Age vibes.

Perhaps you were even like the dear sister who was a trained and professional Reader. She was delivered from reading horoscopes, and then happened to overhear "some of the Christian leaders say that adultery is okay sometimes."[82]

It is not the fact that people are "slipping" that bothers you, in particular. It is their lack of shame over these matters, altogether. It is as though there exists an unspoken rule that, so long as we all agree, are laughing together, and no one "gets hurt"— all is fair in love, war, and matters of the Christian faith.

What with ministers continually being caught in sexual scandals who are continually "gracing" our awareness —either with the secretary (of their own sex, or the other)

—will it some day be alright to cuss and swear—even within the church, because "everyone is doing it"?

I can remember, as a child, never going into a church where a woman wore slacks. It was considered a denial of her femininity. Today, such is a very common place. We have, in fact, shifted the moral framework (and dress code) of our culture. As Chinese women have been wearing pantaloons (or its equivalent) for centuries, the same is now common within the West. It may, in fact, be *hypocritical* to expect otherwise at Church fellowships, today. Is this to be our pattern of *moral* conduct, as well?

Will "alternative life styles" soon be the norm, with no one the wiser (or offended) for the shift, within the Church of Jesus Christ?

Muslims, and non-Christian observers, commonly chide and even comfort themselves about "those hypocrites" in the Christian Church. Yet correcting the problem within the fellowship of believers is not so simple as it may at first seem. Christian fellowship and conduct are much more about relationships, than about strict guidelines composed of "dos and don'ts."

Within the New Testament there is wide latitude for personal conduct and belief. Even on matters that affect the way Heaven views our conduct, members are allowed to make allowances for the way we live our lives. Consider, for example, an issue that some within the more conservative camp may take exception to: women praying in public. Paul makes an interesting comment, in regard to personal dress code and conduct when a godly woman is engaged in public prayer. I realize that the subject of "woman's lib" is hot today, but this is not the point within the following example.

Instead, please note with me just how much latitude the apostle allows—even within the perspective of offending angelic observers, who are now ministering to the saints.[83]

> For as woman came from man, even so man also comes through woman; but all things are from God.
> Judge among yourselves. Is it proper for a woman to pray to God with her head uncovered?

Does not even nature itself teach you that if a man has long hair, it is a dishonor to him? But if a woman has long hair, it is a glory to her; for her hair is given to her for a covering.

But if anyone seems to be contentious, we have no such custom, nor do the churches of God.

I Corinthians 11:12-16

The apostle's real reason for making the above statements, regarding covering the heads of women while praying, is given in the verses immediately preceding the ones just quoted above, where he notes that we should have an eternal perspective. Essentially, from Heaven's perspective, where all is in godly order, the angels expect for the same to be true among believers. —For the woman was created out of/and for, the man.[84]

Yet Paul acknowledges that men are born to women (and so both are mutually dependent). So, although angels would prefer to see women in obvious subjection as an expression of their faith (not of inferiority),[85] the apostle allows latitude for those whose culture does not understand such customs.

In another place, the apostle notes that believers should structure their conduct with a serious consideration for how our actions will affect the consciences of onlookers: particularly when those onlookers are Christians, themselves.

So then each of us shall give account of himself to God.

Therefore let us not judge one another anymore, but rather resolve this, not to put a stumbling block or a cause to fall in our brother's way.

I know and am convinced by the Lord Jesus that there is nothing unclean of itself; but to him who considers anything to be unclean, to him it is unclean.

Yet if your brother is grieved because of your food, you are
no longer walking in love. Do not destroy with your food the
one for whom Christ died.

Therefore do not let your good be spoken of as evil;

Romans 14:12-16

The specific situation referred to in the above comment was
that of eating food offered to idols. Within a culture coming out of
obvious physical idolatry (or entering the same, with American
idols . . .) such may easily be misunderstood as a breach of the
faith: committing sacrilege with what has been obviously recognized as a violation of Christian worship.

A modern application might apply, for example, if I were researching a certain custom, to determine its viability within the
Christian community (whether I want for my family to engage in a
particular practice or not—in the viewing of a particular movie, or
media event, for example)—if an onlooker took offense when immediately recognizing a New Age[86] influence from which they'd
been delivered, and expressed the same to me—I would have to
immediately halt the viewing of that video.

The human conscience is the watchdog of the soul. We dare
not play with it, nor violate it with activities we intrinsically feel to
be wrong. Even the prophet Ezekiel, when told to engage in a pa-
gan practice that would visually demonstrate a future defilement of
fellow Israelites—was allowed to alter *God's instructions*, in order
to avoid offending his own conscience (Ezekiel 4:12-15).

So, where do we draw the line? What forms of conduct, or
policies held within the fellowship of believers are undeniably offensive to the Lord? What conduct, or policy directive, when engaged in, will result in a diminishing of Christian experience, regardless of whether or not we feel it is "done in love"?

This is one of the purposes for the Lord giving us His letters to the seven churches.

Keeping in mind the premise presented in the previous chapter, of the dangers of group think, we now bring forward by way of third party, a historical outline of the Christian church from the time of Christ, to the present. This is not a detailed view, mind you, but will suffice for our example, for we seek to convey those same broad strokes that these original seven letters made use of: forming an outline of church's rise, diminishing, and rising again in a manner almost similar to the rise and fall of Israel's faithfulness in the history of the Old Testament, but in a much more compact manner.

There are a few surprises here (so, what else is new) so that we really must be on guard against group think. Within the fires of tribulation, the views expressed here will be refined, and further appreciated. By way of example, we may expect the serious reader to gain a better *heavenly* perspective on the Roman Catholic Church, for example: neither affirming the "Fundamentalist" perspective—nor Rome's. Nor will we find a blanket endorsement of either Protestant or Roman Catholic positions. Sorry, but we really *are* pursuing a Heavenly perspective, here.

Our purpose therefore, is not to study church history, but to gain an appreciation of the way Heaven has viewed the changes taking place within the church, down through the centuries.

→In John's first letter to Ephesus, for example, we peek in from the outside at a church that is both powerful and prevailing under persecution: newly minted from the day of Pentecost, and victorious up to the day of the apostles' passing into Glory. Its understanding of things both temporal and eternal were conveyed by the

Holy Spirit of God, and would be puzzled over for centuries, by succeeding church epochs not so completely surrendered to the same *Holy* Spirit.

Yet with all of the above attributes, the Lord presents us with a red alert for a possible "heart attack" in the Lord's concern for His people: similar to what James says regarding the Holy Spirit's earnestly desiring our hearts and affections.[87] For he reminds us that the Lord is indeed a jealous God. He requires our deepest loyalty and affections, regardless of professed access to either ecclesiastical, or spiritual power. Says our Lord to the church at Ephesus:

> "I know your works, your labor, your patience, and that you cannot bear those who are evil. And you have tested those who say they are apostles and are not, and have found them liars;
>
> "and you have persevered and have patience, and have labored for My name's sake and have not become weary.
>
> "Nevertheless I have this against you, that you have left your first love."
>
> Revelation 2:2-4

Such advice reminds us of Paul's admonition to the church at Corinth—after posting guidelines on Holy Ghost conduct among those filled with the Spirit and exercising spiritual gifts, while speaking in tongues. "—Earnestly desire the best gifts," Paul says, "And yet I show you a more excellent way"[88]—after which he pens the glorious passage on the love of God, in the thirteenth chapter:

> Though I speak with the tongues of men and of angels, but have not love, I have become sounding brass or a clanging cymbal.
>
> And though I have the gift of prophecy, and understand all mysteries and all knowledge, and though I have all faith, so

that I could remove mountains, but have not love, I am nothing. . . .

I Corinthians 13:1,2

Thus, we have been introduced to the first of our seven church epochs; the Apostolic Church. All seven church periods, will now follow in their own order:

The Apostolic Church — AD 30 - 100

The Persecuted Church — AD 100 - 313

The Imperial Church — AD 313 - 476

The Medieval Church — AD 476 – 1453

The Reformed Church — AD 1453 – 1648

The Modern Church — AD 1648 — 1948

Two things are now immediately evident (or not so evident) to some. For one, I've taken the liberty to "cap" the "Modern Church" at Israel's returning to her land, for the listing given above comes from a popular book on church history also studied in Christian Bible schools, entitled THE STORY OF THE CHRISTIAN CHURCH. It was originally copyrighted in 1918,[89] several decades before the nation of Israel was re-founded. We may finish our listing therefore, with:

7. The Last Day Church — AD 1948 – Christ's 2nd coming.

In all honesty, we have yet to meet one other facet of God's work within the terminal generation, but will have to wait until next chapter to be introduced to the sons of oil. For now, we will content ourselves with announcing the existence of this Last Day

Church corresponding to the seventh church (Laodicea) and . . . the sleeping virgins.

We may now line up our seven letters, for the reader's consideration, so that independent study may also be enjoined, after having been introduced to these matters. The chapter and verse numbers are included in the brackets [ ], for the readers further study. They are:

- Ephesus [2:1-7][†] –the apostolic church, with a loss of fervent love for the Lord

- Smyrna [2:8-11] –the persecuted church: poor, but rich in faith.

- Pergamos [2:12-17] –the church where Satan's seat dwells: maintaining its distinction as a Christian fellowship, but allowing encroaching heresies. This was the church of Constantine's era, past the edict of toleration, wherein the Roman empire "flipped" in its policy towards Christian faith, essentially making it the official religion of the empire.

- Thyatira [2:18-29] –the church where particular heresies fully take hold: this is where Jezebel dwells, in a church that will one day be called "Babylon the Harlot." Of particular interest, is the contrast between this church (having the roots of the Roman Catholic Church) and the next (with Protestant beginnings). For while Sardis is doctrinally sound, Thyatira actually has more commendable works (compare 2:19 with 3:1). . . .

[†] Here, only chapter and verse notation is utilized. In this case denoting Revelation 2:1-7.

- Sardis [3:1-6] – the church that has a name of being alive, but is dead. This fellowship has not yet discovered the fullness of the Holy Spirit. As the body without the Spirit is dead, so with this fellowship: doctrinal correctness notwithstanding. From modern day "Sardis" we hear such pronouncements as, "The Mark of the Beast is only symbolic"—an excellent example of denominational blindness: "If our group denies it, forget about what God is actually doing, in the world around us(!)"

- Philadelphia [3:7-13] –the church with the open door, of freedom, having a "little strength." It is important to realize that little strength will not suffice at the Boiling Point. – The biblical definition of "little strength" is given by Solomon: if you faint in the day of adversity, your strength is small (Pr. 24:10) This church exits before the Midnight Cry (Rev. 3:10) . . . .

- Laodicea [3:14-22] – the lukewarm church: overly tolerant, and lacking the fire, she is in danger of being *vomited* from Christ's mouth (Rev. 3:16). One opportunity exists for redemption: making it past the Midnight Cry. Christ's exact wording, in regard to this matter:

"Because you say, 'I am rich, have become wealthy, and have need of nothing'; and do not know that you are wretched, miserable, poor, blind, and naked;

"I counsel you to buy from Me gold refined in the fire, that you may be rich; and white garments, that you may be clothed, that the shame of your nakedness may not be revealed; and anoint your eyes with eye salve, that you may see. As many as I love, I rebuke and chasten. Therefore be zealous and repent."

Revelation 3:17-19

Note that "gold refined in the fire" is a reference to great trial and hardship (I Peter 1:6,7).

→ Christian Churches operating within our present generation have roots extending to one of these past seven church eras—with the "sons of oil" also having the potential of being a special case of the first church age, restructured for the end time. (More on this, next chapter.) An example of applying this principle to a well known evangelical fellowship, would be to equate the Southern Baptist Organization with the church of Philadelphia. However, have you detected who the church of Sardis represents? If the church at Pergamos represents the time of the church on earth at the time of Constantine's edict of toleration (313 AD) and that of Thyatira represents the Roman Catholic institution, fully elevating Mary (contrary to Jeremiah 7:18,19) [†]—who then is the church of Sardis, which follows directly after . . . in the Reformation?

It would be an interesting study, for the reader, to investigate the beliefs of the Reformed Brethren, and of others who trace their roots into this era, to discern who it is that:

- Denies that Israel is still under the covenant promises of God (accessing a doctrine termed "replacement theology"). We'd expect such things from Rome, but from those within Protestant ranks?

- Often takes a Preterit view of prophecy (placing all prophetic fulfillment *in the past*).

[†] Is this false Mary, then, the woman alluded to in Thyatira's reproof—who "calls herself a prophetess" (Rev. 2:20)? Is this why she has so many apparitions?

→ By this time, any with eyes to see may easily discern why, although C.I. Scofield (and others) were quick to consider the view that the letters to the seven churches do represent seven general church epochs —few dare actually teach on the subject. It steps too firmly on everyone's toes. Only those in the fire of persecution, firmly rooted in the fellowship of the sufferings of Christ (not in a monastic asceticism, or artificial flagellation, but simple holy living)—come out unscathed.

Such was the church of Smyrna (and of some, today, in the third world . . .).

These observations are particularly cogent, for a church that has obviously entered the Laodicean era which, by the way, has the potential of infecting any (and all) who encounter wealth and affluence within the freedom of Christian faith: sons of oil, or not.[†]

I am well aware that, some who are reading this material already feel "persecuted" but, believe me, we haven't seen anything yet! Further, early repentance is much preferred over terminal blindness, and eternal regret. The ultimate purpose of our study is not to "oogle and awe" over the fulfillment of Bible prophecy, but to produce a virgin's cry from deep within. We need to prepare ourselves by fully reaching out to our Beloved; our wick fully lit, with love's flame burning brightly, at Christ's appearing.

For, only the truth can set us free.

Before we leave this chapter allow a few serious observations concerning the first, through the fourth, church eras. We have already mentioned Jezebel, whose children the Lord said, He would kill with death (Rev. 2:23). The Medieval Church lasted from 476

[†] Just a hint of things to come, in our discussions on the *sons of oil.*

– 1453 by Hurlbut's estimation, within a world very much slower than our own. The Black Death (Bubonic Plague) took place in 1347 AD.

Of particular interest to us in this closing hour, is a specific error mentioned by the Lord to two of the first three churches. Two of the first three recognized the problem. From the fourth church epoch on, it is no longer mentioned at all—not because it has been abandoned, but because it has become *embedded*. It will have to be judged at the end, in other words. We want to avoid it, for it will send millions into Hell.

It is, I believe, the ultimate danger presented by "Group Think" and the primary reason for admonishing all of God's faithful to come out of the compromised religious system of the end times (Rev. 18:4).

This is the doctrine of the Nicolaitanes.

"But this you have, that you hate the deeds of the Nicolaitans, which I also hate."

Revelation 2:6

This quote is the first time this infestation is mentioned. Note that it is within the Apostolic (Spirit filled) church, that this doctrine is mentioned, and is shunned. It's wording is reminiscent of the Lord's statement regarding His hatred of divorce (Mal. 2:13-16), and its context, is similar to Peter's admonition to husbands (I Pet. 3:7) where he warns that such activity hinders a person's prayers from being answered. Serious repentance is thus enjoined.

Repent; or else I will come unto thee quickly, and will fight against them with the sword of my mouth.

Revelation 2:10

Earlier, this error was shunned in the Apostolic church. Now, within the fledgling spiritual harlot (typifying the church of the end time apostate system[90]) this particular doctrine starts to take root, and flourish. Pergamos:

> "And to the angel of the church in Pergamos write, 'These things says He who has the sharp two-edged sword:
>
> "I know your works, and where you dwell, where Satan's throne is. And you hold fast to My name, and did not deny My faith even in the days in which Antipas was My faithful martyr, who was killed among you, where Satan dwells.
>
> "But I have a few things against you, because you have there those who hold the doctrine of Balaam, who taught Balak to put a stumbling block before the children of Israel, to eat things sacrificed to idols, and to commit sexual immorality.
>
> "Thus you also have those who hold the doctrine of the Nicolaitans, which thing I hate.
>
> Revelation 2:12-15

When Constantine issued his edit of toleration in 313 AD, he placed Christian persecution in the past ("Antipas *was* my faithful martyr, . . .*was* killed among you"). The place of Satan's seat (the Roman emperor's domain) became the seat of power for the church and, as such, a doorway for opportunists looking for political clout and influence. Needless to say, the "called out" nature of the church was quickly evaporating.

The Church was no longer the place of the called out faithful, separating itself from the vices of the world, as a dedicated and chaste bride to her husband—but as an undisciplined adulteress, within a mixed multitude of true and many false believers, bringing confusion and corruption into the fellowship. It was no doubt (to some persons' way of thinking) in reaction to this encroachment that the Nicolaitan error flourished—as celibacy might, in a general over reaction to wide-spread perversion within society.

This tendency, to over-react, and to over compensate, would mark this, and the next church era down through the centuries, fostering the inception of monasteries and convents, for example. However, the solution that so few would then embrace, and which Christ and the New Testament writers repeatedly enjoin, is not an increased asceticism or forced discipline—but complete submission to the indwelling work of the Holy Spirit.[91]

It is within this context, and this compromising environment, that the Lord warns the brethren of that church and church age:

> "Thus you also have those who hold the doctrine of the Nicolaitans, which thing I hate."

The official definition of this Nicolaitan error is:

> One of a sect in the ancient christian (sic) church, so named from Nicolas, a deacon of the church of Jerusalem. They held that all married women should be common to prevent jealousy. They are not charged with erroneous opinions respecting God, but with licentious practices. Rev. ii[92]

It must be noted that, while this explanation may seem to fit the context (of sexual immorality) –that such activity, of living within a Christian community where wives are so little respected that a swapping spouses is condoned—would be unprecedented within the New Testament, or the Bible itself. Further, such an admonition, without some prior definition having been furnished to give a clear indication within Scripture itself, of what is being reproved—gives cause to suspect that this is but one more an instance of John's Apocalypse forecasting a coded message *into the future.*

Which it certainly is.

The term "nicolaitane" is actually a transliteration[93] of the Greek word found within the actual text. In other words, the translators were so uncertain of what it actually means that they simply transferred it to the text without defining or interpreting the word. It is made up of two root words: "nikos" – victorious (translated "victory" in Matt. 12:20, I Cor. 15:52, 55...) and "laos" – from which we get the word "laity," representing the rank and file of membership within the church.[94]

So that what this really refers to is the instituting of an elite ecclesiastical class of individuals, who rule over the common people "for their own good." Before we so quickly condemn such a practice, however, we would do well to consider the perceived advantages of maintaining a strong and centralized, organizational structure. For example, it presents us with the ability to standardize belief systems and speak with a unified voice. One of the reasons that the Roman Catholic institution can wield such an incredibly powerful influence within the world in which we live, today, is because of its well defined organizational structure.

With carefully designated areas of authority.

Any organizational entity, whether government, business, or especially the military needs a strong and definable leadership. Humanly speaking, maintenance of a large body of people, in an orderly manner, seems impossible without such organizational structure.

Unless, that is, there were a supernatural aspect of leadership, maintained by the Holy Spirit Himself. Further, we may later recognize this point in our discussion of the US in prophecy—reflecting on the freedom found in Christian faith—which fosters a greater freedom within this area, as well. Failure to resist the temptation to enforce a regimented ecclesiastical structure upon the body of Christ reminds me of an Old Testament command that was also overlooked by the nation of Israel: the year of Jubilee.[95]

It also was an issue of liberty.

Every seven years slaves were to be set free, and country-side lands were to be returned to their original owners. It was a great command, something obviously reflecting a Heavenly community—but it was never quite followed. Regarding the matter of equality within the body of Christ, Jesus enjoined:

> . . .saying: "The scribes and the Pharisees sit in Moses' seat.
>
> "Therefore whatever they tell you to observe, that observe and do, but do not do according to their works; for they say, and do not do.
>
> . . .
>
> "But you, do not be called 'Rabbi'; for One is your Teacher, the Christ, and you are all brethren.
> "Do not call anyone on earth your father; for One is your Father, He who is in heaven.
> "And do not be called teachers; for One is your Teacher, the Christ.
> "But he who is greatest among you shall be your servant.[96]
>
> Matthew 23:1-3, 8-11

—And because we are interested in Heaven's perspective, we are compelled to point out to our brethren pointing the finger at our Roman Catholic friends: You, Reverend so-and-so . . .

Reverend is God's name (Psalm 111:9 AV).

By the way, I did not tell you why the Nicolaitane error will send so many into Hell, did I? It is because of the incredible influence these leaders have at their disposal. They are essentially above correction. You see, within the original (early) church, everyone was subject to examination and measurement by the Word. In this light, even the great apostle Paul (although, in this case obviously falsely accused) felt it necessary to defend himself against accusatory members within the Corinthian church. What is most interesting, is the way he characterized the "honor" sometimes conveyed upon the apostles within local assemblies. We would do well to remember this, even among the sons of oil.

> For I think that God has displayed us, the apostles, last, as men condemned to death; for we have been made a spectacle to the world, both to angels and to men.
>
> We are fools for Christ's sake, but you are wise in Christ! We are weak, but you are strong! You are distinguished, but we are dishonored!
>
> To the present hour we both hunger and thirst, and we are poorly clothed, and beaten, and homeless.
>
> And we labor, working with our own hands. Being reviled, we bless; being persecuted, we endure;
>
> being defamed, we entreat. We have been made as the filth of the world, the offscouring of all things until now.
>
> I do not write these things to shame you, but as my beloved children I warn you.
>
> For though you might have ten thousand instructors in Christ, yet you do not have many fathers; for in Christ Jesus I have begotten you through the gospel.
>
> I Corinthians 4:9-15

Here is your "father" in the gospel: a *brother* like ourselves.

But when today's (and tomorrow's) Bishop tells millions, "Don't worry about it. This can't *possibly* be the mark of the beast! (chuckle, chuckle)" How many will take the Berean route, crack open their Bibles, and check the matter out, for themselves? Ah! Now you see what I mean. We really do need to be students of the Word, for ourselves. Our eternal souls will depend on it!

How can I sign on to any fellowship that has me promise that I *must* do what leadership prescribes regarding matters of conscience? If I can't find it supported in the Scriptures, why should I jeopardize my eternal soul?

We need to be like the Bereans.

So, how are we to maintain order within the body of Christ? In the same way a free and democratic society used to maintain order in the founding of this nation: by maintaining the integrity of its members.[97] In other words, by nurturing the fear of God and comfort of the Holy Spirit,[98] as we search the Scriptures daily —we become persons who are trustworthy, and act responsibly.

For it is through the Holy Spirit, that the true body of Christ operates in its fullness, and no one, operating in the power of the Holy Spirit, may do so

without effective and fervent prayer . . .

Chapter 11:

FROM GOD'S TEMPLE:
TRUMPETING FROM THE HEAVENS

So the seven angels who had the seven trumpets prepared themselves to sound.

The first angel sounded: And hail and fire followed, mingled with blood, and they were thrown to the earth.

Revelation 8:6,7a AV

Behold, I tell you a mystery: We shall not all sleep, but we shall all be changed;

in a moment, in the twinkling of an eye, <u>at the last trumpet</u>. For the trumpet will sound, and the dead will be raised incorruptible, and we shall be changed.

I Corinthians 15:51,52 [emphasis added]

Prayer is the membrane moving between earth and Heaven. Through it passes the faith of those on earth, to connect with the Lord in Heaven. Properly exerted, it becomes a two way exchange, between this awesome God of Eternity, and the needy upon earth.

Yet, in the year 2000, the Southern Baptist Convention drew severe criticism and ridicule over specialized prayer guides, which directed prayer heavenward for the purpose of targeting specific groups of people in (gasp) other religions, such as Hindus and Moslems. My first reaction was, "Huh? What on earth . . .?" Why should *non* believers (or liberals who don't really believe in the power of prayer) care about how Christians pray?

Forget the arguments over tolerance. They couldn't care less what you think of them. (Or, perhaps they do. Big Brother would now put us in jail for thinking incorrectly. That's what "hate crimes" are, you know. Hatred is in the heart. We would now jail people for incorrect *attitudes*. Yes, I am black, but I am a Christian first. I value freedom, more than comfort.)

The point is, that our Southern Baptist brethren hit upon something, here: strategic praying. By targeting specific groups, at specific times, they provide prayer covering for those working within difficult mission fields. Hm-m-m-m wonder why the outcry. Sounds to me like Hell was starting to lose some ground here . . . .

Therefore, before we proceed any further we must realize that there are some aspects of prayer that the modern church has largely forgotten: that prayer may be utilized as a *weapon* in spiritual warfare, for the salvation of souls. Further, that this warfare is not always "pretty," politically correct, or without consequence! Even the imprecatory nature of some of the Psalms, ("Let their table become a snare before them, And their well being a trap . . .") may be effectively utilized, within the spiritual realm, when seeking to interdict demonic activity.

We do not, however, wish to find these same weapons being redirected back *at us* from Heaven! Note, if you will, other remaining verses from the psalm quoted, above. Some verses following read:

Let their eyes be darkened, so that they do not see; And make their loins shake continually.

Pour out Your indignation upon them, And let Your wrathful anger take hold of them.

Let their dwelling place be desolate; Let no one live in their tents.

For they persecute the ones You have struck, And talk of the grief of those You have wounded.

Psalm 69:22-26

"Let their eyes be darkened . . ." --Could this also apply to . . . *sleeping virgins??* Or, can you see a possible connection, in the above verses—to the foolish virgins, napping, perhaps? What of those "Judas priests" who turn on the faithful, to ostracize and criticize (or worst) those seeking to warn them of the impending judgments of God?

Thus, some will not only stay in the boiling pot, some will also stoke its flames, and agitate the witches brew . . . .

In other words, we must cast off the "sewing circle" mentality of praying, as we approach Heaven's prayer chamber. For what we will find here is not something pretty; designed for the delicate ears of the politically correct.

Further, when we understand that even the petitions mentioned under one's breath may take flight as requests before God, we more readily understand the nature of what we are about to en-counter (and the reason we should take care to avoid cussing and swearing – Matt. 5:34, James 5:12). Such requests should be made carefully, after much care and agony, before the Lord.

For such judgments, Isaiah assures us, can create a sense of urgency that even the most hardened sinner finds it hard to ignore

(Isaiah 26:9,10)—and is, in fact, absolutely necessary within the life of all true believers (Heb. 12:6). Even though within the present climate of tolerance (or pacifism) such activity may be unconscious, or even unintentional, it may still have a devastating impact, nonetheless. (No wonder Big Brother is concerned with hate crimes! He is really concerned with our secret prayers!) In fact the apostle Paul informs us that within true prayer there is an unconscious aspect in which the Holy Spirit petitions the Father with "groanings that cannot be uttered" (Rom. 8:26). Perhaps this is what James is referring to, when warning wealthy business owners to be careful of how they treat their workers, for example, in light of their responsibility, before God. James warns:

> Come now, you rich, weep and howl for your miseries that are coming upon you!
>
> . . .
>
> Indeed the wages of the laborers who mowed your fields, which you kept back by fraud, cry out; and the cries of the reapers have reached the ears of the Lord of Sabaoth.
> You have lived on the earth in pleasure and luxury; you have fattened your hearts as in a day of slaughter.
>
> . . .
>
> Therefore be patient, brethren, until the coming of the Lord. See how the farmer waits for the precious fruit of the earth, waiting patiently for it until it receives the early and latter rain.
> You also be patient. Establish your hearts, for the coming of the Lord is at hand.
>
> James 5:1,4,5,7,8 [emphasis added]

A similar warning, and outcry, we have already heard sounded from the saints after the fifth seal is broken, as they cry out under the altar,

> "How long, O Lord, holy and true, until You judge and avenge our blood on those who dwell on the earth?"
>
> Revelation 6:10

We may remember Stephen's noble prayer—that the Lord not pay back those who were stoning him to death (Acts 7:60)! Yet, as the church age draws to a close, and the indignation of God's wrath builds up, the created universe does indeed sense that we are reaching a boiling point, so that even the natural world, itself, begins to look forward to the day in which all of creation will be redeemed and Paradise is restored (Romans 8:22). The faithful, who do not sleep, must certainly understand this (it is the only way we may grasp what we are about to encounter, as well as the call of the "two witnesses").

Knowledge that serious petitioning (prayer) towards the God of Heaven continues to terrorizes the liberal establishments of this world, to no end. It troubles them to think that God does, indeed, "interfere" in the affairs of men. I seek to avoid the mention of "liberals" when speaking, because we must not distinguish them in particular (all have sinned[99]). Yet any with eyes to see must realize that many find this aspect of God's nature a source of great discomfort (with good reason!) It is a severe disturbance to any embracing the secular mindset.

→For the secular point of view, you understand, *insists* that God is inactive within our present world. Yet we Christians must do all

181

within our power not to placate, or to water down, the danger in which those who blaspheme God will soon find themselves.

Put another way, God does not laugh with the comedian who uses His name in vain. Nor does He wring His hands at the vulgar diatribes of the wicked. Quite the contrary: Scripture describes an utterly awesome God, in complete control of His universe. He is in no hurry to vindicate Himself. It is only because of His great love for us, that He has not already atomized despotic empires, and eradicated evil from off the face of the earth.

Thus, we must understand that God is not "stressed" by either our indifference or rebellion. Scripture presents the picture of the world being in great peril, with impending danger, utterly at the mercy of this almighty Lord of Heaven and Earth. This is, no doubt, the real reason for secular concern over "global warming" and the like. It is not the melting of ice caps that they really fear: it is the heated wrath of God. It is not "Armageddon" (the movie), Star Trek, or UFO aliens that we are really confronting. It is God, Himself.

> Why do the nations rage, And the people plot a vain thing?
> The kings of the earth set themselves, And the rulers take counsel together, Against the LORD and against His Anointed, saying,
> "Let us break Their bonds in pieces And cast away Their cords from us."
> He who sits in the heavens shall laugh; The LORD shall hold them in derision.
>
> Psalm 2:1-4

The Lord, along with those about His throne, laugh at the clenched fists of (post) modern man. Angelic hosts are fully aware

182

that should God's wrath be unleashed, completely, all of earth would be utterly destroyed. Consider what might have happened in a lesser instance: in the Cuban missile crisis, for example. What if the US in its swaggering response, and because of ignorance concerning the advanced nature of the weapons actually on hand— had actually been attacked by those nukes, so that some of our cities had been reduced to rubble? We are still recovering from hurricane Katrina, what about the radioactive fallout of a nuclear confrontation?? Yet we are headed for a far greater conflagration, and confrontation with the living God.

It is within this context that Christ admonishes us to *love* our enemies, and to *pray for* those who despitefully use us, for truly, those who touch God's people touch a nerve in the heart of God. He is jealous for His people. Certainly this is what first greets us as we are introduced to the prayer chamber in Heaven (actually, to the altar upon which our prayers ascend, as incense).

> And I saw the seven angels who stand before God, and to them were given seven trumpets.
>
> Then another angel, having a golden censer, came and stood at the altar. He was given much incense, that he should offer it with the prayers of all the saints upon the golden altar which was before the throne.
>
> And the smoke of the incense, with the prayers of the saints, ascended before God from the angel's hand.
>
> Then the angel took the censer, filled it with fire from the altar, and threw it to the earth. And there were noises, thunderings, lightnings, and an earthquake.
>
> Revelation 8:1-5

It is important, when studying these events marking the sounding of the seven trumpets, to pay close attention to the direction from which judgments fly. Notice, also, Heaven's reaction to the prayers of the faithful. There is a direct interaction between the prayer, and the Presence of God. The prayers *ascend* along with the incense, before the Lord. In the Lord's response to these petitions, however, it is *from* the altar of God, and *from* Heaven that they fly, towards/into the earth. Remember the "falling away" mentioned by Paul?[†] Yes, it is true that such is a translation, quickly drawing a picture with words, of the church going into apostasy. Yet here, in John's Revelation, we see an even more graphic presentation of God's answer to this apostasy, as He begins unleashing His judgments out *onto* a wayward world (and church) without many of us at first noticing its effect. Yet from Heaven's perspective, the results are ominous. "Many waters cannot quench love, Nor can the floods drown it. . . ." for our God is a consuming fire (S of Sol. 8:7, Heb. 12:29).

→Note that, in the context of the verses just quoted, fire denotes two key attributes of God: both His love, and judgment attributes. The Scriptures say that God is both "love" (I John 4:16) as well as a God of judgment/justice.

> Therefore the LORD will wait, that He may be gracious to you; And therefore He will be exalted, that He may have mercy on you. For the LORD is a God of justice; Blessed are all those who wait for Him.
>
> Isaiah 30:18

[†] II Thes. 2:3

Waiting for God's *execution* of justice (i.e. His judgments) is exactly what the saints are doing, as their prayers ascend up to Heaven (Rev. 6:9, James 5:1-8). What we are allowed to see here, is that even before the world-at-large acknowledges that God is, indeed, taking note of the saints petitions—He is already beginning to answer.

Yet, it is God's love that actually acts as a catalyst for this judgment: for it strikes the match that ignites His jealousy—both for His name, and for His people.[†] When the wrath of God grows full, there is a release of fire. As the fire is discharged, it attacks/affects the object of His holy vengeance. Thus, in each of the first four trumpets there is a release of fire *away from* the altar: denoting a cooling down, as the furnace of God's wrath continues to heat up. Judgment is going forward, yet the wrath of God continues to store up behind it, to the breaking point. Thus, we are introduced to the first four trumpets, in Revelation chapter eight. We will give a shocking (and very politically incorrect) example of the result of these judgments, after reaching the fifth trumpet. At the sixth trumpet, the dam breaks. At the seventh, He returns to personally clean house . . . .

You will have to meditate on the seemingly "insignificant" developments that will at first be outlined. They proscribe and define fundamental changes of attitude and heart within the church. Doctrines are involved, yes, but the attitudes truly make the differ-

---

[†] Jealousy, which springs from a clear expectation of faithfulness to our Beloved, is clearly reflected in the Scriptures. God is a jealous God, in both Old and New Testaments "For the LORD your God is a consuming fire, a jealous God." (Deut. 4:24)— "Or do you think that the Scripture says in vain, 'The Spirit who dwells in us yearns jealously' "? (James 4:5).

ence, here. Humankind's fundamental attitude towards God is changing. By the time Antichrist arrives . . . men will openly *hate God.*

For now, let us start at the beginning.

- In the first trumpet, we see that fire is mingled with hail and *blood*.

This is a cooling down of the church, in essential doctrines. Men have cast off the blood of Christ (Acts 20:28, Rev. 12:11), and fear of God (i.e. the *fire* of God -Heb. 10:29).

- In the second, a great mountain, burning with fire, is *cast down*

This denotes an increase of lawlessness (Matt. 24:12) —the mountain represents Mt. Sinai, where the Law was given by Moses (Heb. 12:18, I Tim. 1:9).

→Note the underlined scripture reference: This text, spoken by Jesus in the context of His returning, notes that **when lawlessness abounds, the love *of God* grows cold in the hearts of men and women** (check original Greek). This is directly related to the next trumpet.

- In the third, a star (that has fire in itself) is cast down, called *Wormwood,* making waters bitter:

The fire of emotion has now separated from true love in the heavens. A false fire (false love) now descends. In the context of that sentimental self esteem/selfishness now follows an emotional advance of lawlessness—as many *within the church* boast of how bitter they are . . . with God. BEWARE (Heb. 12:6-8)!

- In the fourth trumpet—the sun itself is blocked (darkened), as well as the moon, and stars

So devastating is the falling away of many within the church, that people begin to get **a warped view of God**, Himself (this is what the Sun represents).

→And of the moon (representing the *reflection* of God's glory: the Church)

A most obvious example of this last point might be the proposal to make homosexual marriages legal –or, even acceptable, within the church. Many contend that great damage is being done to the home, by such unions. *What of humankind's view of God?*[100]

→Thus, the very ability of men and women to see the glory of God (represented by the symbolism of the Sun) is perverted by the darkness of the age, and weakness within the church.

As the fourth trumpet comes to a close, we brace ourselves for the fifth, for we hear a warning in Heaven, saying, "Woe, woe, woe to the inhabitants of the earth, because of the remaining blasts of the trumpet of the three angels who are about to sound!" [101]

Then it happens.

- In the ninth chapter of Revelation, we are introduced to the fifth trumpet, where the number "five" bears a particular relation to judgment, for it was for five months that Noah floated on the waters in his ark (Genesis 8:3) and it was in the fifth month, that Israel went into captivity (Jeremiah 52:12). With this fifth trumpet, the perspective shifts from Heaven, to earth. From this point on, the message concerns how much direct authority Hell will be given over a world that had formerly been increasingly dominated by an ever increasing outreach, and influence, of the gospel.

In other words, we have now firmly shifted out of the Philadelphian church age, into the Laodicean (lukewarm) era—this church era, in the dominant part of the Christian world, has largely forgotten that we are at war in the spiritual realm (or plays "war games").

What strikes me the most, in this regard, is the new shift in perspective by the world, at large. When attending elementary school, in the 1950's, I can recall even secularists revering the power of the sun to bring forth life upon earth (looking up, and noting our dependence upon sunlight). –No more. The emphasis, now, is upon the earth itself: the secular world's view is now *downward*, into the earth. It is now vogue to see the planet, itself, as our Source and "Mother"—which is also an offhanded denial of our Father, God.[102]

A limitation placed, upon the fifth angel:

With the sounding of the fifth angel, the shift in perspective from Heaven to earth intensifies, allowing it to focus its affections on the occult and witchcraft, as our world continues to dig deeper into the Night. Yet, within the grace of God, we also see a restriction placed upon Hell's power.

In fact, this judgment cannot touch those walking in the Spirit. Let us back up, for a moment, to read John's vision more carefully:

> Then the fifth angel sounded: And I saw a star fallen from heaven to the earth. To him was given the key to the bottomless pit.
>
> And he opened the bottomless pit, and smoke arose out of the pit like the smoke of a great furnace. So the sun and the air were darkened because of the smoke of the pit.
>
> Revelation 9:1,2

The amazing thing about this unleashing of darkness, with its shifting reference point, from Heaven to earth . . . is that God sees fit (at this point) to limit the powers of this Darkness. They are obviously demonic, for they are called locusts—yet are *unable to consume grass or foliage* (vs. 3)! Thus, as these special demons arise out of the pit, they have only the power to *torment* men and women.

They may not render a fatal blow. They can only *harass*.

One obvious point, in this present phase, is that the power of the "born again" experience is still holding. The new birth still produces wide spread deliverance. As the influence of the Laodicean age progresses, however, so does the cooling down Christian experience . . . along with the ability to resist these forces (Isaiah 59:1,2). Sorry, I know that many do not want to hear this, but for those "foolish virgins" without the oil (and sealing[103]) of the Holy Spirit, these "locusts" are a major issue. . . Oh, Lord Jesus, ever connect me to Your Pipeline!

> They were commanded not to harm the grass of the earth, or any green thing, or any tree, but only those men who do not have the seal of God on their foreheads.

> And they were not given authority to kill them, but to tor-
> ment them for five months. Their torment was like the tor-
> ment of a scorpion when it strikes a man.

> In those days men will seek death and will not find it; they
> will desire to die, and death will flee from them.

> Revelation 9:4-6

These are demons of *stress*. And their description?

Dare we take a look?

> And they had hair as the hair of women, and their teeth were
> as the teeth of lions.
> And they had breastplates, as it were breastplates of iron;
> and the sound of their wings was as the sound of chariots of
> many horses running to battle.
> And they had tails like unto scorpions, and there were
> stings in their tails: and their power was to hurt men five
> months.

> vss 8-10

Feminism, violent speech, hard hearts, and a love for warfare
and contention (rebellion)—all inflamed by tails that look like ser-
pents (tongues).[†] In other words, when resisted, they threaten to
up-end, and to utterly disturb, all of society. You cannot resist
these spirits without going to war against them. Such will require
a full-court press.

[†] Scripture describes an ungodly tongue as a world of iniquity, . . .set on fire of Hell
(James 3:6).

190

In simple terms, these fellas can make you want to "pull your hair out!"

Yet, Scripture promises that those within the body of Christ may be totally immune to the effects of such attack (vs. 4).

So, why are many Christians continually being "chewed up" here (Galatians 5:15,16)?

Again, because of the falling away: Men (and churches) turn away from the fullness of God's Spirit. Years ago, the greatest thing that could happen to a believer was to truly experience the new birth, and be "born again." It is a truly *holy* experience, in a transaction taking place within that membrane between Heaven's courts, and His womb (of true Christians) upon earth. In those days, also, Christians gloried in being Spirit led. Now, many prefer being purpose driven, co-dependent, or in twelve step programs where God is reduced to a psychological rabbit's foot.

No, no, no. Please, no excuses. There is a definite difference between a generic *herd mentality* of those driven—and of the lowly sheep, being led by my loving Shepherd, the Lord Jesus Christ (Psalm 23).

With Him, I shall not want. Without Him, no matter what the name: whether in (so called) spirit leadings, or preacher shenanigans, I will definitely be found wanting at midnight.

Yet, there is hope for those, throughout the Christian world, who embrace the pipe-line now being made available within the evangelical/charismatic community, just so long . . . as we don't sell out.

Chapter 12:

Merchandising the Temple

And He found in the temple those who sold oxen and sheep and doves, and the moneychangers doing business.

When He had made a whip of cords, He drove them all out of the temple, with the sheep and the oxen, and poured out the changers' money and overturned the tables.

And He said to those who sold doves, "Take these things away! Do not make My Father's house a house of merchandise!"

John 2:14-16

He seemed so out of character, turning those tables over, and yet as we notice, more carefully, who it is that Jesus rebukes while "upsetting things" –something begins to dawn upon us.

It was not those selling oxen and sheep, nor was it the exchanging of money that particularly disturbed Him. No, it was those who sold *doves.* Again, it was those *selling doves* whom He addressed, with earnest rebuke. Now doves . . . represent the ministering of the Holy Spirit, for it was as a dove, that the Holy Spirit descended upon Christ, after His baptism, preparing Him to go forth as the Messiah (Matt. 3:16-4:1).

Just how serious is this matter of merchandising the Holy Spirit's power? Did God have another plan? This is something that we simply must not overlook, as we consider God's power at work among His people. Remember:

We have earlier noted that the foolish virgins had no oil (Holy Spirit power) in their lamps. We have also noted that the wise did, and that the "sons of oil" are connected to the pipeline. Is it not significant, then, that an outflow of power now come just at the point in history when we'd expect the church to be going into total recession: within the Laodicean church era? Just as lukewarm attitudes (and sleep) started to reign in the West, and the door of freedom yet remained open—did God have another plan? Is it now in process?

Further: we must remember the devastating conclusion to our last chapter. IT IS ONLY THROUGH THE POWER OF THE HOLY SPIRIT (those sealed with the seal of God – Rev. 9:4, Eph. 1:13) that we become immune to, and may overcome, the locusts of the fifth trumpet!

So now, we simply must ask, where *are* the two witnesses? Are they not the *sons of oil*?

Firstly, to be fair, we must ask where they were, in Old Testament times, when the original prophecy was given to Zechariah. For the "sons of oil" were then cited to exist in the *present tense*. "These are the two anointed ones, who stand beside the Lord of the whole earth" (Zech. 4:14). If you take the time to read that fourth chapter of Zechariah for yourself, slowly, you will notice that this is *not* the first time that the prophet Zechariah had been introduced to these sons of oil. In fact, they were mentioned earlier within the same chapter along with another description, that seems more appropriate for New Testament believers, than for Zechariah, in the Old Testament.

Why?

Because it has a reference to (what we now call) Pentecostal power.

Please, *please,* keep these concepts straight in your mind. Review the earlier chapters, if necessary, before going on. What we are about to uncover is extremely important! Further, be prepared to be challenged (again)–for what we are about to uncover will touch virtually all branches of the Christian Church.

Yet, we are doing judgment work, here. The purpose of this book is not to promote particular churches or denominations, but to prepare those few and rare individuals who desire to awaken early, and be prepared for the Midnight Cry. This will require some soul searching, for us all.

Seat belt buckled?

John the Baptist & Charismatics: Déjà vu:

Now let us turn to look, and remember the timing of this revelation concerning the two witnesses: it is at the opening of the Laodicean church era. Satan fully expects for the church to be relaxed and become comatose in its laid back condition, waiting to be raptured out of here.

Then, something happens—God's Spirit begins to move. In fact, He had already started preparation, going before the physical restoration of Israel, much as John the Baptist had, before Israel's physical Messiah (Jesus) had arrived upon the scene, the first time.

John ministered before Jesus, much as another move of God preceded the restoration of Israel. In John's case he was:

"The voice of one crying in the wilderness: 'Prepare the way of the LORD; Make His paths straight.'"

And John himself was clothed in camel's hair, with a leather belt around his waist; . . . .

Matthew 3:3,4

194

Notice, if you will, the similarity in both John's appearance and motif, with the description of the two witnesses of Revelation eleven ("clothed in sackcloth" – vs. 3). Now, reminding ourselves once more that this eleventh chapter is, indeed, a spiritual chapter[*] we will also consider the fact that when this prophecy was first fulfilled, it was generally misunderstood within that generation, as well.

> And His disciples asked Him, saying, "Why then do the scribes say that Elijah must come first?"
>
> Jesus answered and said to them, "Indeed, Elijah is coming first and <u>will</u> restore all things.
>
> "But I say to you that Elijah has come already, and they did not know him but did to him whatever they wished. Likewise the Son of Man is also about to suffer at their hands."
>
> Matthew 17:10-12 [emphasis added]

Please notice the almost cryptic comment in verse thirteen and then eleven, "But . . . Elijah *has* come already . . . ." –in verse 13

while leaving open future ministry, in His the earlier quote: "Elijah is coming first and *will* restore . . ." –in verse 11. Now, John the Baptist had just been beheaded, a short time before —thus leaving room for a *future fulfillment*, within the context of John's two witnesses.

Again: Remember that when this ministry initiates, it is difficult to discern, if not prayerfully observant (as was the case with John the Baptist's ministry).

---

[*] As was first emphasized, in chapter 4. . .

One point more, to chew on, before returning to the Old Testament prophet, Zechariah. In John the Baptist's case, Herod merely *arrested* the prophet to silence him, for he was but one individual. In the larger projection of Revelation eleven at the end of the age, it takes a *war* to silence two witnesses (Rev. 11:7 – ??). Why does the *beast* (Antichrist: the ruler of the world) need to launch a *war* to silence two people(??). It is because the two witnesses are not two *individuals*. The two witnesses are . . . a movement.

We're ready for Zechariah(!)

Now, let us go back to Zechariah's prophecy, and to the angel's *first* explanation of the two sons of oil.

> So I answered and spoke to the angel who talked with me, saying, "What are these, my lord?"
>
> Then the angel who talked with me answered and said to me, "Do you not know what these are?" And I said, "No, my lord."
>
> So he answered and said to me: "This is the word of the LORD to Zerubbabel: 'Not by might nor by power, but by My Spirit,' Says the LORD of hosts.
>
> Zech. 4:4-6

Now, Zerubbabel *was* rebuilding the temple (Zech. 4:9), yet in Revelation (and through Acts 15) we have seen that the temple is *already* being built. Therefore, no such notation occurs in Revelation eleven, of temple reconstruction. However, the mention of Holy Spirit power *is* clearly implied in John's two witnesses:

> "And I will give power to my two witnesses, and they will prophesy . . . clothed in sackcloth."
>
> Revelation 11:3

You will note that I have intentionally omitted mention of the 3½ clock, covered earlier. Here, we are focusing on the power . . . and on the sackcloth. I can always tell those who are unprepared to indulge in this ministry by their resistance to this simple (even childlike) mention of trial, pain, and endurance: the sackcloth.

<u>Through thick & thin:</u>

The wise man builds his house upon the Rock

The wise man builds his house upon the Word

The wise man builds his house, right <u>now,</u>

           whether or not

The blessings have already come down.

For we shall wear a crown

         After our Lord has touched the ground

We shall wear a crown

    forevermore . . .

To remember the simplest, and most obvious moving of God in recent times, we must turn to observe the opening of the 20th century, where there was an experiencing of Pentecostal power and Charismatic renewal. There have been abuses, this is true, yet I believe that this is where we see evidence of the Holy Spirit's anticipation of the coming renewal of both the Church and Israel, mid century. As with Israel, so with these brethren, as we have often seen infractions impinging upon their covenant, and covenant rights. As Israel had to be repeatedly chastened and warned, so too with the Pentecostal movement. For, whom the Lord loves, He chastens (spanks) and strongly punishes for the sake of reinstruction (Heb. 12:6-11).

At first the Pentecostal movement had great success and influence as millions were swept into its ranks, within the US (see "God's Generals" by Roberts Liardon,[104] written in general charismatic tones.) Presently, there is also an incredible move of God in the third world, frequently within countries where the door of freedom . . . is not open. Wise virgins, within the West, are investing heavily in this treasure trove of third world believers: sending them Bibles, assistance, and encouragement whenever possible.

This is one of the wisest things that any believer, within the West, can do in preparation for the Midnight Cry. Scripture gives particular encouragement, and assurance, to those who so care for their persecuted brethren, around the world:

"All the nations will be gathered before Him, and He will separate them one from another, as a shepherd divides his sheep from the goats.

"And He will set the sheep on His right hand, but the goats on the left.

"Then the King will say to those on His right hand, 'Come, you blessed of My Father, inherit the kingdom prepared for you from the foundation of the world:

'for I was hungry and you gave Me food; I was thirsty and you gave Me drink; I was a stranger and you took Me in;

'I was naked and you clothed Me; I was sick and you visited Me; I was in prison and you came to Me.'

"Then the righteous will answer Him, saying, 'Lord, when did we see You hungry and feed You, or thirsty and give You drink?

'When did we see You a stranger and take You in, or naked and clothe You?

'Or when did we see You sick, or in prison, and come to You?'

"And the King will answer and say to them, 'Assuredly, I say to you, inasmuch as you did it to one of the least of these My brethren, you did it to Me.' "

Matthew 25:32-40

Also not to be ignored, is a general promise to those who assist the downtrodden:

Blessed is he who considers the poor; The LORD will deliver him in time of trouble.

The LORD will preserve him and keep him alive, And he will be blessed on the earth; You will not deliver him to the will of his enemies.

Psalm 41:1,2

My brothers, and sisters, as we consider going into the time of tribulation, the above promises hold much more value than money in the bank (literally)!!

Back to our anticipated move of God, through the "sons of oil." For when they arrived, Satan did a back-flip (almost like a "pre-emptive strike") performing a special tactical maneuver that hurt him to his heart: he started to bless these power brokers in the Kingdom of God, with money. For some of the greatest delusions, and most difficult to overcome, are those which are positive (that's what a bribe is, after all—a temptation to do wrong, for what appears to be a "good" reason).[105]

At this point, although a warning was issued earlier to "buckle your seat belts" I must reissue this warning again, with a special caveat to those who do not identify themselves as Pentecostal — I've had a word for you, as well. Do not gloat.

In order to dig into this next arena I will have to rely upon some personal experiences to illustrate the point of danger that is here described. I don't really relish this approach but, since these are matters of the soul and spirit (and I am, and have both) my own experience will have to serve as a test tube for some of these powerful ingredients.

I was raised in a holiness fellowship, became an atheist for a period of approximately six years, and returned to the Lord with all of my heart and soul at the age of eighteen years. At that point I was no longer a "second generation Christian." I was running for my life, and seeking the Lord for myself. "Churchianity" had no appeal to me, and I set out to seek, and to know, the Lord like the people described in the Bible. To me, reading through the book of Acts obviously included (and still includes) the baptism of the Holy Spirit.

To this day I have little, or no, respect for those who say that the day of miracles is past. Such is totally illogical for anyone who says that they believe in the Bible. Or in the God of the Bible. You may never see a miracle (or recognize its occurrence) *in your entire lifetime*, but this in no way means that you could not experience one, given the proper conditions. Queen Esther lived in a time when faith was at such a low ebb that the name of God was not even *mentioned once* in the book bearing her name. And that book is in the Bible! Yet, does this mean God was not active in her day?

Does it mean that God had stopped speaking to prophets, in her day? Did it prevent Simeon, and Anna (two witnesses) from knowing in advance that the Messiah was in their midst *supernaturally* (Luke 2:25-29,36-38)?

No! It only means that her environment had so suppressed personal faith, that God could not trust these people with a personal encounter, or bridge the gap into their conscious world.

However, this does not mean that simply because God has spoken to someone . . . that they are "home free." No, if anything, it places an even *greater* burden of responsibility upon them to keep their lives clean, and their attitude humble.

I have sat in assemblies where the power of the Holy Spirit is evident. Yet, the minister goes off on a rabbit trail, chasing monetary blessing, and the atmosphere in the room turns into one of obvious covetousness. God has been turned into a money machine. People get excited, women may swoon, and children have visions of grandeur. In some cases there are visions that are hard to ignore or deny. The case of one minister (who has passed on, I'll not give his name) experienced a trip into hell and back and afterwards converted. He had many miracles and experiences to his name. Yet, when speaking about money he would poo-poo those who were afraid of becoming ensnared in its.

As I sit in such assemblies, quite frankly, my head swims. Oh, the dreams of power! But as I walk away from the meeting, I feel like I've had my pocket picked. . . .

When going back to my Bible, as well, something is wrong. Where is the lowly Jesus, the Lord of glory, who made Himself poor, so that we might be made rich? What of His very first statement in His most famous sermon?

Blessed are the poor in spirit: for theirs is the kingdom of heaven.

What of his second, and third, axioms for living?

Blessed are they that mourn: for they shall be comforted.

Blessed are the meek: for they shall inherit the earth.

Matthew 5:3-5

What of Christ's clear warning concerning the deceitfulness of riches?

And He said to them, "Take heed and beware of covetousness, for one's life does not consist in the abundance of the things he possesses."

Luke 12:15

"Now he who received seed among the thorns is he who hears the word, and the cares of this world and the deceitfulness of riches choke the word, and he <u>becomes unfruitful</u>."

Matthew 13:22 [emphasis added]

Yet, how can someone possibly become unfruitful within the Kingdom of God when there are thousands of people attending their assemblies, and (apparently) worshipping God? Or—perhaps we should turn the question around, and ask:

How could Jesus have objected to so many people worshipping God, and selling doves, in the temple?

How is it possible? Simply because of wrong priorities. When I seek Him first, He *does* provide for me,[†] but when I make those provisions my aim—I am mercenary, and turn the church into a money machine.

[†] Matthew 6:33

And if I am wrong, then accept my apologies, great Money Preacher, as you guide your congregation past the (very) narrow gate

of the Midnight Cry.

In the mean while, let us encourage our precious Pentecostal brothers and sisters who are servants of God, indeed—and let us remind ourselves that God yet has everything under control.

And now that we have done our "house cleaning" it is time to again revisit, and to examine more closely,

the spoiler: The Green Horse. . . .

Chapter 13:

BEHOLD, A GREEN HORSE
The spoiler . . . Ishmael's "descendents"

> When He opened the fourth seal, I heard the voice of the fourth living creature saying, "Come and see."
>
> So I looked, and behold, a **[green]** horse. And the name of him who sat on it was Death, and Hades followed with him. And power was given to them over a fourth of the earth, to kill with sword, with hunger, with death, and by the beasts of the earth.
>
> Revelation 6:7,8 NKJV
>
> My people are destroyed for lack of knowledge. Because you have rejected knowledge, I also will reject you . . .
>
> Hosea 4:6a

We now come to the issue that had to be confronted, once realizing that many translators had "missed it" by interpreting this passage [in brackets] as a "pale horse," instead of literal green—as the original Greek suggests.   Yet it is a criticism that may seem overbearing, given the reason for the translation—for who has ever seen a *green horse*? In this sense, it is a tribute to translators expecting both truth and transparency within Scripture. For since Scripture is life-giving and practical, it is generally expected that a correct application leans towards a pale (vice greenish-grey) creature of death-like appearance. For since green skin seems rather radical and strange—the translators felt justified in seeking to avoid the overtly bizarre, while sticking to what is more easily identified.

After all, John's Revelation has enough "bizarre" symbols, as it is!

However, the word *chloros* does come from the same Greek root word from which we get the word "chlorophyll." This green wonder allows the transformation of carbon-dioxide into oxygen within living plants. Yet while green plants convey the idea of healthy vegetables, green animals are on a different order, altogether. *Chloros,* in other words, is much more accurately translated "pale-green" or simply "green"[106] and is most certainly an appropriate label for a horse whose chief attribute. . . is Death itself.

Now is the time to finally catch up to that prophecy. After 9/11 our world has changed, and so has our perspective. We may not like to admit it, and we may wish to insist that the "radicals" who drove the commercial airliners into the Twin Towers did *not* change our world, or affect the way we look at the future—but we all know they did. The families and friends of those who perished in those towers know this to be especially true.

As do our soldiers now fighting in Afghanistan, and Iraq.

Praise God, the Scriptures have been ahead of that trauma, all along!

Yet, why blame Islam for this distinction? Is not the "green lobby" (environmentalism) also a strong influence within our world, today? Indeed it is, as we have noted with prior horsemen, particularly in relation to the Kyoto treaty. Yet, the distinction John makes of its being a horse having the ominous name of

"Death". . . most easily identifies it with the Islamic threat, and its suicide bombers. It was the *suicidal* aspect of 9/11, after all, that caught us most off guard. The very idea that such an attack might be attempted at peril of one's own life, really did startle the average onlooker. Conventional warfare takes great pains to inflict casualties, while insuring the survivability of its soldiers. Americans mourn the loss of every soldier, within a conflict. Islamic terrorists, however, actually see suicidal attack as a form of martyrdom, and therefore something to be desired.

Islamic warriors embrace death—and green, is the color of choice, within Islam. Notes the online cultural cyclopedia (wikipedia) of this color's association with Islam:

> The color green has been associated with Islam for many centuries. . . . In the Qur'an (Surah 18:32), it is said that the inhabitants of paradise will wear green garments of fine silk. While the reference to the Qur'an is verifiable, it is not clear if other explanations are reliable or mere folklore. Regardless of its origins, the color green has been considered especially Islamic for centuries. Crusaders avoided using any green in their coats of arms, so that they could not possibly be mistaken for their Muslim opponents in the heat of battle.[107]

Islamic Jihad attacks have been engineered "outside of the box" and have already coaxed unconventional responses from the West, as well: the most notable being a pre-emptive strike, from the US. A more serious response, however, will affect our freedoms more directly, at the Midnight Cry . . . .

9/11 has become the suicide bomber's "poster child" – literally, with large posters hung up in terrorists hide-outs. Like it, or not, this disaster has put Islam on the map. Even within a world of gross intellectual denial and "dumbing down" of personal faith, Islamic fundamentalists have presented modern day pundits with something they were hoping to put behind us, in our present-day world: persons whose primary self image is defined by their beliefs, instead of personal and physical wealth. For, like it or not, up until this point it was generally assumed by the nations of the world—that any serious threat to the up, and coming, World Order could be "bought off" if we were willing to pay a high enough price. With Islam, however, the price

is conversion.

Are *you* for sale?

We will find out, at the Midnight Cry.

As Muammar Qaddafi suggested, even before the turn of the century, to Lebanese Christians confronting the fragmentation of their country because of civil war that was being waged as an extension of the jihad:

> I hope there is a new generation of Lebanese
> Christians who will wake up one day and realize
> Arabs cannot be Christians and Christians cannot
> be Arabs, so then they will convert to Islam and
> be true Arabs.[108]

In other words, this is an essentially religious war (that's what jihad is about, after all . . .). Nor can the irony long escape the observer that from the perspective of John's Apocalypse, this is exactly what the final conflict is really all about: religious fervor, and what we *really* believe in. The reason so many find themselves being "bought off" is because their real god *is* green, is it not? —But we are examining the Islamic faith.

There are many excellent books on this subject, written by converted Muslims who, at peril of their lives, have graced us with their warnings. They have long since renounced the Green Horse, and worship of the dollar. Within these pages, however, we will confine ourselves to the roots of Islam, to find its:

- Spiritual identity within Scripture

- Place within prophecy

- Ultimate destiny.

In order to accomplish the above aims, we will have to identify exactly what Islam is, and what it teaches, at least at the most fundamental level. Then, we will look into the Scriptures to find spiritual markers on present and future events, so that we may be able to identify their activities, not only in the Revelation (with the Green Horse) but elsewhere within Scripture. Finally, we will examine what the Bible says of the ultimate destiny of this particular belief and sect.

As may be expected, its judgment will be sure, and absolute.

For, as powerful as the Islamic religion, world, and culture is—it is no match for the living God.

Becoming a Muslim is not difficult, at all. As with many powerful dogmas cherished within the souls of many, it is the simple heart cry of the individual that forms the fountainhead of its conviction. Most central to this particular belief system is the recitation of the <u>Islamic creed</u>, which states:

→ "There is no god but Allah, and Muhammad is the messenger of Allah." (Or, as I have heard it stated: "There is no god but Allah, and Muhammad is his prophet.").

Following this, the true Muslim must accept five main articles of *Iman* (faith):

- Belief in Allah as the one true God.

- Belief in angels as the instruments of God's will.

- Belief in the four inspirited books: Torah, Zabur, Injil, Quran, of which the Quran is the final and most complete.

- Belief in the twenty-eight prophets of Allah, of whom Muhammad is the last.

- Belief in a final day of judgment.[109]

I have chosen these five tenets, over Islam's five pillars (recitation of the creed, prayer, alms giving, fast of Ramadan, and pilgrimage to Mecca)—because these five articles of faith will assist us more fully in identifying Islam's place within prophecy.

Please note, in particular, its reference to the Scriptures: the Torah, Zabur, Injil, and Quran. In simple English, these are: the Old Testament (Torah & Psalms of David) as well as:

> . . . the Injil (Gospel) of Jesus, and the Quran . . . (Although Muslims talk about the Torah, Psalms, and Gospel, they do not mean by those terms the same Old and New Testaments that Christians have in their Bible. They believe that the original Torah, Psalms, and Gospel have been corrupted and lost. . . .)[110]

Here, we immediately detect a problem. For Scripture states that God has exalted His word above His very name (Psalm 138:2). Further, the Bible states that God created the Universe by speaking it into existence (Genesis 1) and that Jesus, the Son of God, is the

Word that "became flesh" (John 1:14). If God cannot preserve His Word, therefore, how can we believe that He would be able to speak the universe into being, by using that same power?

Further, since Jesus is identified as the Word, become flesh (as a man), and Jesus is God[*] . . . how can we condone such a belief system, at all?

Already, therefore, we have a *major* discrepancy. For by stating that Scripture has been corrupted, and proposing that the Quran is the last word, on God's will, Islam also confesses that:

- The Gospel, and Old Testament, were here before the Quran.

- The Quran is clearly in disagreement with the Scriptures.

- Allah *cannot* be the same god as Jehovah, of the Bible, whose word will not return to Him void, nor be altered– although Heaven and earth pass away (Isaiah 55:10,11, Matthew 5:18, 24:35).

> "The grass withers, the flower fades, But the word
> of our God stands forever."
>
> Isaiah 40:8

One point more, which we will have to make use of, when locating this movement within Scripture: for since Islam knows of, but rejects, the Scriptures —Islam has effectively forsaken the way of Scriptural covenants, and done violence to the promises contained therein.

This last point proves extremely useful, when identifying the "trigger point" of Antichrist's unveiling, as revealed in Daniel's

---

[*] Already covered, in the previous section.

prophecy. For at the time of the end, just as the Midnight Cry is about to break, the one who will become known as the Antichrist will "return in rage against the holy covenant, and do damage. So he shall return and show regard for those who forsake the holy covenant.

> "And forces shall be mustered by him, and they shall defile the sanctuary fortress; then they shall take away the daily sacrifices, and place there the abomination of desolation."
>
> Daniel 11:30,31

Now, if you remember our opening comments, near the start of this book, you may recall that this "abomination of desolation" is exactly what Jesus warned about, in the twenty fourth chapter of Matthew (24:15). Note, with me, what happens *just prior* to initiating this action: he will confer with those who *forsake* God's covenant. Of course, this includes apostate believers of all stripes, but also. . . the sons of Ishmael.

The sons of Ishmael?

As incredible as it may seem from a biblical perspective, whether through ignorance or design (or divine design) Muslims actually identify with the rejected line of Abraham. For in Scripture Abraham had more than one son. Christians and Jews identify with Isaac: the son of promise, and of faith. Abraham had to believe God, in order to receive that son. However, Abraham was not infertile by any stretch of the imagination. For he eventually had two wives, a concubine, and eight sons.[111]

However, Scripture focuses on the contest between the son of the promise—whom Abraham had to trust God for—and Ishmael, who was born to Sarah's maid (Abraham's concubine, also called "the bondwoman" in the New Testament).

Having a child by natural means was no big deal. The whole point of Abraham's life was the miraculous intervention of God. Isaac could not have existed, unless God had personally intervened in regard to Sarah's dead womb. [†] When Hagar the Egyptian (the concubine, just mentioned) started to mock the miracle performed by God to give Sarah a child at the age of 90 years,[112] the reaction was severe. Sarah demanded that she, and her child, be disowned.

> Nevertheless what does the Scripture say? "Cast out the bondwoman and her son, for the son of the bondwoman shall not be heir with the son of the freewoman."
> So then, brethren, we are not children of the bondwoman but of the free.
>
> Galatians 4:30,31

Another ancestral line which the Arab world identifies with "came from Jacob's twin brother, Esau, according to Genesis 36."[113] Esau, you may recollect, is the fellow who sold his spiritual rights to Abraham's blessing for a bowl of soup (Genesis 25:31-34). It is Esau, who is also identified as "Edom" and with Mt. Seir (the place of their abode) in the general writings of Scripture, and of Bible prophecy.[†]

What does the Bible say will ultimately become of this seemingly unstoppable force within our world? Although Islamic jihad does seem to be unstoppable, at present, the day will come when this movement will be remembered . . . with disdain, at Christ's returning.

[†] Romans 4:19

[†] "Esau is Edom" – Genesis 36:8

"Thus with your mouth you have boasted against Me and multiplied your words against Me; I have heard them."

'Thus says the Lord GOD: "The whole earth will rejoice when I make you desolate.

"As you rejoiced because the inheritance of the house of Is-rael was desolate, so I will do to you; you shall be desolate, O Mount Seir, as well as all of Edom; all of it! Then they shall know that I am the LORD."'

Ezekiel 35:13-15

However, one very important corollary may be derived from our observation concerning Ishmael, and the issue of jihad. It re-lates to a blessing (and curse) pronounced upon him within Scrip-ture, prior to his birth. This pronouncement came just after Hagar had been "thrown out of the house" by Sarah, on an earlier occa-sion. On that occasion bitter fighting had broken out, just after Hagar realized that she was able to produce what her mistress could not. (Oh, the wisdom of having only one wife!)

Thrown out into the wilderness to fend for herself (and die) the angel of the Lord intervened, and commanded her to return to her mistress, and submit to her. He then gave her this prophetic promise regarding the son she was about to bear.

And the Angel of the LORD said to her: "Behold, you are with child, And you shall bear a son. You shall call his name Ish-mael, Because the LORD has heard your affliction.

He shall be a wild man; His hand shall be against every man, And every man's hand against him. And he shall dwell in the presence of all his brethren."

Genesis 16:11,12 [emphasis added]

Mark Gabriel (an assumed name, to protect family and friends) was beaten and tortured to within an inch of his life—just for considering contradictions within the religion of Islam. After his eventual conversion, and because of his extensive training within that culture (in the "Ivy League" universities of the Muslim world) he writes with authority, regarding the cultural roots of Islam. He writes, of seventh-century Arabia:

> Being courageous and violent was a sign of manhood in seventh-century Arabia. The people of this culture considered being quick to fight as a necessity for survival. Only the strongest survived; therefore, these tribes fought constantly as a way of existence. This mentality was manifested into a basic lifestyle.
>
> Defend your own tribe and its territory.
>
> Plunder the possessions of those you defeat. Many individuals and groups would invade others to gain position and wealth.
>
> Islam did not change any of these characteristics or influence the behavior of the Arabs. Instead, Islam embraced the Arab mentality and used it to accomplish its agenda. . . . Islam called on the Arabs to act out their courage and violent ways.[114]

Within this chapter, we have examined the engine "under the hood" of the Green Horse. It is turbo-charged by powerful forces of violence, rage, and more that we have not examined here.[115] We have noted briefly, as well, that the Lord "has the number" of this rider. Its remaining days of power and influence are certainly numbered, and will soon come to an end.

Since we are here examining the spiritual roots of Islam, however, some further explanation is called for, in relation to its claims to authenticity, in comparison to the Christian religion.

Islam, a New Dispensation?

Islam states that Mohammed is the "seal of the prophets"—in other words, the last and the best of them all. Within the biblical, and Christian, way of thinking Islam proposes nothing less than a dispensational change. That is, it proposes that we actually change the way we look at, and worship, God.

By way of experience, the Jews point to only two such occurrences within human history (through Abraham, and Moses). Christians may point to one other (Christ).[116] The apostle John outlines two of these occurrences by simply writing that, "the law was given through Moses, but grace and truth came by Jesus Christ" (John 1:17). You may not have thought about it, but what Jesus clearly taught when He came to earth was, to the Jewish way of thinking, utterly outlandish. Who in his right mind claims equality with God? Read through the eighth chapter of John's gospel, and try to imagine a mere man walking into your local assembly, and making these claims, as Jesus did:

> "I am the light of the world. He who follows Me shall not walk in darkness, but have the light of life." (vs. 12)

> "You are from beneath; I am from above. You are of this world; I am not of this world. Therefore I said to you that you will die in your sins; for if you do not believe that I am He, you will die in your sins." (vss. 23, 24)

"Most assuredly, I say to you, if anyone keeps My word he shall never see death." (vs. 51)

"Most assuredly, I say to you, before Abraham was, I AM." (vs. 58)

Clearly, Jesus was calling for a major shift in the way we view, and worship, God. The idea that God has a Son (only hinted at, in the Old Testament – Prov. 30:4, Isaiah 9:6) was now to be brought up, front and center, within the hearts and minds of serious believers in Jehovah.

Dispensational changes that *do* alter the way we relate to, and worship, God are very serious matters. For the sake of order, and the avoidance of confusion, it is logical to expect that the true God will warn those who follow Him of any such changes that are to be expected in the future. Christians know and expect, for example, just such a change after Christ's second coming. We will have new bodies. We will live and reign with Christ. Nor will we be subject to temptation, sin, or physical death any longer.[117] Yet some would seek to preempt these promises, with a false hope— especially towards the end, just prior to His return. "Take heed that no one deceives you," Jesus warned, "For many will come in My name, saying, 'I am the Christ,' and will deceive many" (Matthew 24:4,5).

In the Bible, whenever there is a *dispensational shift*, there is an explosion of the supernatural to let the faithful know that, most certainly, God has come on the scene to certify these changes. This is what He did with Moses, when delivering a nation of slaves out of the hands of the world's premier superpower (Egypt) through a series of ten plagues, and later by feeding them miraculously for forty years from the heavens, while carrying them through the wilderness.

When Jesus came, He healed the sick, fed thousands from simple lunch buckets, and raised the dead. All of these things were done without "smoke and mirrors" and in broad daylight (or in evening light, if the day drew long and the demands of the crowds pressed on). Yet, from Mohammed we have no such miraculous certification. Mohammed rose to prominence by the edge of the sword. When you read the story of Mohammed's life, it seems somewhat reminiscent of the life of King David. He was a great strategist, and devoted to his beliefs. Yet we must remember what is being proposed there: that people change the very way they view God.[118]

Islam is not respected in the West because its beliefs are cogent, or appear to be true. Western intellectuals no longer accept the concept of truth. As we have noted earlier, truth demands a commitment. Truth must rule the life of the man or woman who recognizes it as such. Truth always relates to God (or the god) in one's life.

Thus to answer our question honestly, we must acknowledge that Islam has gotten the attention of the West because of two very convincing "arguments:"

- At the point of a gun (through Jihad, principally involving suicide bombers engaging in "asymmetric warfare"[119] and terrorist acts).

- Through its influence in the Middle East, via vast oil reserves.

If you think about it, it hardly seems possible to structure an argument more compelling to post modern man. These two issues are most urgent within the minds of any thinking individual living in the West. Of what use is your SUV if you have no gasoline to power it up? —And as 9/11 has demonstrated, even with all the denials and deconstruction going on within our universities, we still have a healthy appetite to stay alive!

<u>Resist, in love:</u>

Although it is important to resist Islam, however, let us remember that these precious people have eternal souls. Many of them, even as you read this material now, are discovering the love of Jesus Christ "below the radar screen"—through covert missionaries, and especially by means of satellite broadcasts and the internet—and even through divine intervention, and miracles.[120] Let us love these people, and hate the evil. Let us pray fervently for the salvation of their souls.

The "War on Terror" can be won, this is true (so long as we have not passed the point of no return).

But only in Jesus' name.

→ It is now time to turn the page . . . and to look more closely at Israel, and current events through that amazing twelfth chapter of John's Apocalypse:

time to start connecting the dots.

Time to see the Woman in the Sun.

The Nations rising:

C0NNECTING
THE
DOTS

"And at midnight a cry was heard: 'Behold, the bridegroom is coming; go out to meet him!"

Matthew 25:6

For us, there are only two (2) dots:

The first, when Christ walked on Earth,

The second,

After the cry, at midnight . . .

BETWEEN THESE TWO "DOTS"

ALL THESE EVENTS

MUST "FIT IN"

Terms to ponder in Section III:

- "The beast" – the global federation, that morphs into an experience focusing on a man: the Antichrist.

- The fear of God – an attitude and commitment that places God first—knowing that our actions do have consequences.

- Big Brother – a term made famous by George Orwell's all seeing eye (camera): seeing everyone and everything.

- RFID – Radio Frequency Identification: electronic tracking devices, most commonly used as anti-theft devices—now being tested, to track people.

- A "gray world" – a mental outlook that defines right and wrong so carelessly—that we are unable to *do* what is right.

- The Midnight Cry – when believers will have to wake up and either lose everything, material —or everything, spiritual

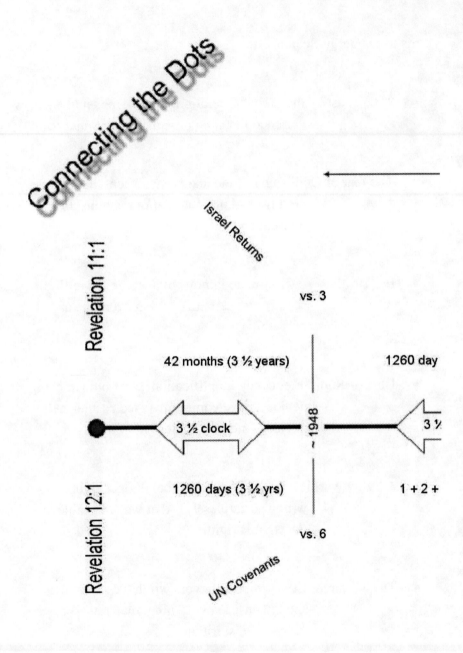

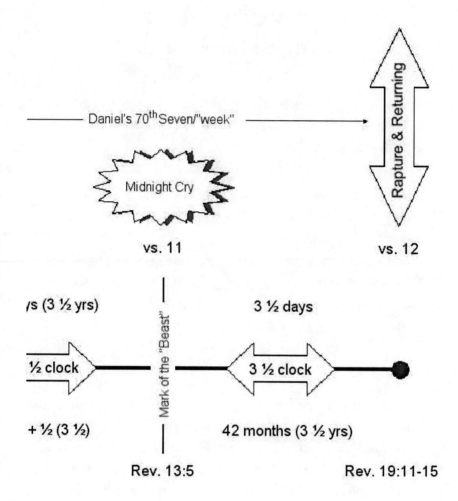

Daniel's 70th Seven/"week"

Midnight Cry

Rapture & Returning

vs. 11

vs. 12

/s (3 ½ yrs)

3 ½ days

Mark of the "Beast"

½ clock

3 ½ clock

+ ½ (3 ½)

42 months (3 ½ yrs)

Rev. 13:5

Rev. 19:11-15

Chapter 14:

WOMAN IN THE SUN
(Nation of the Son)

Now a great sign appeared in heaven: a woman clothed with the sun, with the moon under her feet, and on her head a garland of twelve stars.

. . .

But the earth helped the woman, and the earth opened its mouth and swallowed up the flood which the dragon had spewed out of his mouth.

And the dragon was enraged with the woman, and he went to make war <u>with the rest of her offspring</u>, who keep the commandments of God and have the testimony of Jesus Christ.

Revelation 12:1, 16,17 [emphasis added]

The woman in the sun is the nation of Israel. She is the woman of destiny. She has a definite future that will soon affect all of humankind. Deny it, as we may, the world keeps beating a path to the doorstep of this heavenly footprint in the sand. Enemies and proponents, of 9/11 alike, eagerly point in her direction while either accusing or grieving. . . the loss of a truly Promised Land and hope in the sun (Son). Yes, 9/11 delayed the announcement[121] of its partitioning into a "Palestinian State" –yet the latest evangelical President, on record, has persisted and insisted on going down this dangerous road, even after recovering from the attacks. Was 9/11 more than an attack from the Green Horse? Did

Heaven allow this assault as a wake up call to the evangelical community; alerting us to beware of the dangers of playing fast and loose with the Holy Land? The Lord knows (so should we).

We do know that this special nation, mentioned in John's twelfth chapter, really *is* the nation of Israel. We have clearly stated this, earlier, within our study. Being committed on this matter, let us now go back and review a few prerequisites for utilizing our "two gun" approach to unlocking this section of John's Revelation by making use of our two greatest time pieces in the terminal generation: the 3½ clocks, and Israel herself.

Within this chapter, these two concepts will once more come together, and merge, into a larger picture . . . .

One point that has continued to dawn upon us, since considering the "onion skins," is the tendency of the overlaps to *increase in detail* as we progress through John's Revelation.[†] This is particularly evident in the overlaps we are about to explore in Revelation's twelfth and thirteenth chapters. Providing we identify the symbols correctly, we will not only detect Israel's destiny as outlined from the New Testament era leading into the twentieth cen-

---

[†] Please remember this point, when reading through the thirteenth chapter. It will prove significant when seeking to understand that chapter's 3½ clock. In the thirteenth chapter of the Apocalypse, the forty-two months represent a literal three, and one half, years.

tury, but also be able to view the general historical outline of the Church of Jesus Christ as well. These are the "offspring" referred to in the last verse of John's twelfth chapter (above). These offspring include both Israel and the church itself. This is one more reason to consider the apostle John as the "other apostle to the Gentiles." For while Paul points out that the Gentiles are "joint heirs" in the Messianic Kingdom of God (Romans 8:17) John pushes the issue by calling Israel . . . our common mother.

Again, this is an attribute common to John's writings, and is evident in the way he writes about "the Jews."[122]

What the twelfth chapter of John's Revelation does for us, is to put all of the most crucial elements of spiritual warfare: God Himself, the Lord Jesus Christ, Israel and her offspring—as well as the devil and his angels—into stark perspective. After reading through this chapter we will not find it difficult to understand Paul's reference to the battle for men's souls as not being with "flesh and blood."[123] In fact, what we see here is the main reason for the birthing of the Dark Ages[124]— as the church turned aside to pursue temporal power, and largely neglected true spiritual warfare for the deliverance of human souls.[125] (Is this a problem, today, as well . . .?)

→The result was centuries of human history, largely lived in spiritual darkness—without the gospel, as the Bible lay chained to altars of pretty buildings and cathedrals. Thus, the politically incorrect term "Dark Ages" does seem most appropriate when referring to this period of time spanning the years of western history that start from the time of the emperor Constantine, up until the Protestant Reformation. Further, had the Lord not ordained a final wrap up, in the manner we will soon explore, there is little doubt but that we would soon once more descend, into a new "Dark Age."

226

This last point should not surprise us at all for, as we have seen in our review of Revelation 8 & 9, our present rate of decline is both a direct result of neglected prayer within much of the Christian community—as well as the petitions of the oppressed. The "progress" of the "Prosperity Movement" within many charismatic circles may also be seen as a "new approach" towards temporal power: seeking the power and glitter of this world . . . over that of eternity (while profusely denying such to be the case, of course. But actions speak louder than words . . .).

→One of the most devastating effects of the Laodicean era upon our world, has been a loss of a gracious prayer covering. Our reach in prayer becomes narrower, and our effectiveness in the world in which we live, much more diminished, as we begin to focus on personal prosperity within this world.

Say what you will about the Islamic world, one of the principle reasons for its devastating impact, is its ability to project an influence well beyond personal concerns. *The Green Horse rides most effectively because of its otherworldly perspective.* Indeed, this is one reason that it is so appropriate for that horseman to be so designated as the "green horse." Who ever saw a *green* horse? Do we not speak of "green men" when referring to those outside of our world?

Yet, is this not also to the way Christians are to live? Did not Jesus pray:

". . .the world has hated them because they are not of the world, just as I am not of the world.

"I do not pray that You should take them out of the world, but that You should keep them from the evil one.

"They are not of the world, just as I am not of the world."

John 17:14-16

227

It used to be that ministers wore turned back collars, for example, as a sort of protest to being secularized. Today, ministers "dress down" to minister. Are we also dressing down, in our spiritual armor? Today's Christians have largely become integrated into the present world-centered mindset. In this, we have increasingly lost our saltiness[126] and distinction. Yet, all of this will change, at the Midnight Cry. Forgive the diversion.

Back to our examination of this amazing chapter.

The layout of Revelation, Chapter 12:

The scope and layout of this chapter may be noted by the number of verses needed to describe the entire lifespan of Jesus Christ, while He lived here on earth.

> . . . And the dragon stood before the woman who was ready to give birth, to devour her Child as soon as it was born.
> She bore a male Child who was to rule all nations with a rod of iron. And her Child was caught up to God and His throne.
>
> Revelation 12:4,5

His entire life in just 1½ verses! The first half of verse four deals with Satan (the dragon) leading a revolt in Heaven wherein he influences one-third of the angels to follow him in rebellion against God. Later, he will lead these demons to launch an attack in the heavenly realm that will leave the world very dark indeed (vss. 7,8). To do this, he will project a cloud of spiritual interference very similar to that experienced by Daniel when seeking further revelation from God.[127]

228

—And the time compression increases! For after this child (Jesus) is caught up into heaven the woman who represents Israel, goes into her diaspora (dispersion into all the world) as was foretold by Christ:

> "And they will fall by the edge of the sword, and be led away captive into all nations. And Jerusalem will be trampled by Gentiles until the times of the Gentiles are fulfilled."
>
> Luke 21:24

This is our first 3½, is it not (when Jerusalem is trodden down of the Gentiles)? Yes, and this is where we need to again remember our "clocks." For this time the diaspora is called "the wilderness" and the clock is not designated as 42 months, but as 1260 days. Next verse, in Revelation twelve:

> Then the woman fled into the wilderness, where she has a place prepared by God, that they should feed her there <u>one thousand two hundred and sixty days</u>.
>
> Rev. 12:6 [emphasis added]

Why does the Lord utilize *days* in this instance, instead of months as in the previous chapter? Perhaps because days seem longer, when enduring tribulation (remember, the second 3½ clock of the eleventh chapter, with 1260 days, referred to the witnesses *in sackcloth*). When prisoners are serving a sentence, they don't count the months, they count the *days*.[128]

Our next "clock" is not so easily discernable, but should be very exciting for those of us living within the US. For this is the first mention we will make, in this book, of the eagle's wings.[129]

This instance is a direct reference to the US in Bible prophecy. —
And here it is that I begin to see the hand of the Lord in guidance,
concerning the layout of this book, for we would normally *start*
with the eagle's wings, since it is most dramatic. From this vantage point, however, and because we have detected aspects of
judgment and the spiritual underpinnings in the founding of the US
government, it is hopeful that the reader is more prepared to address what we are about to uncover.

(The US in Prophecy)

It is very important that we clearly accept the fact that the
United States is, indeed, displayed within Bible prophecy. How
can it otherwise be? Consider the matter from the outside (without
any prior knowledge of what we have uncovered). If God has indeed projected future events, and these events are to deal with the
nations at the end of the age, how can it be that the United States of
America, the sole remaining super power on the face of the earth,
not be mentioned within prophecy?

There is only one of two ways such a possibility may exist,
either:

- The US is previously annihilated, or,
- This country has been reduced to a banana state (become
  inconsequential).

In either case, the US meets with judgment!

Read your Bible, and search the Scriptures, God *always* deals
with the super powers. He dealt with Egypt, Babylon, Rome, and
every other power that touched or had an influence in the world
that affected Israel. Always.

There is only one way (only one) that we can discount the appearance of the US in Bible prophecy for any reason other than

those cited above:

If we wish to remain ignorant, and refuse to awaken.

There is no other way. We may simply prize our pet interpretations, inherited from our fathers who had no need to understand these end time prophecies, more than we treasure the truth. Yet, allow me to forewarn you. Every minister who insists on keeping his mouth shut on this issue will answer to God, and to his parishioners, at the Midnight Cry! Of course, I may be wrong. Maybe there will be no Midnight Cry, after all (but don't bet your soul on it)!

The Prayer War:

So the war in the heavens, which we may more accurately describe as the "prayer war," continued until the Lord brought enlightenment, and the evangelical prayer cover was once more effective. There were the Waldensians: persecuted, and driven into the hills in the twelfth century, John Wycliff: protected by nobles as he translated the Bible into the English tongue in the fourteenth, John Huss the Bohemian: martyred in 1415, along with William Tyndale and many others in the sixteenth century, as they started to cry out to the God of Heaven for enlightenment and deliverance. The source of this cry, I believe, may be traced to a particular judgment executed throughout the tail of the fourteenth century wherein the "black death" laid waste many, throughout Europe, and caused many to reevaluate their relationship with God (and need for Him).

There are also those who will credit the rise of humanism (not an atheistic humanism, but a man centered philosophy) and the intellectual Renaissance with the emergence of the West from the middle ages. I do not. If you look at a map of Europe, and notice carefully where the lines are drawn between the Protestant Reformation and regions where the Renaissance took hold, you will notice that the areas of humanism center about Rome and the Papal See. In other words, where Papal power was strongest, and most unforgiving, a less aggressive reform was taking place.

All of these earth shaking (and heavenly influenced) changes came to a head, of course, with the emergence of a victorious reformation ignited by Martin Luther's 95 thesis, at the council of Worms. From then on, the "genie could not be put back into the bottle." In fact it was no genie at all, but a work of the Holy Spirit. The prayer war was breaking through:

> And war broke out in heaven: Michael and his angels fought with the dragon; and the dragon and his angels fought,
>
> but they did not prevail, nor was a place found for them in heaven any longer.
>
> So the great dragon was cast out, that serpent of old, called the Devil and Satan, who deceives the whole world; he was cast to the earth, and his angels were cast out with him.
>
> Then I heard a loud voice saying in heaven, "Now salvation, and strength, and the kingdom of our God, and the power of His Christ have come, for the accuser of our brethren, who accused them before our God day and night, has been cast down.
>
> "And they overcame him by the blood of the Lamb and by the word of their testimony, and they did not love their lives to the death."
>
> Revelation 12:7-11

From then on, and for as long as men were willing to pay the price (and pay they did, at the stake, through hardship, crossing oceans, and while braving the extremes of weather and infirmity)—there was a new experience of living upon this earth as the "kingdom of our God, and the power of His Christ" became ever more evident and prevalent, within our physical world.

Yet, let us not forget the "otherworldly" perspective of these brethren who were strong, and did exploits for the Lord (verse eleven, above). They were conscious of:

- The blood of Christ Jesus, shed for our sins.

- The importance of the Word of God, and of clean Christian living (their testimony)

- Being willing to seal their witness with their own blood.

All of these components will once more return, with great clarity in the near future, for they are the necessary ingredients to making it past . . . the Midnight Cry.

Even as I write these things I cannot help but be notice how bland and timid the church has generally become within our western environment. It seems that the Green Horse has frightened Christians into timidity; fearful of being thought of as "fundamentalists,"[†] or of being too forceful in our faith and love towards our Lord Jesus Christ. Yet, it is specifically because the Christian church *is* in retreat that the Green Horse now springs into the vacuum, claiming victory within a world hungering for truth, as it is plainly taught within the Word of God: the Holy Bible.

Continuing our pursuit of the two streams of God's beloved: the nation of Israel, and the church of the living God, we again ad-

---

[†] believing the fundamentals of the Christian faith

vance to our next quote from Revelation twelve. Here, we will note that Satan, having now lost his quest in the heavenlies, to deny masses of humanity access to the throne of God through the blood of Christ (i.e. through believing prayer and repentance[130] I Timothy 2:5) —now sets out to persecute the nation/woman who brought forth the Messiah.

In our next account, we see Israel preparing to exit her diaspora. We also note the first mention of the US, in its originally generous appeal to foreign immigrants, acting as a home-away-from-home for the Jews. Yet, we must be very careful in our consideration of the following text, for it bears reference to the second 3½ clock. It's reference to the US, therefore, is not to the Jewish presence or influence within the US, *but to the present ability of the Jewish community within this nation—to nourish the fledgling nation of Israel.*[†] For it was not until recently (2005-2006) that the nation in possession of the greatest concentration of Jews, became Israel, itself. Before 2005, that greatest concentration of Jews could only be found . . . within the US.[131] Thus, after the Protestant Reformation emerged, Satan set out to redouble his efforts to persecute the Jews of the world. Eventually, this attack would also focus on the US. For now, let us take our next quote from this amazing prophecy, found in the Holy Bible:

> But the woman was given two wings of a great eagle, that she might fly into the wilderness to her place, where she is nourished for a time and times and half a time, from the presence of the serpent.
>
> vs. 14

[†] Remember: the second 3½ clock emphasizes restoration.

234

Yes, those eagle's wings do denote an aspect of the US spirit of freedom and (earlier) faith. We will soon explore this area, as well. For now, however, let us continue our discovery within this chapter. For in truth, we have not yet encountered the most amazing part of this section of Scripture. For if we consider all that we have discussed so far to be plausible, we may also recognize that we are now progressing through the twentieth century. Two world wars took place within that century. The second gave birth, at its close, to the nation of Israel with the founding of the United Nations and issuance of General Assembly Resolution 181.[132]

> So the serpent spewed water out of his mouth like a flood after the woman, that he might cause her to be carried away by the flood.
>
> But the earth helped the woman, and the earth opened its mouth and swallowed up the flood which the dragon had spewed out of his mouth.

vss. 15, 16

This water "like a flood" refers to the mass of humanity (mustered during WW II) utilized to attack the woman (and those who would assist her). This agrees with Revelation seventeen's description of massive bodies of water being referred to as, "peoples, multitudes, nations, and tongues" (17:15). In the context of World War II, it may also represent the fact that the war spanned great oceans (both the Atlantic and Pacific, for example) . . . .

Incredible!

But wait, did you notice something unusual about the above text? What is this notation about the *earth* opening its mouth to assist the woman?? Is not the woman Israel? Is not Israel Satan's sworn enemy and prey to be devoured by him, at all costs?

Is not Satan the "god of this world" (II Cor. 4:4 AV)?? How

can it be, then, that Satan's minions would assist his arch-foe?

God ordained it. The Lord of Heaven did a divine "override" of Satan's authority, to give birth to this incredible miracle: the re-birth of the nation of Israel. No wonder the next verse states that "the dragon was wroth with the woman, and went to make war with the remnant of her seed" (vs. 17)!!

Just in case you were wondering, that's what all the bloodshed in the middle east is all about,

Today.

It is also what the Midnight Cry will be about.

Of course, . . . there is also the matter of the world's one lone super-power. Where did we come from, anyway? Could it even be possible . . . (could it? Possibly??)—that our very origins are forecast within Scriptures?

Come and see. . . .

Chapter 15:

WINGS OF AN EAGLE . . .
HEART OF A MAN

"And four great beasts came up from the sea, each different from the other.

"The first was like a lion, and had eagle's wings. I watched till its wings were plucked off; and it was lifted up from the earth and made to stand on two feet like a man, and a man's heart was given to it."

Daniel 7:3,4

As we round the corner in the final phase of this study, we must take a breath and ponder a question: Is judgment really predetermined, or merely the result of human sin and weakness? Calvinists,[133] I am certain, will have a field day answering this one, when considering the trumpeting judgments of Revelation 8 & 9. It is evident in the final analysis, after all, that God *does* have everything under control. For it is *from the heavens,* that the trumpet judgments are issued. So, let us consider another angle: how may humankind be redeemed?

We must consider this one more carefully, before answering. Christians understand that redemption is "buying back" what has been sold into slavery or bondage. It is because we had violated God's word, in the Garden, that we have fallen and become cursed. For the payback for sinful living is death (Romans 6:23a).

And the gift of God?

What is the gift of God, in relation to judgment and damnation?

It is a reversing of the curse, while turning history and human destiny on its head. It is the Hindu karma *broken* to smithereens. It is death and despair given new hope, and resurrected. It is the impossible, becoming

Reality.

And, What of the US of A?

We have already started to explore the concept of the Lord's redeeming His covenant people, both physical and spiritual: both the nation of Israel, and the church. What if God were to plan the redemption of an entire Gentile national system, within His program of the ages? What if He planned for a nation to arise which would –after having paid a terrible price, this is true—succeed at doing what no other nation in the history of the world has even come close to accomplishing (short of Israel, in the Old Testament)?

I believe this to be *exactly* what God planned for the United States of America (and this in no way diminishes what God has, and is, doing in other nations, even today. The nation that honors the Lord, or sees a significant percentage of its people do so *will* be blessed. Period. If you don't believe this, take a closer look at the Christian revival taking place, even now . . . in Red China.[134] Is this not a factor in China's becoming an economic powerhouse? Is it not unusual for a *communist* state to be so economically prosperous?![135])

Peter Marshall and David Manuel, in their historical classic, *The Light and the Glory* [136] posit that the original founders of the "American Dream" were really . . . here, let us quote their brain storming, directly:

> "The Puritans really believed it," Peter mused, breaking the heavy silence . . .
>
> "Believed what?" asked David, ...
>
> "they actually believed," Peter answered, . . . "what few people have, before or since: that the Kingdom of God really *could* be built on earth, in their lifetimes. . . . They knew that they were sinners. But like the Pilgrims, they were dedicated to actually living together in obedience to God's laws, under the Lordship of Jesus Christ." (emphasis in original. p. 145)

Yet from a purely Heavenly perspective, what the American colonists proposed, was against the rules. Christ had stated clearly that His kingdom is not of this world. "If My kingdom were of this world," Jesus said, "My servants would fight . . ." (Jn. 18:36). Further, Solomon clearly warns not to seek the overthrow of organized government.

> My son, fear the LORD and the king; Do not associate with those given to change;
>
> For their calamity will rise suddenly, And who knows the ruin those two can bring?
>
> Proverbs 24:21,22

To which the apostle Paul seconds:

For there is no authority except from God, and the authorities that exist are appointed by God.

Therefore whoever resists the authority resists the ordinance of God, and those who resist will bring judgment on themselves.

Romans 13:1,2

All of the co-signers of the Declaration of Independence understood what was at sake, and prepared to pay a high price either with their lives, fortunes, or both (some sacrificing their sacred honor as well, when charged with treason against the Crown). George Washington, himself no slacker, could be found placing himself in harms way, at the head of marching columns to steady his men and to build morale, and yet –he was spared wounding or death (Ibid. p. 318). Thus was our fledgling nation afforded a man of great character, and resolve, to lead her in the turbulent (and tempting) days of infancy. "He was the man who could have been a king but refused a crown and saved a republic."[137]

What is now important to realize, from the vantage point of our study at the close of the age, is that the American Revolution was about much more than what we commonly call "freedom." It was about doing things in a manner that mirrored the very Kingdom of God, upon earth. These colonists, if you will, sought to bring about the fulfillment of the (commonly designated) Lord's Prayer. —That God's will be done, on earth, as it is, in Heaven.[138] It is important to realize this, for when the Green Horse rides, many issues tend to become clouded. Yet it is not *self-sacrifice, alone*, that makes one's convictions valid. We must always ask, "Is it true?"

Is it true, what you believe in?

240

Do you believe *the truth?*

We have noted earlier, that the Green Horse represents Islam, and the Islamic world. Is there a representation for the West, as well? What of the White Horse, within that sixth chapter? Perhaps we may gain better perspective by first comparing it to the Lord's horse . . . .

> Now I saw heaven opened, and behold, a white horse. And He who sat on him was called Faithful and True, and in righteousness He judges and makes war.
>
> Revelation 19:11

It is obvious within this context, that this "white horse" does refer to Christ returning in power and glory to execute judgment upon the world (see the verses that follow, where the Rider is called "the Word of God."-compare with John 1:1. . . .)

This horse rides at the final trumpet after the angel declares, "The kingdoms of this world have become the kingdoms of our Lord and of His Christ, and He shall reign forever and ever!"[139] Now, let us compare our Lord's white horse with that of the first horse, of the four horsemen:

> And I looked, and behold, a white horse. He who sat on it had a bow; and a crown was given to him, and he went out conquering and to conquer.
>
> Revelation 6:2

The exact identity of this rider is not given. Nor is his character so clearly defined. It is almost as if there were something missing here: as if he started out to create a glorious realm, and settled for . . . a secular state.

I believe that this points to the world's sole remaining superpower.

As was noted earlier, many of the founders of the US republic were desirous of its being created as a Christian nation. Such an admission seems anathema, today, within our present secular climate. Yet it was a commonly accepted axiom in the past, and was so declared by the Supreme Court in 1892 when ruling in the case of *The Church of the Holy Trinity vs. United States,* which read in part:

> There is no dissonance in these declarations. There is a universal language pervading them all, having one meaning; they affirm and reaffirm that this is a religious nation. . . .

> The form of oath universally prevailing, concluding with an appeal to the Almighty; the custom of opening sessions of all deliberative bodies and most conventions with prayer; the prefatory words of all wills, "In the name of God, amen"; . . . These, and many other matters which might be noticed, add a volume of unofficial declarations to the mass of organic utterances that this is a Christian nation.[140]

Although there be "no dissonance" in the fact of what was originally formed within these United States—It still remains true that, from Heaven's point of view, the settlers were in clear rebellion to the Crown. What the founders of this republic sought was an exception, and special consideration from Heaven, to be allowed to worship God freely. This they requested from the God of the Bible both humbly and repeatedly. For as we have briefly demonstrated, the founders of this republic were in possession of a genuine desire to establish a godly kingdom upon earth, although the price be ever so high.

The Counterfeit Kingdom:

We must force ourselves not to forget all that we have been studying thus far, however, and keep firmly within the our awareness, the warning given since the chapter on the onion skins: That Antichrist's "Paradise" will seem to prosper immediately after the Mark is issued, for a short time. In other words, there will be a *counterfeit kingdom.*

Do you remember what Christ said, of the time directly preceding His returning? "Many will come saying I am Christ," (Matt. 24:5). Now, this may be taken many ways, not the least of which is to have many *counterfeit* kingdom principles, building up a false empire very similar to what Christian founders envisioned for the US at its birth.

In other words (fasten your seat belts, again—tightly) "Democracy" may be utilized to advance Satan's kingdom, as well. What will ultimately greet the Lord at Armageddon will be the remnant of a once proud and prosperous empire. The greatest disaster, however, will be the loss experienced by multitudes who have succumbed to temptation, after having awakened at midnight. Further, as difficult as it is to accept the concept, *the White Horse leads* the way into the darkness, after it has forsaken its original calling. . . .

What was this "original calling"?

It was Christian, within the kingdom of God.

Such is the way of Christ, applied to all of Christian living (Colossian 3:17). We are designed to be the head, and not the tail.

We must take care however, where we are leading others!

The White Horse leads:

Faith is a natural engine for science, technology, and the business world— for all of these endeavors must deal with the unknown. The white horse (White Horse) of Revelation six, therefore, most naturally represents this Christian world view leading the way into the realm of unprecedented wealth and prosperity, as has been experienced in the West for the past century, or more. What follows the White Horse. . . is disdain.

The terminal generation soon takes the blessings of God for granted. They say, "Our hand is high; And it is not the LORD who has done all this." (Deut. 32:27).

> Why do the nations rage, And the people plot a vain thing?
> The kings of the earth set themselves, And the rulers take counsel together, Against the LORD and against His Anointed, saying,
>
> "Let us break Their bonds in pieces And cast away Their cords from us."
>
> Psalm 2:1-3

God's reaction to this rattling of sabers, and shaking of fleshly fists, upon earth—is to laugh (vs. 4)!

This means that the White Horse rider does not remain . . .untainted. Notice, if you will, that the rider has something in his hand.

> And I looked, and behold, a white horse. He who sat on it
> had a bow; and a crown was given to him, and he went out

244

conquering and to conquer.

Revelation 6:2

What an interesting thing for a rider to carry: a bow. What on earth does this symbolize? Why use the symbolism of a "bow"???

Why, indeed. For a bow has *two* meanings: one positive . . . and the other, with a potential for evil. A bow, you remember, calls to mind our Lord's promise to Noah. "I do set my bow in the clouds . . ." (Genesis 6:13) This first bow, is the bow of Promise.

Its second meaning, conveys great evil. It symbolizes the cowardly attacks of Satan. It was the "stand off weapon of choice" within the Old Testament. This is how ancient kings were killed: by archers handling a bow (I Kings 22:34, II Chron. 35:23,24). In the same way, as we shall see, this symbol of a bow will change (and is now changing) from its good, to evil symbolism, within the analogy. . . of the United States, as we study it. Yes, there is much to pray over, within this book, and very much, for the virgin saint to cry out to God for.

FAST FORWARD:

We are going to do something, right here, that we have not done so far within our study. We are going to actually *fast forward* our study, for a page or two, to wet the reader's appetite for what is about to be unveiled. Actually, there is good reason for this, for if the reader is anything like myself (considering yourself a good Christian voter) the issues you are about to read in this, and the following chapter, may seem to haunt you—until going to prayer.

You are about to share in concepts that have taken me many years to digest and come to terms with. Further, the more you love this country, the more you will feel the need to intercede for our country, president, and government leaders. For what we are about to show is that the US is *not* innocent in the turn of events about to unfold in the rising of Antichrist and the governing of the world body. (Actually, if love were not so blind, this would seem rather obvious. Have you noticed which nation is actually housing the UN headquarters . . . ?)

Within the next chapter we will come very close to concluding our study. We will look squarely at the Midnight Cry, and rise of the New World Order (so called—for only Christ's return will bring a *truly* New Order, with peace for this troubled planet).

Within the next chapter, as well, we will carefully show how to arrive at the firm conclusion that the US is indeed within Bible prophecy—yet there, we will also focus on the second aspect of the US in prophecy . . . after the bow "changes colors" and transitions into the Night. (Not pretty, not pretty . . . but we need to know the truth. Only then can we be truly *free*.)

→ Ultimately, it will be shown that the US is the "wingless lion" – the nation that arose out of British roots (the noble lion) and had the wings of an eagle upon its back (Daniel 7:4). The noble bald eagle, of course, is the national symbol of the United States of America (look on the back of a one dollar bill). This "lion with eagle's wings" ultimately has its noble wings plucked—in the same manner as the rider on the White Horse has a change of heart, while morphing his bow of Promise—into a bow of destruction.

The republic that started out with the heart cry of an eagle (rising on wings of faith) ends up with the heart of a man: changing from a Christian nation—into a Humanist state. We will have to pursue this further, next chapter. . . .

The New World Order, first made public by George Bush, Sr.

saw the US lead a UN coalition into the Middle East to rescue the world from the throes of Saddam Hussein—now largely imperiled by the Green Horse. You may not have seen it this way, but there is an aspect of Middle Eastern policy which has attempted to finish off what was first started during Operation Desert Storm. If you can remember back that far, you may recall that the Berlin Wall had fallen, a short time before. As we shall see, there is symbolism within the two main systematic prophets (Daniel & John's Revelation) pointing towards an amazing cooperation between these two super powers, in what is destined to become known as the "beast."

This is a strange name to give to those leading us into a brave new world where we'd hoped to find rest and comfort, from the conflicting tensions of the Cold War. We had marched into a world in which the US and Russia—and the rest of the world, appeared to finally have the potential of living in peace and harmony.

For a very short time it really did seem that we had no need for a nuclear defense. Peace was on the horizon.

Swords were being ground into plowshares.

And then . . . 9/11.

It may be too early to tell, but I do believe the fall of the twin towers may have been forecast within Scripture. I say that it may be too early to tell (although each passing year makes it evident that it has, indeed, been foretold) because the prophecy we are about to quote could easily be swallowed up within an apocalypse of many such events. In other words, if no other comparable disaster takes place prior to Antichrist's arising, such would allow this particular prophecy of towers falling, to stand out, on its own. Its significance will then be better appreciated.

As will be its promise of revival.

> There will be on every high mountain And on every high hill Rivers and streams of waters, In the day of the great slaughter, <u>When the towers fall</u>.
>
> Moreover the light of the moon will be as the light of the sun, And the light of the sun will be sevenfold, As the light of seven days, <u>In the day that the LORD binds up the bruise of His people And heals the stroke of their wound</u>.[141]

Isaiah 30:25, 26 [emphasis added]

The reference to rivers of waters on "every high hill" refers to those in the ministry of the sons of oil, on the mountain peaks of faith. There, will be found revival—in the sackcloth. The two verses which follow immediately after these, are an Old Testament reference to the Midnight Cry.[142]

As was stated, 9/11 seemed to mess up everything. It demonstrated to persons in the West that the Green Horse is indeed a serious threat to world peace and security. No longer could we think of Islamic Jihad as "something going on, over there." President George Bush has appraised this as a threat having much wider implications than a mere local, middle eastern, occurrence—and he is correct. The Green Horse is out of the bottle.

The New Order however, which emerged at the close of the Cold War, is not backing down. Western leaders are determined not to surrender the 21st Century to Sharia law. The "great iron teeth" of the wingless lion's 'head' (which we will examine next chapter)—are powerful, and world leaders are quite happy to allow us to use those teeth to do the dirty work as effectively as possible, to bring Islamic third world nations "back into line."

Further, the increasingly wide use of digital technology, to track everything, everywhere, is the Humanist response, answer, and solution—to keeping the lid on religious movements—while

248

still maintaining a semblance of freedom within the Western hemisphere.

I hope you understood what you just read. You may have to ponder this one, for some time. **Big Brother is emerging as the only alternative to the Green Horse.** Without him, secularists reason, there is no way to maintain order within society while also maintaining a semblance of "freedom," at the same time. They hope to quietly monitor the actions (and, if possible, the thoughts) of everyone within our societies with the purpose of preserving order. We may rant and rave about lost privacy and freedoms, but in all honesty there is no other real solution, save one.

Shouting back up to Heaven.

So now, once again, we have an impetus to return to the only real alternative there is, by returning to that prayer chamber in Heaven, with the original spirit of petitioning and supplication that birthed this nation.

For without serious revival, our next stop *will be* 1984 . . .

Chapter 16

1984 *in* 2014
Accelerating change?

> He causes all, both small and great, rich and poor, free and slave, to receive a mark on their right hand or on their foreheads,
>
> and that no one may buy or sell except one who has the mark or the name of the beast, or the number of his name.
>
> Here is wisdom. Let him who has understanding calculate the number of the beast, for it is the number of a man: His number is 666.
>
> Revelation 13:16-18

To date, most of the Christian world has portrayed the cry at midnight, as well as our current tendency towards increased citizen surveillance, as an almost harmless event: as "a bump in the road" on the way to the Lord's returning, and as innocent devices for tracking financial transactions. The *worship* aspect of 666 has not yet stared out at us. Our only concern, thus far, has been with buying and selling. This benign concern could change rapidly at any moment, however, as the Green Horse launches its next major assault. Such may suddenly accelerate the movement of prophecy, and turn many freedom loving Americans into very frightened pawns, looking for the comfort of a big brother. . . .

George Orwell in his classic science fiction thriller "1984" envisioned a day wherein everyone, everywhere, would be under the constant surveillance of Big Brother. In everything you did, and in every place you visited, Big Brother was there watching your activities. This Orwellian dream, driven by fears of terrorism and other security concerns within the commercial industry, is similar to plans already being enacted by Great Britain to further empower its ever present surveillance of motor traffic in the greater London area. With plans to link its thousands of CCTV (closed circuit TVs) to developing software, it will soon be able to monitor the movement of every licensed vehicle within the metropolis: from point of origin, to its destination.[143]

Already such technology has reaped dividends, you may recall, in the British investigation into subway bombings carried out in 2005. It was no accident that they were able to track the bombers, and to catch them on camera. "Candid Camera" is a way of life in that city. Similar technology is now laying wait for all "global citizens" of the twenty-first century: laying the ground work for completely tracking the movement of every individual by the year 2011, give or take a few years.[144] The proposed tracking device will be considerably more sophisticated than the highly visible closed circuit television, however. It will most likely involve some variation of the now common RFID tagging system seen almost everywhere in our clothing and department stores, by making use of a skin implant similar to the one already developed by Applied Digital Systems.[145]

On the US government end, President George Bush, on May 11th of 2005 has *already* signed a military appropriations bill into law which included a legislative addendum entitled "The Real ID Act." This incidental legislation effectively mandates that *every US citizen* be in possession of a National ID[146] within two years of the bill's implementation (i.e. by 2008). Its means of tracking US citizens, will be a very simple tool: using a revamped, state-of-the-art, driver's license (and non-driver ID)—having the distinguishing characteristic of linking its information into a national data base[147]. . . ultimately giving it the ability to be shared with other nations within the global community. Even if repealed, officially, the technology and trends that are moving in the direction of this Orwellian dream are already being supported by existing technologies. RFID technology (Radio Frequency Identification), for example, is already being incorporated into US passports.[148]

We are all familiar with recent developments, wherein it was revealed that the US National Security Agency has been monitoring ("mining") international and domestic phone calls via sophisticated electronic technology: listening in on domestic phone calls, by way of sophisticated digital systems that allow agents to analyze voice communications on the fly; quickly flagging voice changes in order to single out persons conducting suspicious activities.

What every born-again Christian should be concerned about, however, is that all of this technology is arising at a time when other activities (and still more, to be revealed in this chapter) are converging within the same time frame. It is like walking into a room with the intention of stepping into a heated swimming pool in the dead of winter, only to discover loaded guns pointing at you from all directions. The door behind you has closed, and there is no turning back. The temperature in the water no longer seems comfortable. We have been set up for the issuance of the Mark of the Beast.

By the time the Mark arrives, micro electronic tracking will be so pervasive, that personal human identification will be only one of several collateral annoyances. Says Katherine Albrecht of "Spy-Chips…" —there are actually industries that are now *planning* to make available personal reading devices that will allow your

252

neighbor to spy on your personal belongings, through covert tagging devices already being implanted in our clothing. Says Albrecht, "They call their patented vision the Real-World Showroom. We call it the pervert's best friend. Here's how [the company] says it will work:

> With the Real-World Showroom, consumers have immediate access to a wireless, always-on shopping channel. The showroom is, quite literally, the everyday world. If someone walking down the street sees something they like—say, an article of clothing on a passerby—they can . . . [point] a PDA—one with a permanent wireless connection to the Internet—at an item, it can be called up on the screen. Users can instantly find out more about the item and even purchase it."[149]

Presumably, they will soon be able detect if the person they are monitoring . . . is in possession of the Mark, or not, as well. If you haven't figured it out, already, this is the Midnight Cry. The slow simmer, which we have been demonstrating first initiates as an act of judgment from the heavens—is now coming to a rapid boil within the world in which we live. World events are accelerating towards the day wherein the prophecy given by the angel, to the apostle John on that little island in the Icarian Sea (called "Patmos") will to be completely, and literally, fulfilled.

→ Israel is back in her land, the church is in a condition of apathy (with most who hear about this developing technology, noting its emergence: in highway pass cards, or "EZ Pass," and other means of highway surveillance, for example—and dutifully going back to sleep—or sleep walking after the dollar, either in a "church," or via TV).

→ At the same time, government agencies now work furtively at locking the door of freedom behind terrorists, while also making it impossible for honest citizens to return to "the good old days."

So serious is the ramification of the decisions being made at the Midnight Cry, John tells us, that *angels* will be commissioned to issue the appropriate warnings—almost as if to say, "We must not leave this up to sleepy virgins. Let's make sure that the word gets out!"

Just in case you thought that last statement leaves us with nothing to worry about, consider this, that the previous warning issued by an angel, is described as "the everlasting gospel" (Revelation 14:6). So, what is so unusual about this "gospel," that an angel must declare it? Here, read it for yourself.

> Then I saw another angel flying in the midst of heaven, having the everlasting gospel to preach to those who dwell on the earth; to every nation, tribe, tongue, and people;
> saying with a loud voice, "Fear God and give glory to Him, for the hour of His judgment has come; and worship Him who made heaven and earth, the sea and springs of water."
>
> Revelation 14:6,7

Did you notice anything unusual about the angel's message? When last did you hear a sermon on the *fear of God?* How many do you know . . . who *practice* this virtue? Why, the very term is virtually anathema (so that many would supplant its concept with a "reverence" for God.[150] Yet, the original Greek makes use of the term *"phobeo"* from which we get the term, "phobea" –in. *Photophobia*, the fear of light, for example, an increasingly prevalent malady, today. . . ..)

Do we even appreciate what the fear of God accomplishes,

anymore? Quite simply, it means that we take God seriously, and realize that there are very real consequences to our moral decisions. Without it you lie, simply because it is convenient to do so, never considering that the Word says that all liars spend eternity in Hell (Rev. 21:8). Even church goers now "sleep in" with their "friends" (lovers) in an arrangement, because "everyone is doing it"—and then wonder why STDs are spreading like the plague, or AIDS is pandemic.

Scripture states that any society that is so careless, will bring down a curse upon itself. As can be easily demonstrated, Scripture clearly teaches that atheism, homosexuality, and the morally careless condition we now associate with "sit-coms" and soap operas are all part and parcel of the same package (Romans 1:27-32). The fires that heat the kettle for judgment, in other words, are deeply imbedded within the framework of our every day lives.

It is the church's job to act as the moral conscience and restraint upon a nation, but when this mandate is abandoned—for whatever reason, whether it is because newsmen and pundits call us quacks, narrow minded, or divisive (or *really* persecute us)—the Lord is not impotent, or without recourse.

The Final Test of Worship:

Prophetic warnings point to all of human society being presented with a very simple, and definitive, test of professed faith and belief in the God of the Bible. This is where the issue of worship will ultimately display its pass-fail criteria. It's "final grades" will be issued soon after the cry at Midnight. This final test of allegiance and worship will involve what is commonly referred to, of course, as the Mark of the Beast.

Then a third angel followed them, saying with a loud voice,

"If anyone worships the beast and his image, and receives his mark on his forehead or on his hand,

"he himself shall also drink of the wine of the wrath of God, which is poured out full strength into the cup of His indignation. He shall be tormented with fire and brimstone in the presence of the holy angels and in the presence of the Lamb."

Revelation 14:9,10

Oh well, so much for nit-picking over doctrine! Either you do, or you don't! What I firmly believe, is that by the time this event takes place, Antichrist and his minions will be *flaunting* their flagrant demands—even *reminding* Christians of what Scripture warns against (daring us to obey God, rather than man).

Either cast off all that "Jesus stuff" and fanaticism—or act irrationally, to be targeted by the War on Terror (or some other popular agenda we may be attacked by). We have already effectively crossed the line into accepting a national ID. We've done this as a reaction to 9/11. How will we react to another terrorist act, upon our soil? Or

→To the unleashing of a nuclear device, or "suitcase bomb" within a major city?

Who could resist the temptation of allowing further human tracking and identification —for the preservation of our "freedoms" and prosperity—via biometric implants and the physical marking of individuals?

One better: who could resist a call to pledging allegiance to world peace and prosperity—or to an international call for the cessation of terrorist acts, and a belief in human dignity, etc. Yet, how far is a "belief in man" from . . . worship?

The Green Horse is pursuing us.

We can only go on. In this case, "outward" from established society ("Go out to meet Him!")—or give up, and stay in the pot, to boil alive—and burn, forever.

Garden of Eden: "Take 2"

What we have shown in this book is that preparation for events soon to transpire have not simply "happened," nor do they emerge to dominate us "over night." It takes time: time that the church has been giving to the enemy, as Laodicea sleeps . . .

We are indeed headed for a repeat of the original temptation, in the Garden. We are witnessing a re-converging of human choice that will be a "re-make" of the Garden of Eden experience. This defining experience will demand that we obey one single command, effectively determining the destiny of every human being upon planet earth. We will either refuse the Marking of the Beast and live eternally, or accept his lie and again bet on a Paradise of our own, hoping that the Lord will be unable to continue to fulfill His word—and be lost forever. The compulsion to "fall into line," to say the least, will be overwhelming to all but those having the "extra oil" (or pipeline) that enables us to resist.

As Adam and Eve lost Paradise, by disobeying a single command, many will forfeit eternal life, by failing to give heed, to the final command of the age: to refuse Satan's marking.

But . . . what of the United States? What part do *we* play in this end time scenario? There are some who furtively hope that the US will be exempt from such activities. Sorry—excuse me? Sir?

Yes, you, the one with your head in the sand?

How can the nation that is leading the way into wireless technology, and the war on terror, possibly hope to be exempt from these things?

OK, so you say the country is *not that bad.* Granted, we have a few more stages before the Mark is issued: actually, only one or two. We have to witness the morphing (transformation) of two major organizations in the near future. One is already in process. Yup, you guessed it.

It is now possible to unlock the line up of nations, proscribed by Scripture, designating the geopolitical alignment of the nations at the time of Antichrist's rising. Those familiar with Evangelical teaching may be familiar with the line up of nations going down to the final battle, at Armageddon (given in Ezekiel 38). Do you know the line up, *before* Antichrist arises?

Although I must confess that I do not yet understand all of the secrets contained within these Scriptures (or of the others, we just passed through)—I do know that the ramp-up, leading to the rise of Antichrist, is nothing less than remarkable. This, alone, gives me encouragement and impetus, to anticipate our Lord's soon returning.

In Scripture, Antichrist is called "the beast."

Ramping up, for "the beast:"

The "beast" first appears as a federation of nations. Then, as John's thirteenth chapter progresses, its symbolism morphs into that . . . of a man (the Antichrist). An earlier transformation, of a beloved nation we are all familiar with, takes place within this same process. It is extremely important to realize that we are, and will be until the Midnight Cry, *already* within this period of trans-formation. Our first transition does occur within this nation (re-member, the White Horse *leads*) to be followed by the interna-tional community. The world's affections and hopes will then shift its eyes more firmly towards Europe and to a man, resulting in per-sonal exaltation, and intense worship. Antichrist descends into the middle east from the north (that's where Europe, Russia and friends reside . . .).[151] Once we reach that point, we have reached the point of no return. The Midnight Cry will become apparent. The Antichrist will be revealed.[152]

Some will wonder how all of this could have simply slipped under the radar. "Have any of the 'important people' believed this?" they will ask –just like when Jesus came the first time.[153] It really does seem that God takes pleasure in confounding the "bril-liant thinkers" of any given age.[154] For we will make use of com-mon, every day symbols, and apply them to prophecies issued thousands of years ago—to unlock a world of fulfillment many never even thought possible. As promised, we will make use of Daniel's seventh chapter to unlock John's remarkable thirteenth. It is here that observations made in the book's opening comments become much more than mere curiosity, for:

→We must never allow the simple things of this world to trip us up, or to rob us of the ability to see God's truth (I Cor. 1:28,29).

We will refrain from debating whether the symbols of Daniel's seventh chapter were originally intended to represent the nations comprising his original dream in his second chapter his prophecy. I will note only that the first symbol (of eagle's wings) was also utilized by the Roman empire. Therefore, if we were to project from the time of Daniel into the future, the sign of the Roman empire should arise . . . last: not *first* as it does in this seventh chapter. Within the very next chapter of Daniel's writings (chapter eight) symbolism does appear which is specifically cited with reference to Media, Persia, and Greece (Dan. 8:20,21). It does appear, therefore (as we will soon see born out) that this seventh chapter is a very special interlude, designed to link up with another prophecy, *in the end time*.

The whole beast . . . in its parts:

Most interesting within the context of Daniel's seventh chapter, is the observation that while John's Apocalypse describes the beast in its completed order, Daniel describes it . . . in its component parts. In other words, Daniel describes the *individual nations* that make up this final global federation. John, however, describes the relative position and function of the component states *within that federation* of nations—now composing (what we call) The New World Order.

Further, Daniel describes these nations in their natural order of emergence. Each facet of these emerging international powers have a specific role, purpose, and capability. Not all of their activities are pleasant to note. This, of course, is one aspect of Bible prophecy that differs from the way in which we would desire to view the future . . . or most would desire to teach it. We must again, firmly buckle our seat belts, therefore, because there are some truths contained here that may "make [our] stomach bitter."[155]

With gall.

No wonder so few have explored these prophecies! For us, at this closing hour, however, it may make all the difference between life and "death"—in the ages to come, eons and eons, from now. . .

We go now to Daniel's seventh chapter, as it opens for him in a vision, or dream. In this dream he sees events taking place in the future. Different creatures are displayed that make use of *national symbols*. We will first quote it, in its entirety.

"I saw in my vision by night, and behold, the four winds of heaven were stirring up the Great Sea.

3. "And four great beasts came up from the sea, each different from the other.

"The first was like <u>a lion, and had eagle's wings</u>. I watched till <u>its wings were plucked</u> off; and it was lifted up from the earth and made to stand on two feet like a man, and a man's heart was given to it.

5. "And suddenly another beast, a second, <u>like a bear</u>. It was raised up on one side, and <u>had three ribs in its mouth</u> between its teeth. And they said thus to it: 'Arise, devour much flesh!'

"After this I looked, and there was another, like <u>a leopard</u>, which had on its back <u>four wings of a bird</u>. The beast also had four heads, and dominion was given to it.

7. "After this I saw in the night visions, and behold, a fourth beast, dreadful and terrible, exceedingly strong. It had huge

iron teeth; it was devouring, breaking in pieces, and tram-
pling the residue with its feet. It was different from all the
beasts that were before it, and it had ten horns."

Daniel 7:2-7 [emphasis added]

Verse two is included in our quotation so that we may realize
that the "sea" from which these nations arise is, indeed, the mass of
humanity, as earlier noted from Revelation 17:15.

The American Eagle:

If you remove an American Dollar bill from your wallet, or
purse, you will notice our first symbol: the American eagle. This
"eagle" symbol has been given to international super powers, down
through history (see Ezekiel seventeen). Whether our founding
fathers realized the power of this symbolism when choosing our
national symbol, I cannot say. Most interesting, however, is the
"small detail" added about this nation having its wings coming *out
of the sides of a lion.* —So that the nation depicted is actually a
lion, with eagle's wings.

The lion, itself, is actually the national symbol of Great Britain
(check its coat of arms).

Yet the US sprang from its mother country, Great Britain. To
this day, we bear her mother tongue. Most interesting, as well, is
the fact that English is an international trade language. This point
of information will be important to remember, when bouncing
back from Revelation's thirteenth chapter, where the nations are
interrelated within a federation (like the UN . . .).

Exposing the next part of verse four brings to light why so few
have ventured to describe this symbol as representing the US. For

an eagle's wings denote nobility. Those who wait upon the Lord, Isaiah says, will mount up with wings, as do eagles (Isaiah 40:31). These wings point to a nation arising on wings of faith. So then, what does the symbolism of these wings being "plucked" designate?

→We can approach the answer from two points of view: from the text, or by looking at the US while acknowledging what is already happening. We return to the text:

Here we note that the lion with its eagle's wings plucked, is made to stand "on two feet like a man." Thus, we see a basic change of both *characteristic*, and of *heart*. At first this nation could fly. As it became lifted up with pride (as the "mighty United States") it then landed upon its feet, and became dependent upon human wisdom and understanding: determining that it will now make its stand *as a man*. Yet, in this new "standing" we have now lost the fuller weight and influence of our Chief Benefactor, while fighting the (so called) War on Terror . . . .

→To say that the symbolism of this fourth verse indicates a change of *nationality* is certainly to dodge the issue. It most certainly denotes *the same nation*. If you have one of your arms amputated, do you become a different person? No, you have simply been changed. You now have changed characteristics, but you are obviously the same individual.

The same is true of the symbolism used to represent this nation. In fact, for those with eyes to see, the United States is indeed morphing into a humanist state, before our very eyes. This is what the ACLU, and company, are fervently pursuing day and night: eradicating memories of our nation's Christian past, while replacing it with a humanist future and perspective. Humanism, if you have eyes to see, is the basis of all liberal philosophy. It is the only "doctrine" allowed to be pursued within our public schools. Yes, you may "teach the Bible" –but only from a Humanistic perspective.

Yes, you may speak about religion in the public sector, but only from a *secular* point of view. We would dissect God, and (if possible) place Him in a test tube. Never worship Jesus. This is why there is such resistance to simple believing prayer, in our public schools. Prayer (and simple worship of God) violates America's new heart: Humanism. The US has already surrendered its wings, to be able to "stand upon its feet as a man."

If this incredibly accurate symbolism were the only illustration of prophetic accuracy contained within this chapter, it would indeed be sufficient to convince an unbiased onlooker that the Bible's ability to forecast the future, is indeed amazing. In fact, if I were making such predictions, I would certainly "quit while I'm ahead." Not the Lord, however, He has no qualms about forecasting future events for He does, indeed, see the end from the beginning. Thus, the detailed description of our present day world continues. The very next verse, describes the world's number two great military power: the former Soviet Union.

The Russian bear (vs. 5).

It has three ribs in its mouth. What on earth for? The former Soviet Union was an incredibly powerful nation, was it not? For what purpose would it need "three ribs"? In fact, bears do not normally have ribs protruding from their mouths, at all. Ribs are normally a part of their body proper. That is, they are a part of the mother land. . . unless they be surrogates, and actually extensions of the main body. Hm-m-m-m. Did not the former Soviet Union have three surrogate nations, and "partners in crime" within the third world during the Cold War, spreading its poisonous Communist brew?

—Cuba

—Nicaragua

—Lybia

With these nations she subjugated the third world. When she deviated from the plan, she met with less success. Case in point; the Russian excursion into Afghanistan.

Wow! That is truly amazing! Two international symbols, with defining details denoted millennia before they actually came upon the scene. Truly, O Lord, Your word is truth. Yet there is more. For as powerful as the first two illustrations are, this upcoming third symbol is a continual "thorn in our side" whenever negotiating resolutions at the (you guessed it) United Nations. This next beast is indeed a most unusual creature (a spotted leopard— with four heads!).

The third world, . . . leopard:

Quite appropriately, this next creature has never before existed on the international scene. Daniel describes it as:

> another, like a leopard, which had on its back four wings of
> a bird. The beast also had four heads, and dominion was
> given to it.

Vs. 6

In this case, I prefer the Authorized Version's translation which describes these wings as those of a "fowl." Yes, the term

265

"bird" fits the bill (pun intended). But we tend to miss the point there. This is a *common* creature. Its Chaldean word (pronounced *owph*) appears in one other place in the Bible (Dan. 2:38) denoting regular birds of the air. In other words, as a human metaphor it represents the scattered and varied peoples of the world—as pictured by its *four* heads (for four corners of the earth – Is. 11:12).

Those who have lived through the 1960's may recall the "Black Panther" movement, so named because Black Power radicals related to its powerful frame, and beautiful black fur coat. Our text is far more general. This is a *leopard*, having multicolored spots, thus denoting all the varied peoples of the third world. But wait, what is that little note, added to its description?

The text states that "dominion was given to it." Collectively, and even on an individual sphere (we have now seen two black Secretaries of State in the US, to date) the members of the third world have been allowed to exercise ever increasing levels of influence. The Civil Rights movement, in other words, has been ordained of God. Its time had come.

Just like the automobile; if Henry Ford hadn't developed it, someone else would have. If Nelson Mandela hadn't fought against apartheid, someone else would have. If Martin Luther King Jr. hadn't lived, someone else would have had the dream. This is not to demean the accomplishments of these men. It does mean that their efforts were driven on, and supported, because the wind of prophecy was in their sails.[156]

What is most interesting is that the God of the down trodden, and underdog (as is often evident within Scripture—see I Corinthians 1:26, 27) has forecast the emergence of an international power to be reckoned with: an organized third world. For although not allowed to sit on the UN's Security Council, was not Koffi

Anan (and now his successor) from the third world? Do they not wreak havoc with UN resolutions regarding Israel? But, perhaps, we are again getting ahead of ourselves.

—Or, are not going fast enough. It is time to begin our wrap up: to connect the dots, and to bring all of these concepts together so that believers in the twenty-first century (and the citizens, thereof) may easily understand where we are, and how we've arrived at this point—as well as where we are going. We will consider society from a slightly different angle, than formerly accustomed to: from the side of the demonic. Before we do so, however—for this implies some of the same activity within the church, as well—allow me to present the reader with a concept that may not have (even within these pages) occurred to us:

that a foundational premise of the gospel has been lost in the simple omission of a Christian doctrine (only hinted at).

I know, it seemed that we had it all covered in our study of the eighth and ninth chapters of John's Apocalypse: the degradation of doctrines, the cooling down of Christian faith. Even . . . the corruption at the altar.

Wait, we didn't cover that last point?

Forgive me. That is the omission.

For how may we have a habitation of demons within fellowships that have been cleansed thereof? How may such things be possible? Where have we erred? Can it be possible . . . that all of excessive tolerance has first emanated from the church, itself? Yet, why are people coming down to the altar, to begin with?

Yes, why *are* they coming to the altar?

Is it to be saved? From what?

Or are we coming "just as we are"—to go away . . . in the

same condition?

Repentance, my friend. That is the missing ingredient. The basics, again. We have forgotten how to repent, at the altar. We think we're OK—so long as our self esteem is intact. Is this what God had in mind for Adam, in the Garden? That we be His puppets—and He, our Sugar Daddy?[157]

> "Because you say, 'I am rich, have become wealthy, and have need of nothing'; and do not know that you are wretched, miserable, poor, blind, and naked; . . .
>
> "So then, because you are lukewarm, and neither cold nor hot, I will vomit you out of My mouth
>
> . . .
>
> "Behold, I stand at the door and knock. If anyone hears My voice and opens the door, I will come in to him and dine with him, and he with Me."
>
> Revelation 3:17, 16, 20

No wonder Jesus is standing on the outside, knocking.

For, in spite of all denials to the contrary, we still live in God's black-and-white world.

Chapter 17

DEVIL IN MY WINDOW

And he cried mightily with a loud voice, saying, "Babylon the great is fallen, is fallen, and has become a dwelling place of demons, a prison for every foul spirit, and a cage for every unclean and hated bird!

"For all the nations have drunk of the wine of the wrath of her fornication, the kings of the earth have committed fornication with her, and the merchants of the earth have become rich through the abundance of her luxury."

Revelation 18:2,3

The Bible teaches that we live in a black-and-white world—not in fleshly tones of white man, black man—but in spiritual hues of life and death, with terms dealing with good and evil, right and wrong: the righteous and unrighteous. Yet for many within our present day world, particularly within the West, our world has become one that is both gray and undefined. It is a world made as comfortable with lying (without getting caught) and consorting with prostitutes . . .as with sitting down to laugh with holy men and preachers. All is one and the same. Nothing is perceived as endangering our welfare, or of challenging our belief system, just so long as it doesn't touch our pocket book.

Thus, when the US intelligence community seeks to evaluate powerful Muslims around the world, they now face an enigma. Because we tend to see the world about us through the glasses we ourselves wear, and tend to "mirror and project" our belief systems upon others we consider our equals—even measuring their equality by the amount of money they have. We expect the sheiks in Arabia, for example, to secretly think as we do, because they are rich, and have free access to things, and gadgets. When this turns out to be false, we have great difficulty coming to grips with what drives and motivates them. We either adapt our belief system to theirs— or are forced to label them in a derogatory manner (which, within the politically correct world of the bland West means that we officially "don't understand" them). *US News & World Report* recently revealed, for example, that the Iranian president Mahmoud Ahmadinejad "remains a bit of a mystery to official Washington."

> A U.S. intelligence profile, *U.S. News* has learned, depicts him as seeing the world "in very black-and-white terms" yet also possessing the capacity to "change quite quickly."[158]

Be advised, it is not his ability to "change quite quickly" or even to slither like a snake, that chagrins those in Washington. Such attributes are signals to westerners that there is "play" within the belief system of the one we are dealing with. We live in a day wherein officials have happily negotiated with the likes of a Yassar Arafat, and other fellow terrorists, just so long as they have yielded assurances and concessions that placate or support our agenda. No, it is not his changeable nature that bothers them. Such persons, they realize, may be reasonably bought off—even if only for a season.

No, it is that extremely "black-and-white" quality: the thing we used to call "conviction." *That* is what bothers them. Such conviction is what causes persons to turn their backs on all offers to buy out their souls, while turning their face into the wind, thus allowing their lives to be forfeited for a higher goal. Christian men and women of this stripe are rightly labeled "fundamentalists" (more accurately, "saints") and are most certainly dangerous within the domain of an emerging World Order where all is gray, and truth really doesn't matter (we think) just so "we can all get along"—whether you be an angel . . . or demon possessed. Just so long as one's values do not prevent them from being short changed (miss a monetary "blessing").

Or adversely affect our comfort zone.

Yet, this is exactly where the Lord, as well, draws the line in the sand, is it not? This is what set Daniel apart from his fellows, within the land of ancient Babylon: and the reason that the God of heaven could reveal secrets to him, in spite of the fact that he lived in the place of compromise, subjected to pressures that would seem to us unreasonable. So unreasonable, in fact . . . that it was even *prophesied* that the Jews would compromise themselves, without compunction. It was on this occasion, that Ezekiel balked, protesting to the Lord, when told to give a living demonstration of defilement.

> So I said, "Ah, Lord GOD! Indeed I have never defiled myself from my youth till now; I have never eaten what died of itself or was torn by beasts, nor has abominable flesh ever come into my mouth."

So the Lord allowed Ezekiel to keep his life, and experience, clean by performing a modified demonstration of eating defiled bread. Yet the Lord had already given a warning that, "So shall the children of Israel eat their defiled bread among the Gentiles, where I will drive them." (Ezekiel 4:14,13). In other words, within Babylon, compromise would be the order of the day. —So much so, that it would be fully expected for God's people to lay down their dietary laws and commandments, to accommodate the environment in which they found themselves. When in Babylon, do as the Babylonians do.

Then Daniel came along, in "Compromise City" itself: within the king's palace of Babylon, *refusing* to bow.

> But Daniel purposed in his heart that he would not defile himself with the portion of the king's delicacies, nor with the wine which he drank; therefore he requested of the chief of the eunuchs that he might not defile himself.
>
> Daniel 1:8

Daniel drew a line in the sand. That's the point. *He* took the initiative, and sought God early, searching his own heart and ferreting out those areas of compromise *within* that would make him unfit to stand in an hour of trial.[†]

For this diligence in faith, Daniel was not only given favor with God, but with the officials within Babylon, as well. His was not an experience without trial and testing, this is true. Moreover: three others, who associated with him (close friends) were also thrown into a furnace that was so hot that even the men hoisting them for destruction, were consumed by the very flames designed for their execution. Nor did Daniel escape the testing (for the possible tasting) of hungry lions.

Yet the God of Heaven: the God who truly sees our world in terms of "extreme black-and-white" was pleased with Daniel and his friends. This was the man to whom the angel came describing

---

[†] See also II Cor. 10:3-5!

272

the few, and the brave, who will not sleep at the end of the age. These are persons who cannot be bought,

Being willing to gladly pay a price

to wear the sackcloth.

These will do great exploits for God.

"And forces shall be mustered by him, and they shall defile the sanctuary fortress; then they shall take away the daily sacrifices, and place there the abomination of desolation.

"Those who do wickedly against the covenant he shall corrupt with flattery; **but the people who know their God shall be strong, and carry out great exploits**.

Daniel 11:31,32 [emphasis added]

Their cultural context is that of the abomination of desolation, which we now know represents none other than . . . the Mark of the Beast. We are now able, more readily, to discern it clearly upon the horizon, and understand how "flattery" might easily be employed in such a time. Many will tell these brethren how truly "wise" and "strong" they can be: thinking for themselves, and "providing for your family." (Echoes of trials in the Garden . . .).

To the faithful, however, a different paradigm and pattern for life exists. They see the world differently, and march to Heaven's tune, preferring to tread on the battlefield of the soul and spirit, while taking crucial ground—before the world has to meet the Lord, Himself,

in the skies over Armageddon.

Thus it is not Antichrist, alone, that must be resisted: it is the corruption all about (and even within) ourselves. It is our tendency to do as the Jews did when Christ came the first time: to side with the errors of religious leaders, even in the face of clear evidence to the contrary. Such will be obvious, for example, in the lives of foolish virgins seeking to accede to the wishes of the religious elite arguing prodigiously that the marking system of the Antichrist *cannot possibly* be what the Bible speaks about, when warning not to take the Mark of the Beast in our right hand or forehead.

—Even while the chips are being injected, within those very same parts of our very bodies: both arm and/or forehead.

For this reason, I believe the Lord will make the marking system blatant—even "in your face" with the enemies of the Lord actually mocking believers, whenever possible, and essentially daring us to resist. They will play cat-and-mouse with the sensibilities of a people totally unaccustomed to conflict or confrontation, until Satan's Kristallnacht, once again breaks out into the open; lighting a thousand fires, and causing saints' blood to flow in the streets— even as regular church goers run back to their sealed sanitariums – er, sanctuaries, to comfort themselves within safe havens.

They will be singing their hymns ever louder, while seeking to quietly pull the covering over their heads, for a final good sleep in the Night (they think).[†] All of this, bearing a strange, and even troubling, similarity to the way the Church reacted during the first Holocaust.[ω]

> "And then many will be offended, will betray one another, and will hate one another.
>
> "Then many false prophets will rise up and deceive many.

[†] Amos 5:21-23, 6:5,6

[ω] Scripture forecasts tribulation, to the Jew first, and then . . .to the Gentile (Romans 2:9)

"And because lawlessness will abound, the love of many will grow cold.

"But he who endures to the end shall be saved."

Matthew 24:10-13

It is then that most will gladly "speak lies in hypocrisy" because their consciences are seared (sealed off) at the bottom line of economics: so afraid to lose all they have, that they cannot see what the Lord has waiting for us

in Heaven.

* * *

"That man doesn't know God!" I said aloud, to no one in particular.

"What's the matter?" my wife's voice came running.

"This man doesn't know God! He says that all events in the real world, have a bad ending!"

"Wha--?" she wanted to know, "Calm down . . ." (Keep your shirt on. . .!) She knows better than to accost me with humanist jargon and ideas. This is especially true regarding movies and television viewing. Once, after viewing a video in the college classroom, I spent days agonizing over it. The class was supposed to be Christian, and promoting a Christian world view—but the movie (in spite of Christian sounding names, like "Trinity") obviously had something wrong with it. It seemed demonic. In fact, its entire focus was so consistently evil that its overall projection was that of a perfect negative: the good guys lived in the dark, and the bad guys in the sunlight. Truth was found through a blue pill, and the heroes lived deep in the earth, near to where its (very) warm. The movie, of course, is THE MATRIX.

I've told people that serious unlocking of Bible prophecy started, for me, after the pastor of the church I was attending (Dave Wilkerson, of Times Square Church) forecast a dive in the Stock Market. A key ingredient in his personal discipline has been the elimination of TV from his household (see THE CROSS AND THE SWITCHBLADE, opening discussion). Actually, that was a principle reason for my attending his fellowship—for I had already come to realize the dangers of modern media. In fact, while in the military, I had actually taken our television out of the house, to throw it into a creek. A police officer saw what I was doing, followed me home, and returned the set to us. That was the first time I tried to get rid of it. . . .

I finally decided that it really is the Lord's will for me to make use the media as a "window" into the heart and soul of society. . . .

But it can be a very dangerous "window."

Recently, while researching for this book, I came across an interesting note made by a reputed Bible scholar who also holds the post-trib position. It was not his position on prophecy that caught my attention (I was familiar with him, already)—it was his revelation regarding the culture then existing at the time of the apostle John's writing. It relates to certain activity, then practiced, within the Roman empire, regarding how stone statues were often used within idolatrous worship. In this particular case, this Roman custom does have great bearing on our quest for insight:

I quote from a footnote on page 238 of Van Kempen's book on Bible prophecy, THE SIGN. This quote relates to his interpretation of how the right-hand man of Antichrist (commonly called the false prophet) will bring about compliance. First, John's Revelation, and then the Bible scholar's assessment. John's vision:

> He was granted power to give breath to the image of the beast, that the image of the beast should both speak and cause as many as would not worship the image of the beast to be killed.

> He causes all, both small and great, rich and poor, free and slave, to receive a mark on their right hand or on their foreheads,

Revelation 13:15,16

Now, the quote:

> Dr. Gundry strongly emphasized interpreting this passage in light of the culture of John's day. In order to control the diverse peoples and nations of their vast empire, and to promote some degree of unification, the Romans erected statues of, and temples to the caesar, or emperor, in the cities of the lands they conquered. . . . Certain historical records report that some priests in pagan temples employed a form of ventriloquism to make it appear that the worshiped statues themselves were speaking.[159]

Looking back at the passage from Revelation thirteen, we suddenly notice that the only human-like characteristics mentioned, are:

- the fact that it has an image

- the image has the ability to speak.

Does this piece of cultural information lend any insight into the culture of our day? What of technical infrastructures, already in place? Can it help us to identify a popular tool, presently in production and utilized on a broad scale, to unify the many paradigms and thought processes already present within our world, today?

Taking another look at still another passage, earlier given, within John's Revelation we note that after the devastation of the sixth trumpet, the writer mentions that:

> the rest of mankind, who were not killed by these plagues, did not repent of the works of their hands, that they should not worship demons, and idols of gold, silver, brass, stone, and wood, which can neither see nor hear nor walk.
>
> Revelation 9:20

Note the interesting inclusion of the idols not being able to see, hear, or walk—but the omission of any ability to speak. This fits the pattern, then, of an image that *is* able to speak. When we compare these descriptions with that of our modern day society we suddenly realize that there *is* a "modern day miracle" available within the living rooms of 99% of American households. In addition, its hold over the public is now so powerful, that it is actually being officially classified as a form of personal addiction. Notes a website on the connection between TV viewing and personal health:

> Millions of Americans are so hooked on television that they fit the criteria for substance abuse as defined in the official psychiatric manual, according to Rutgers University psychologist and TV-Free America board member Robert Kubey. Heavy TV viewers exhibit five dependency symptoms—two more than necessary to arrive at a clinical diagnosis of substance abuse. These in-

clude: 1) using TV as a sedative; 2) indiscriminate viewing; 3) feeling loss of control while viewing; 4) feeling angry with oneself for watching too much; 5) inability to stop watching; and 6) feeling miserable when kept from watching.[160]

If you have a business, or means of getting things done, the preferred means of conveyance for the businessman's dream (or pusher's adrenalin) is the addict, who can't say "No" to your product line. Such is the power of modern television. It's ubiquitous presence, even within areas where the quality of life is substandard and far below the poverty line (as in third world ghettos, and depressed areas of the middle east, where the satellite dish remains an almost universal appendage) testifies to the power of this media. I love to give to SAT 7, a Christian ministry capitalizing on the constant presence of satellite dishes as a mainstay of middle eastern life—also used as a means of getting the gospel past the gate keepers of closed societies.

—Which also means that its lust and perversion are able to get past our own gates, if we're caught "napping." Another web site, monitoring the effects of TV viewing upon the populace, notes that (among other things):

> • In a sample of programming from the 2001-2002 TV season, sexual content appeared in 64% of all TV programs. Those programs with sexually related material had an average of 4.4 scenes per hour. Talk of sex is more frequent (61%) vs. overt portrayals (32%). 1 out of every 7 programs includes a portrayal of sexual intercourse.
>
> • Portrayals that included sexual risks (STDs or

becoming pregnant), abstinence or need for sexual safety was depicted in 15% of the shows with sexual content. Hence, sexual content on TV is more likely to promote sexual activity among US adolescents than it is to discourage it.

• Factors positively associated with initiation of intercourse among virgins are: Watching Sex on TV, having older friends, getting low grades, engaging in deviant behavior. Positive factors for virgins to abstain are: parental monitoring, parent education, living with both parents, having parents who would disapprove of adolescent sex, being religious, and having good mental health.

• "In a recent national survey conducted by Nielsen (4/29/04), 78% of American families who had recently been part of the Nielsen 'People Meter' panel wanted more shows 'without profanity or swear words.'

• "In a national opinion poll conducted for TV Guide (8/2/03), 57% of TV viewers said they 'noticed an increase in offensive material on television lately.'" [161]

So pervasive and powerful is the effect of the media on the way we think, that it would be laughable if it were not so serious. I was listening to a program host on the web earnestly dealing with demonic oppression, for example, by a noted minister on the subject (now deceased)—when I noticed this modern announcer introduced his co-host as his "Yoda." Yoda? You are warning people about participation with demons, and identify your co-host with

Yoda?? Where is our discernment, today? I have never felt comfortable watching that demonic image, nor the other little imp,[*] presented in Lord of the Rings. Yet we are raising a generation that can't even detect a demon, if it were to bite them—or if it did, wouldn't know to distrust the sulfurous smell that followed it . . . .

We live in a society that is much more comfortable with demons, than with saints. We prefer the gray netherworld of Hollywood, to the bright light of God's Presence.

> "And this is the condemnation, that the light has come into the world, and men loved darkness rather than light, because their deeds were evil.
> "For everyone practicing evil hates the light and does not come to the light, lest his deeds should be exposed."
>
> —Jesus Christ (John 3:19,20)

How will the terminal generation be able to withstand the peer pressure and moral decline that is being (not so) subtly processed within our present day society? How, indeed. Such would require a serious contemplation of the Bible's admonition not to sit in the congregation of the ungodly.

> Blessed is the man Who walks not in the counsel of the ungodly, Nor stands in the path of sinners, Nor sits in the seat of the scornful;
>
> . . .
>
> And I heard another voice from heaven saying, "Come out of her, my people, lest you share in her sins, and lest you receive of her plagues.

---

[*] Gollum

"For her sins have reached to heaven, and God has remembered her iniquities."

Psalm 2:1, Revelation 18:4,5

Whenever I present such a concept to a fellow believer and
they "poo-poo" the suggestion that there is an inherent danger in
indiscriminant TV viewing I am made painfully aware of the poor
"defensive" posture of the Christian church today. Who would go
into a den of Islamic extremists, fully "belted" with explosives, to
laugh and jest with them? Would it not be evident that you just
might not be able to leave the room, alive?!

Why enter the room, in the first place?

Why enter, with your guard down? For foolishness perverts
the soul, and lowers our guard. Through it, the con man makes his
advance, and the unrighteous paramour, gains inroads into the
good graces of an otherwise virtuous woman (Proverbs 19:3).

Yet many of us now allow easy access to ungodliness, along
with the vile misuse of the Lord's name, into our very living
rooms, without a second thought.

Then said he unto me,
Son of man, hast thou seen what the ancients of the house
of Israel do in the dark, every man in the chambers of his
imagery?
for they say, The LORD seeth us not; the LORD hath forsaken the earth.

Yet the Lord has *not* forsaken the earth. Nor is His hand with-
ered. He can certainly judge this present generation. In fact, this
generation is going down the very path the Lord has warned we

would take, two millennia ago within John's Revelation of Jesus Christ.

For the point of no return, is fast approaching.

And yet —there may yet be, a window of opportunity.

Chapter 18:

WINDOW OF DECEIT . . .
OR OPPORTUNITY ???

> And for this reason God will send them strong delusion,
> that they should believe the lie,
> that they all may be condemned who did not believe the
> truth but had pleasure in unrighteousness.
>
> II Thessalonians 2:11,12

Now that we've completed our introductory course to the keys, we are more prepared to connect the dots, and consider what it is that the Lord is saying to us, within the terminal generation. Yes, God has been speaking to us, though few have paid attention, and we recognize that His voice is getting ever more forceful, as we sense a new urgency in Christ's warning to disciples, "Take heed, that no one deceive you . . ." (Matthew 24:4). We understand that the spin doctors in the window, are actually no doctors at all, but witchdoctors, stirring up the pot. We know, also, that such a brew has not come to boil over night, but must be stoked carefully over the years, across cultures, and even within ourselves, if we doze off. It may sometimes seem that such delusion is simply too deep, and the temptation to doze, is too strong in the shadows. Yet Christ promises assistance to all who are serious about resisting the pull of the Night (I Corinthians 10:13).

As we appreciate the fact that *strong* delusion does not emerge on the landscape, over night, we forcefully turn our hearts towards Home (Heaven) and acknowledge that the strongest lies are those deeply rooted in governments, culture, and . . . religion. We have investigated emotional and religious roots in the first and second sections. The pull of the media was considered in our last chapter, and those of government touched upon in our description of the US and Israel. However, we have not truly come to terms with the gut wrenching reality of one central player in the New World Order (so called) as Scripture has described it. Duty now requires that we come to grips with, and confront the reality of our American involvement, in the ramp-up into the Apocalypse. The door of freedom will close, and the window of Heaven . . . open wide.

Yes, I have again resurrected that unpleasant "Apocalypse" term because, as we have exposed the dual nature of the rider on the white horse (with his dual purpose "bow") so too, we must realize that the US has two diverging destinies, with the last being the most unpleasant, in the end. For the head of the beast *is* this "wing-plucked" lion, that once had beautiful eagle's wings—at least, until the beast begins to morph into the one we will call *the Antichrist.*

Further, the *preliminary muscle* of the beast (NWO) is supplied by . . . this wingless lion.

Finally, the main voice sounded, in subjugating the rest of the world (with its military muscle) is that of . . . the wingless lion. For the *mouth* is in the head, and the head is derived from . . . this same entity. If we dare to continue approaching this matter with open minds, one conclusion becomes increasingly obvious: both negative and hopeful. First, the negative:

Prophetic descriptions of, what we now call, The New World

Order (i.e. the beast, as a global federation) reveal our present involvement within its stark symbolism:

> Then I stood on the sand of the sea. And I saw a beast rising up out of the sea, having seven heads and ten horns, and on his horns ten crowns, and on his heads a blasphemous name.
>
> Now the beast which I saw was like a leopard, his feet were like the feet of a bear, and his mouth like the mouth of a lion. The dragon gave him his power, his throne, and great authority.
>
> Revelation 13:1-3 [emphasis added]

Now, looking more closely at Daniel's description to see how these military powers *interact* within this beast, as a federation of nations—we begin to notice something:

> "After this I saw in the night visions, and behold, a fourth beast, dreadful and terrible, exceedingly strong. It had huge iron teeth; it was devouring, breaking in pieces, and trampling the residue with its feet. . . ."
>
> Daniel 7:7 [emphasis added]

Please note that Scripture specifically states that at the outset, it is the *mouth* (the US) that first subjugates the rest of the world, to bring it into line with the agenda of the New Order. While it is the bear (Russia) that performs the stomping, in the mop up (also outlined in Ezekiel 38 . . .). Yet in between, there is a man (at the end of the thirteenth chapter of the Apocalypse) that humankind finds itself falling in love with, and worshipping: a man whose name amounts to the number 666 (Revelation 13:18).

And now, to consider the positive side:

As unpleasant as the above revelations may be, to American Christians, there is one aspect of this insight that can prove incredibly powerful, especially in light of what we are about to explore within this chapter:

America yet leads.

I said, the US is still a world leader.

Please, all of you who teach that it is the fault of the rest of the world that we are heading towards Armageddon, please remove that blindfold from your eyes! We are not only a "super power" in military might; the US is yet a geopolitical leader, with a definite "voice" in where our world is heading.

Period.

You may deny it, if you will. The world, the devil, and eternity will certainly laugh at you, for you are most certainly living in personal denial. For, consider this: that if the United States of America –not Europe, primarily—were to experience a true revival, the *entire world* would feel its impact. Nor may the third world save our denominations and stave off judgment, but the US might. Every Christian *in the world* should be praying for a revival to take place within these *United States of America!* Now, put that in your pipe—or even under your kettle, and smoke it (I don't smoke, but you get the picture).

Now consider this:

One point at issue is the matter of what lies under the hood of the machine driving the US towards Armageddon. With very little thought it soon becomes obvious that a primary force for conflict within the middle east is not only the Green Horse, but green money, as well. Even politicians recognize this. Monetary pressures are experienced largely through the world's appetite for the energy generated by the consumption of middle eastern crude (oil). However, if an observer were to take notice of just how much oil prices have been fluctuating —and when these fluctuations occur in relation to public response, it just may begin to dawn upon us that the day of "the reign of oil" as a driving force for both geopolitics and international intrigue by the Green Horse, may not last forever.

At least, that's the way some in the middle east may well see it (and ourselves. . ?).

This truth may be discerned by way the middle eastern cartel responds to our reaction to higher gas prices, for example. At present Saudi Arabia, and friends, seem to have a choke hold (or very great influence) on present oil supplies. Let the oil market seem to be threatened, however, or allow an increasingly serious discussion of alternative fuels and sources of energy to take place and—viola! Suddenly, the price at the pump seems to find a way to plummet, a bit.[162]

Why is this?

Because technology is beginning to catch up.[163]

Brazil is already independent of oil pressures, with its fuller use of ethanol, and offshore drilling.

California, and other states, are presently experimenting with making alternative fuels available.[164] It is true, that at present, some of these efforts are stumbling badly[165] —yet, consider the possibility, for example, of new money (not yet allocated) . . . being channeled into developing alternative fuel outlets and distribution points. Combine this with the possibility of hybrid automotive

288

technology—and how long do you think it would take for the US, alone, to become self supporting? Combine this with the Alaskan pipeline . . . .

Truth is (I know this may be considered near treasonous to suggest, but) to date, we simply have not truly demonstrated the will to break the strangle-hold of foreign oil. Political cheer-leading aside, even good intentions are insufficient to enable the White House to institute reform. [†] One energy think tank, quoted in a New York Times article on 2 February of 2006, has proposed that Washington HAS been *purposely* slowing down energy independence for economic reasons (no, not because of personal investments, it's the economy....). Notes this study group on its website:

> In fact, the administration may have avoided measures to aggressively curb oil consumption because it understands such moves might end up weakening American and European oil companies. Since each barrel of oil enters into a global pool that is traded daily, higher-cost producers - in places like the tar sands of Alberta, the North Sea off Britain or Norway, or the Gulf of Mexico in the United States - would be the first to halt production if the United States were to lower its oil purchases and thus ease market prices.[166]

[†] For an inside look at how very good intentions—even how Christian intentions, may easily evaporate into thin air within the White House, read David Kuo's revealing book: TEMPTING FAITH, An Inside Story of Political Seduction. Freedom Press, copyrighted 2006.

There may be other pressures, as well. For Saudi oil dollars are now being heavily invested into the Western economy. We now have a vested interest, if you will, of protecting this flow of capital into our society. Their gasoline runs our cars, and then their "green backs" assist our economy. I know this sounds contradictory, but consider this: If you are a wage earner, consider what would happen to *your* paycheck, if your boss suddenly lost *his* means of support for the company. How easy would it be for him to make a decision to cut ties with a major corporation . . . if they had already gained an interest within his own manufacturing plant? (In other words, if the owner was himself "owned" by Walmart—how quick would he be, to go independent???)

He may huff and puff about being his own boss . . . until the big boys, from Arkansas, "put the arm" on him.

But remember our opening observation, about "strong delusion." You do recall, don't you, that it does sometimes seem that the delusion is so strong that it may not seem fair? So consider this: what if the supply of oil were no longer an issue, at all, any longer?

You say, wha--??? " ' you have a new fuel car that can run on water?"

Almost. Let's just say that the oil I propose using, just doesn't have to be purchased in such large quantities from the middle east, or from Venezuela for that matter, if we so choose. We can get almost all of it, right here, in the northern hemisphere. Now, please understand, I am no oil expert. Nor chemical engineer. My purpose in argument, here, is only to present the reader with possibilities, and spring boards of faith, to open new windows of possibility in the mind so that we may pray in faith.

Further, even with the diffusing of the "oil card" there still remains the very troublesome issue of loose-cannon "nukes."

Iran, in particular, remains an ever present menace to the rest of the world. Her "Green Horse" mentality, coupled with nuclear power, spells *trouble!* (Think about that, the next time you hear about politicians solving our middle eastern problems by pulling out of Iraq. When we pull out, who fills the vacuum???)

My brothers and sisters, there is *much* to pray over, today!!

Yet, it is possible for the LORD to *completely defuse* the middle eastern conflict, and to turn it off, like a man turning off a light switch. My purpose for pursuing this present avenue of discussion, is only to present *one possible scenario* for assisting that event. Those who read this book, and seriously consider what has been said here, should fully understand by now that even if a solution is perfectly logical—there is no way for us to avoid Armageddon, within the next ten years, unless God intervenes. Our world is presently *spring loaded* and "dead bent" towards self destruction. The middle east (in case you haven't noticed) has become *more* unbalanced because of Saddam's demise.

He was keeping Shia Iran in check. Now, we will have to do it . . .
.

Yet, ask yourself why this nation, realizing its heavy dependence upon oil, would be so petty and concerned about disturbing some Caribou (while most Alaskans are not[167])—when there is the possibility of *decimating the entire planet*, through thermonuclear exchange (of missiles): simply because we cannot contain the Green Horse, being fueled by middle eastern oil reserves,

or see past the Green lobby, playing fast and loose with environmental statistics.

Why *not* unleash our reserves?

"Because they will run out," you say.

What if they didn't?

You say, "Wha--?? Frank, stop speaking in riddles!"

OK. I will. Be forewarned, however, that if you attempt to make use of the following information, without first instituting true revival, *it will not work.* Guaranteed. Read that again: *it will not work.* Why? Because the Lord has ordained it. We are presently under a cloud of divine judgment. (I almost hate to give hope, here, because I know some will simply *ignore* the warning, and try to run with what is about to be shared.)

There is good reason to believe that oil has *not* originated from the remains of dinosaur fossils. There is good, and scientific evidence to support the belief that at least some oil sources may actually . . . come from a renewable resource.

In other words, there are areas on the earth where the oil actually renews its reservoirs, as rain renews our water supplies on an annual basis. You heard me right: there are places in the world where the oil *simply does not run out, because it is renewed.* This is one reason why, with all of the billions and billions of barrels of oil being pumped out of the middle east . . . their oil reserves still show no sign of exhausting. (Of course, if you owned one of those oil fields, you might not want for people, elsewhere, to know about that.)

This theory of renewable oil fields is actually held by some scientists and, in particular by Thomas Gold, professor emeritus at Cornell University. You can read about it at <http://www.lewrockwell.com/orig5/crispin8.html>. The Wall Street Journal also printed an article, on its front page,[168] about an oil field that has actually been observed demonstrating this ability to renew itself (Eugene Island) after its output had diminished.

By utilizing 3D seismic technology, scientists were actually able to see the oil being renewed from cracks deep within the earth. They saw it happening (like taking a sonogram, of the earth's belly—see the earlier web link, given above).

"Wow! Wow! And double Wow!" you say. Yes, and Eugene Island actually happens to exist in the Gulf of Mexico, off our coast.

"Triple Wow!"

HOLD ON! Hold your horses. Please. First of all, from what we now know, the Gulf cannot supply the lion's share of our energy needs. –But what if there is (or we were to discover) a section of the Alaskan fields that happened to display this very same attribute? We cannot tell, for we have not yet fully developed this resource. My only real purpose for sharing this information is to present the reader with a viable possibility, and hope, while praying for revival. Again, I most solemnly, and seriously, warn the reader that the information just provided will provide *no relief whatever* to present world conflicts or tensions, without serious revival.

NONE. Nada, nothing. No one will believe you. Yet even if *the US Government* were to believe this, and attempt it (and appeared to *succeed*) without revival—it will not work. NO ONE will be able to do a thing to make use of this information, or halt our rush towards judgment.

NO ONE—unless, there is revival (see Jeremiah 37 for a similar illustration).

God controls our future!

Our premise, from the outset, has been that the God of the Bible has everything under control. He is a holy God, and nothing can simply "slip by Him." Nevertheless, God is also merciful, and Scripture informs us that it is not His will for any to perish, but that all come to repentance. This last comment, concerning the Lord's mercy, was made within the direct context of the timing Christ's second coming. "Where is the promise of His returning," people were saying, "for since the fathers fell asleep, all things continue as they were from the beginning of creation" (II Peter 3:4). Depending on how you read, or read into this text, it does appear that the saints of the first century expected for the Lord to return at any moment—certainly within their lifetime.

Yet, Peter affirms a serious and awesome point, regarding the timing of the Lord's returning: similar to the first warning issued prior to Christ's ascension into Heaven. There is an over-arching plan that God has, that trumps all other considerations upon which Christ's returning is contingent:

the preparation of His bride.

The whole purpose of human creation, and of the Lord's coming into the world, has been to prepare a people with whom He will live, for the rest of eternity. Did you catch that? All of human history is but a parenthesis in eternity—almost like a comma, on an eternal continuum. Before Genesis, there is only God. After the new Heaven and Earth, there is God and His bride (us)!

Whew! Sit down, and think about that one, for a few weeks!

As nice as it would be to see the final wrap up of prophetic events, therefore, "Heaven can wait" in this regard. For, after the Lord returns to earth, the doorway into this privileged position of becoming a child of God,

within the bride of Christ,

will have been closed.

Will He find faith?

Although enlightening, the above point can pose a serious challenge to the believer's faith as we continue pointing our eyes towards the future. It must be assumed that at some point many will simply give up waiting—and then the Lord will respond in a manner not at all pleasing to His almost comatose "bride." This is also an implied reading into Christ's question regarding His *very* serious concern over whether he will find faith on the earth when He returns. The context of His question concerns answered prayer—and of those waiting for their prayers to be answered. Notice how our Lord couches His query, on this very serious issue.

> "And shall God not avenge His own elect who cry out day and night to Him, though He bears long with them?
>
> "I tell you that He will avenge them speedily. Nevertheless, when the Son of Man comes, will He really find faith on the earth?"
>
> Luke 18:7,8

It's the prayer chamber, that He's thinking about: prayers ascending, with reciprocal blessings, judgments, and replies descending towards the earth (see chapter 11).[†]

This text shows that *persistence* is a clear indication of great faith.[*]

[†] p. 177

It also says that the Lord will avenge such persons *speedily,* for He is touched with the pains that we feel, especially since He has already visited our planet as a man and experienced these pains, personally. Yet, He still asks the question, "Will I find faith upon the earth?"

In other words, will the church give up hoping for Christ's returning? Notice, very carefully, that Jesus specifically couches the question within the context of his returning. He asks specifically if, when he returns, He "will … find faith on the earth?"

Conditions of the Wrap-up:

There are times when God's planning for his people is contingent upon our response to His promises. This is not always the case regarding the wrap-up of apocalyptic events and his second coming. In this regard, as we have noted in the chapter on Onion Skins, there are both eventual (circumstances, fashioned by the Lord) and timing factors (evidenced by the 3½ clocks, for example)—as well as matters of faith.

The circumstances required are outlined in the symbols of John's Revelation, through seals, trumpets, and vials (the vials are poured out past the Midnight Cry that this book highlights).

Timing is determined by the 3½ clocks, which themselves are rather flexible—especially in regard to our last point. However, there is a point at which all of these final goals of prophecy are fulfilled. Two of these points are already fulfilled when the mighty angel, who speaks after the mysterious seven thunders (whose message we are forbidden to hear) sounds an alarm:

---

* Observe a very similar, literal case, and the Lord's response in Matt. 15:22-28.

The angel whom I saw . . .

swore by Him who lives forever and ever, who created heaven and the things that are in it, the earth and the things that are in it, and the sea and the things that are in it,

that there should be delay no longer,

Directly after this alarming pronouncement, John notes that in the days of his declaration, when the seventh angel (final trump) is about to sound, the mystery of God is accomplished (10:6). In other words, the gospel mandate is then fully completed (Matthew 24:14).

Two out of three have already been fulfilled. The final condition must now be met. Now, therefore, we must question ourselves on that very touchy question of faithfulness, and of the virgin bride's heart-cry for her beloved. Again, there are times when God's response and preparation for His people is contingent upon our response.

In this case, His is an inverse response to faithfulness, as we shall explain: nevertheless it *is* a response from Heaven. It is not that God has actually gone back upon His word (although the quote that follows seems to imply this) it is only that, since God has called us to be His bride—there are certain points of reckoning that we must cooperate with, for Him to act. If you can accept it; marriage in God's mind is a two-way street. He has the right to expect certain responses from His bride.

Not the least of which, is faithfulness.

So it is that, in the Old Testament "marriage" of the Lord to Israel, the Lord specifically stated that He was married to her (Jer. 3:14)—yet when the children of Israel came to the brink of the

Promised Land (the land of milk and honey: the Honeymoon)—they failed to enter, because they balked, hesitated, and refused to believe God, for what He had clearly promised.

The land promised was a near Paradise: just as the Lord had said. . . but it was a fearsome land, and one in which the inhabitants were so strong that *they thought* that as "mere" Israelites they looked like grasshoppers to those already in possession (Numbers 13:33).

Imagine, they had just seen the Lord *decimate* the world's super-power (Egypt) by speaking ("Thus saith the Lord") through Moses. They had not raised one weapon of war, in defense, to gain release from that iron furnace—and yet now, they proposed; this same God who was still:

- leading them under supernatural cloud-cover (from desert heat) by day,

- warming them at night by a private heating furnace: seen in the fiery pillar that appeared every evening to warm them (from the desert cold, because the desert sands did not retain the warmth)

- and feeding them, continually with food *literally falling from the sky* (manna)

→ would now be unable to deliver them from these *mere mortals,* and give them what He had promised! No wonder the Lord was disgusted, and repulsed, by their unbelief!

It is at this point that the God of Glory, Who placed the planets in their orbits, and spans the universe with His fingers, spoke in anger to these people, whom He had promised that very special piece of real estate. His comment is one of the most telling, awesome, and terrifying in all of Scripture. It is a statement so awesome, I believe, that modern translators have balked at maintaining the language of the Authorized Version, which we now quote.

> your children shall wander in the wilderness forty years, and bear your whoredoms, until your carcases be wasted in the wilderness.
>
> After the number of the days in which ye searched the land, even forty days, each day for a year, shall ye bear your iniquities, even forty years, <u>and ye shall know my breach of promise.</u>
>
> Numbers 14:34 [emphasis added]

Also devastating is the modern translation which notes that after the spies returned, and the Lord pronounced a judgment upon them—of forty years of wandering in the desert, for forty days of (fruitless) investigation—so that the New King James translates the last phrase, above, as "and you shall know my rejection" –reminiscent of the Lord's statement to Laodicea, stating that He will "vomit you out of My mouth" (Rev. 3:16).

Likewise, in a similar way (in a promise to a rebellious "bride") the Lord promises that the church will most certainly find herself in that black hole, after apostasy. This was clearly stated by the apostle Paul to the church at Thessalonica. Paul guarantees the slide before the Lord's returning. "That day" of the Lord's returning, Paul says, will not come . . . until after the church effectively *allows* the unveiling of Antichrist (as we've stated several times over, all ready).

And Blasphemy:

In other words, the world, when looking at the church—will be moved to disdain (blaspheme) God (Rom. 2:24). This is a very serious reason for the church to maintain a godly witness (1Ti

5:14, 6:1 Tit 2:5,8). In fact, if we look at Scriptural reasons for causing blasphemy in each of these texts (the conduct of our women, conduct of our workers, and our personal speech)—while comparing this with John's locusts, in his 5th trumpet, we begin to suspect something: the locusts were chosen, specifically, as a call to revival (compare John's locusts with those in Joel's prophecy). An interesting study would include noting the difference between Joel's members, in sackcloth (lying down –Jl. 1:8,13) and the "sons of oil" (standing before the Lord –Zech. 4:14, see also Psalm 134).

As an insight into this matter, consider the first point: the conduct of young widows. Paul advises us to have them "remarry" so that the enemy will "not speak reproachfully" (I Tim. 5:14). That's young widows. What of Christians . . . divorced??[169]

Blasphemy and God's Honor:

You may not have considered this, but Scripture outlines our final countdown, by defining the "beast" in the close-out of the age, as a social organism riding this wave of blasphemy (Revelation 13:1,5). Blasphemy is the bottom line (rock bottom) of society at large. We have traced the decline of human spirituality, through four trumpets of the Apocalypse—what of American culture, from the 50's to present? Looking through our speaking "window" (last chapter) we saw "Father Knows Best" in the 50's, to be assailed by the "Trivial Pursuit" of the 80's and 90's. Wait a minute.

Excuse me?? Are we, as a society, now basing our dreams on *trivial* pursuits? Is this how we now live our lives? Is life trivial?

Forgive me, that's too deep to consider . . . or is it?

What of our present craze, of voting for an American . . . Idol?

Blasphemy is little understood, today, largely because it is becoming an everyday occurrence—even something to be respected. Evolutionary theory is blasphemous, for example, for it is a slap in God's face, by saying, "Our hand is high, and the Lord has not done all this! We made ourselves! We are our own Creator!"— directly contradicting God's mandate (Deut. 32:27, Ps. 100:3). [170]

We don't seem to hold to the most basic truths, as a society, anymore: that God is our fundamental provider, and the ultimate maintainer of natural resources, for example. The most elementary assertions of Christ—that God does care for the earth's ecosystems, are cast aside. Yes, we're going there . . .

Consider the most basic assertions made to disciples, regarding requirements of faith and believing, spoken in His Sermon on the Mount:

"Look at the birds of the air, for they neither sow nor reap nor gather into barns; yet your heavenly Father feeds them. Are you not of more value than they? Which of you by worrying can add [18 inches] to his stature?

"So why do you worry about clothing? Consider the lilies of the field, how they grow: they neither toil nor spin; and yet I say to you that even Solomon in all his glory was not arrayed like one of these.

"Now if God so clothes the grass of the field, which today is, and tomorrow is thrown into the oven, will He not much more clothe you, O you of little faith?"

Matthew 6:26-30

Stewardship of the earth aside (Genesis 2:15): what does our present "chicken little" ranting and raving over one degree of average climate change—say about our faith in God? One thing that seems incredible to me, is the absence of the simplest of Christian logic, regarding recent weather changes:

→We seem to have discounted (forgotten) the judgments of God. It is so uncommon to respond to the Lord, or trial, with anything *but* whining and self pity today, that we seem to have forgotten how to make use of God's judgments, for personal benefit: to call *ourselves* into account, to search and try our motivations and practices, as we beseech the God of Heaven for His grace and mercy.[171]

I ask you, if God can graciously answer prayer in the affirmative—can He not also do so . . . in the negative? Has it occurred to us that our constant whining and complaining may actually be increasing the tendency towards judgment—so that the "warming trend" actually becomes an explanation to *cover* our eyes, and make us insensitive to God's desire to correct us, as we add "fuel to the fires"?

In other words, when this kettle has reached its "boiling point" our goose is cooked!

To Laodicea, the half baked and lukewarm fellowship of believers who never could awaken enough to climb out of the pot of compromising Christianity, Christ advises:

"Because you say, 'I am rich, have become wealthy, and have need of nothing'; and do not know that you are wretched, miserable, poor, blind, and naked;

"I counsel you to buy from Me gold refined in the fire, that you may be rich; and white garments, that you may be clothed . . .and anoint your eyes with eye salve, that you may see."

Revelation 3:17,18

302

It is because of careless indifference, while wallowing in the gray areas of compromise, that the Lord finds it necessary to re-lease this church, of the final generation, into the black hole of Great Tribulation.

Spared the "black hole"

There have been moments in our recent past, when I believe the die was about to be cast, and we were about to be plunged into that black hole. One instance was immediately after Mikhail Gor-bachev allowed the Berlin Wall to fall when—in an amazing coup attempt—he survived to recover his status as a world figure . . . after subduing three leaders who plotted against him.

At that time, within the framework that we have outlined within this book, Gorbachev could very easily have been attributed with fulfilling the requirements of Antichrist in accordance with both Daniel 7:8 and Revelation 13:3—outlined in an earlier work, posted online.[172]

Another instance appears to have been the Y2K fiasco—which was indeed, a hoax, but appeared to be structured by some to actu-ally dump us into the black hole—but instead, resulted in a church-wide call to serious prayer. I am convinced that the forces of Anti-christ were primed and ready, at that time, as well.

But the church awoke just enough, to start praying.

Coincidence, you say? Yes, I have seen some amazing coin-cidences, given by the Lord to this former atheist. While in the US Navy during the Viet Nam War, I was stationed aboard the USS Blakely (FF 1072) on the east coast. The time eventually came for my ship to shift oceans and lend tangible support to the war effort.

We sailed through the Suez Canal, visited Hawaii, and Subic Bay (Philippines) and entered the northern waters of the war in what was then called the "Line Backer Zone." I had been earlier wrestling with the Navy Chaplaincy over the maintenance of my SGLI (Servicemen's Group Life Insurance)—insisting that it be removed from my records. They thought I was plumb crazy, but as a young Christian I was simply trying to follow the Lord's admonition to avoid laying up treasures in this world (Matt. 6:20,21). In that day, the $20,000 policy looked like a treasure to me. So I requested it be removed.

Today, I do carry some insurance (my mother insisted on it, after I got out. Honor your parents . . .)—but this is not the issue, here. The issue is faith. God honors it. I do believe that this is the reason for what happened next. There are many other stories I could relate (I've been following the Lord for over 30 years, after all . . .) but this one has bearing on our discussion. For you see, that was a dangerous mission, my ship was embarking on: I was stationed on a frigate. It makes for a beautiful peace-time vessel, but becomes a terribly vulnerable target, in time of war (she has a wide superstructure). You don't fire on the enemy, without them firing back. . . .

Yet, on the morning our ship nosed into those waters, and the radar screens, that I was maintaining, started to chart the skies of North Vietnam—there was a cease fire.

It held.

And the war ended.

Today, our country is embroiled in an apparent no-win war. There has been remarkable silence from many, whom we expect should know better, regarding our dependency upon the God who has forecast these turns of events. Yet, the same God who has projected our current situation: the return of the nation of Israel to her land, the rise of the US, Russia, and of the third world—and even the ride of the Green Horse, now threatening to devour one third of humankind through nuclear holocaust—can certainly hold back the hand of judgment.

→We have not been "left behind."

To some Christians, expecting to "be out of here before the fireworks start" these current events have never been a matter of concern, until recently. Yet forming a "Tribulation Force" would be futile. Such would be fighting against Destiny, itself . . . To others, the very question itself strikes them as overly simplistic, and yet I tell the reader very solemnly, that the God of the Bible—who has forecast our destiny, is the only hope for our country and world, today.

Keys to the Apocalypse? Yes, there are keys, but only one Way. Jesus is that Way, Truth, and the Life. No one comes into God's Presence peacefully, without acknowledging Him.

For the individual, Christ is the answer, for all of eternity.

And for America, He holds the only path out of our present dilemma. We need to remember, and to acknowledge, the Lord Jesus Christ, again.

The choice is ours.

There is not a moment to lose.

End Notes:

Chapter 1: Not a Genius

[1] To refresh readers' minds. This reference to three Hebrew boys refers to young men taken into captivity, when the nation of Israel was overrun by the Babylonian empire in approximately 607 BC. The king had set up an enormous golden idol "in the plain of Dura, in the province of Babylon" (Daniel 3:1). Those refusing to bow were to be thrown into an oven. These three young men refused to bow, and were thrown in, but remained unharmed as the Lord appeared in the flames, with them. More can be learned of these young men, of their friend Daniel, and of their bravery, by reading the first three chapters of Daniel's prophecy (Daniel 1 – 3).

[2] Please note that (for the church) this is not "reformation" but, *restoration.* The reformation reclaimed the basic doctrine of justification by faith. What we here refer to as the "restoration" reclaims the fullness of the ministry of the Holy Spirit. There are some surprises here, but they will have to wait until we get further along in our study.

[3] The term "rapture" is derived from the Latin Vulgate translation of

I Thessalonians 4:17. In that translation the snatching away of saints is translated from a word whose Latin root is *rapere.* (from which we also derive the word rape). It is an intense term, denoting the forcible removal of believers from this world "in a moment, in the twinkling of an eye"—literally, *in an atom of time* (I Corinthians 15:52).

[4] For those disturbed by my reference to there being no "secret rapture" mentioned within Scripture, please refer to the ministry web site, for a more complete treatment of this subject, at

< http://www.maranatha-min.net/One2ndComing/home.html>

End notes:

Chapter 2: Welcome to the Kettle

[5] II Timothy 4:4

[6] Acts 20:28

[7] A most interesting note is the fact that, without knowing one another or consulting the other's notes, the Holy Spirit has brought us to the same *conclusions* via different routes of interpretation: that the US is certainly highlighted in prophecy, along with WWII and the Gulf War: Endtime's path is through the 2nd and 5th trumpet, my own is through Revelation 12 and Daniel 11, past verse twenty-one. Careful comparison will also note that we have arrived at the conclusion that we now stand at exactly the same point of reference, on the prophetic time line: just prior to Antichrist's rising, in Revelation 13 . . . .

[8] See the personal note, towards the end of the book. The pastor referred to is David Wilkerson, known for his work with teen drug addicts in the book, *The Cross and the Switchblade*.

[9] I Thessalonians 5:2,3

[10] Job 24:15,16, Matthew 24:43

[11] This application, of changes even within our thinking, and within our immediate environment, is what we will focus on, when exploring Revelation chapters 8 & 9.

[12] Paraphrasing Matthew 16:1-3

[13] Contactless credit & debit cards, sometimes called "tap and go" or the like. These are cards utilizing Radio Frequency Identification (RFID). Such RFID technology is also pending for chip implantation. See Spychips.com.

[14] Revelation 4:1 AV

[15] The time of the Maccabees marked a Jewish revolt led by Judas Maccabeus in the second century B.C. He cleansed the temple that had been desecrated by the

Syrian Antiochus IV (which Chanukah celebrates). An idol, of some kind, had been placed upon the temple's altar of burnt offering, and Jerusalem's inhabitants commanded to worship it.

[16] Christ refers to Himself as the bridegroom, in Matt. 9:15.

[17] See I Thes. 4:16,17. The context is the same as that of Matthew 24. In other words, just as the parable of the ten virgins (Matt. 25:1-10) follows the prophecy of Jesus' second coming —the apostle Paul's advice *not to sleep* follows his description of Christ's returning in the previous chapter.

Chapter 3: Of Paradigms & Onion Skins . . .

[18] This term, "born again," comes from a statement Jesus made to a Jewish leader, while on earth (John 3:1-16). Christ used it to describe a supernatural encounter with God, wherein one departs from the old life, into the new, with God. This experience—beginning with repentance (II Cor. 7:10,11), is what the apostle Paul refers to when saying that Christians have been transferred from the kingdom of darkness, into the kingdom of Christ (Colossians 1:13).

[19] For advanced students: this is an application of I Corinthians 10:1-6 in reverse . We will not devote time to studying this section of John's vision, because it does not focus on the Midnight Cry as forcefully as do the other overlaps. Its main concern is with the reign of Christ, *after* He returns.

[20] <http://en.wikipedia.org/wiki/World_War_II_casualties>

[21] It is also important to realize, that although there are ten toes and ten horns in final empire (of Daniel's vision – Dan. 2:41-43, Rev. 13:1) that Daniel saw the ten toes at the end . . . of two feet. The "orthodox" church is divided into east and west. As we shall see, Russia is also included in the "beast" of Rev. 13. This is something seldom considered . . . .

[22] Revelation 18:10, 17, 19

---

[23] Farah, Joseph. Iran leader's messianic end-times mission. WorldNetDaily. <http://www.worldnetdaily.com/news/article.asp?ARTICLE_ID=48225> . 6 Jan. 2006. 26 July 2006.

[24] Ezekiel 33:11

[25] The "Green Horse" as we will explain later, is a proper translation of Revelation 6:8, where the Greek word, usually translated "pale" is *chloros* from which we get chlorophyll. It literally means, "green."

[26] Margin notes. Young's Literal Translation of the Holy Bible, 1863 version. AGES Software • Albany, OR USA.Version 1.0 © 1996

Chapter 4: What Clocks are These?

[27] For a more detailed discussion of this particular aspect of prophecy, see "PRINCE TO KING" on the ministry website, at < http://maranatha-min.net/TheUPLOOK/2005-7-prince-1.htm#top>

[28] There is some disagreement as to the exact date of Christ's birth (i.e. when our calendar starts, plus/minus three years) –in which case this prophecy might also be fulfilled at Christ's baptism, instead of three years later, at His triumphal entry into Jerusalem. The main point is that Daniel's prophecy points directly into Christ's life-time upon earth.

[29] This concept, of spiritual Israel, is presented very carefully by the apostle Paul in Romans (2:28, 29 & chapt. 11).

[30] John 4:22

[31] Isaiah 9:6,7, Matthew 27:37, Matthew 15:24ff

[32] Genesis 7:11, 24-8:4

[33] Matthew 24:32-34, Mark 13:28-30, Luke 21:29-32 Note the mention of "all trees" in this last reference. This accents the rise of the third world, which we will mention as we cover the rise of the final world order.

[34] Zechariah 4:7—this fourth chapter parallels the description of the two witnesses, in Revelation eleven. Zechariah was intimately involved in the rebuilding of the physical temple, after the Babylonian exile of the Old Testament, and in this seventh verse. He is assured of the success of his endeavor.

[35] Although it was done through the instrumentality of men, the aborting of Paul's activity at this point was indeed Providential. Had he actually offered a sacrifice in the temple at that time it would have been a denial of major New Testament doctrines, most of which were taught by Paul himself, wherein he points out that we are complete in Christ (Gal. 3:1-10, Eph. 4:4-12, 5:2)—and that there is no need for further sacrifice, at all, having being superceded by the *superior* sacrifice of God's own blood (Heb. 9:22-10:4, Acts 20:21)!

[36] Actually, the text does not say that these virgins had "extra" oil (see Matt. 25:3,4). They had *oil with their lamps*. In other words, the foolish virgins had neglected a basic requirement for those who are faithful (Eph. 5:18).

[37] John 10:16

[38] Balaam, although a mercenary prophet, did know the true God. See Numbers Chpt. 22. Balaam paid for selling out, to the heathen king, with his life (Numbers 31:8).

[39] Ephesians 2:14-16

[40] Exodus 25:31,32, 40:24,25

[41] Matthew 5:14-16

Chapter 5: Throne Room of the Universe

End notes:

---

[42] See "CLOSE ENCOUNTERS: A BETTER EXPLANATION" Master Books, copyright 1978 authored by Clifford Wilson and John Weldon. In that work UFO phenomena are carefully compared to other covert phenomena within our physical world—by Christians, who are also scientists. They come to the conclusion that such phenomena are actually the of activities performed by other spiritual beings (identified as demons, within Scripture). . . .

[43] Actually, this is a misnomer. The Scriptures do not support the idea of demon *possession* but of *demonization.* The Greek word, translated "demon-possessed" in Matt. 9:32, for example, is more accurately rendered "demonized" (Gr. Strong's # 1139) which is the verb form of the word pronounced "*daimon*" (demon). In other words, demons attack and seize possession illegally (as a roaring lion – I Pet. 5:8). They do not "own" the person they harass, oppress, or terrorize.

[44] True peace and unity may only be achieved within the bonds of true love (Col. 3:14,15). Thus we now glimpse another reason why God has created two sexes—to draw men and women (though quite different in many ways) into a unity that reflects the spiritual love and union of the Godhead. God is love (I Jn. 4:16), and only such an One as He may be truly united in a holy Trinity.

[45] Death Star A BAD DAY IN THE MILKY WAY. Part 2.
<http://www.pbs.org/wgbh/nova/gamma/milkyway2.html> 9 Jan 2007.

[46] See ONLY THE TRINITY CAN EXPLAIN at < http://maranatha-min.net/Tracts/trinity-1.html >

[47] Here, "have" is used to avoid confusion in the text –as the translators of the Authorized Version did, in the translation of John 4:24 (see next endnote).

[48] Note that in John 4:24, the word "is" is placed in italics in the AV. This is because the Father is outside of time and space. The word "is" (from the verb "to be": He is there. I was there.) —is itself a time reference. Eternity transcends time. This is why the Father communicates most "naturally" with us through the Son, and Holy Spirit. John 12:28,29 remains therefore, as an example of "direct" communication . . . .

Chapter 6: Be Naked, or Saints:

[49] Westminster shorter catechism, question 1:

< http://www.shortercatechism.com/resources/wsc/wsc_001.html> 1 May 2007

[50] I Corinthians 13:7

[51] Christ said, "If you love Me, keep My commandments" (John 14:15).

[52] Revelation 5:8, 8:3, 4, 11:18 . . . .

[53] I John 1:9

[54] Romans 1:7, I Corinthians 1:2, James 4:7

[55] Job 1:6ff

[56] See also Ephesians 6:12ff

[57] For those feeling a need to explore the matter further, consider the reaction of scientists to Al Gore's assertion that the earth's climate is indeed warming (Harris, Tom. Scientists respond to Gore's warnings of climate catastrophe. Canada Free Press. <http://www.canadafreepress.com/2006/harris061206.htm> 12 June 2006. 1 May 2007.) Will the world's oceans rise, as alarmists predict? For students of Bible prophecy, one thing is certain, such would surely be a judgment of God. —Such judgments cannot be legislated away (Lk. 21:25)!

End notes:

Chapter 7: A Few Horsemen:

[58] If one doubts this observation, note the reaction of the inhabitants of the Roman colony, Lystra, where the citizens interpreted the miraculous healing of a man to have been evidence of Roman gods having visited them, upon earth. Although corrected by the apostle, it does illustrate a willingness of even Roman citizens to believe in a supernatural religion (Acts 14:7-18).

[59] This statement was originally quoted by Plato and is attributed to Protagorus, a Greek sophist who lived from 481-411 BC, and is much older than modern socialist/communist thought.

[60] Also known as Marx's dialectic, or Mao's theory of contradictions: thesis, antithesis, synthesis. In other words, two forces in conflict . . . with one winner or solution. Within this mindset, however, even God's domain is up for grabs, if you have enough power. (Sounds like someone we read about in the Bible . . . .)

[61] I John 2:17

[62] For those unfamiliar with these two giants of the faith: The book of Job is the oldest of Old Testament writings, and tells the story of a *very* godly man who is tested by God, as Satan challenges his integrity before God's throne. Satan is allowed to take all he has, even his children, and to strike him with disease—but not to take his life. In the end God doubles all that Job originally had, after noting Job's ultimate, and total, dependence upon the Creator (Job 1-3, 38-42). Abraham is the father of the faith, and of the Jews, after waiting many years for the promise (Galatians 3:7-9, Romans 2:28-30).

[63] This is aptly illustrated in the parable of the laborers in the vineyard (Matt. 20:1-13). The application of the green horse, and measure of wheat for a full day's wage do appear in the NRSV.

[64] See the full text at

< http://www.cnn.com/SPECIALS/1997/global.warming/stories/treaty/ >, or an analysis at < http://en.wikipedia.org/wiki/Kyoto_Protocol> 1 May 2007.

[65] In the eyes of the world, this will be one of Antichrist's greatest failures. It will, no doubt, help to trigger the debacle outlined in the chapter on onion skins . . . .

[66] Note that this does not, in any way, preclude assistance to those *unable* to work. Care for widows and orphans was a church ordained function (I Tim. 5:5-9) originally administered by church deacons (Acts 6:1-6).

[67] Daniel 11:32

Chapter 8: Starting to Boil (a love despised):

[68] II Corinthians 11:2

[69] Revelation 14:4

[70] A more careful explanation of the seven churches, as they relate to church history, is covered in the chapter on the Berean Call.

[71] Ezekiel 33:8,9

[72] It had been proposed earlier, by Christians, that Christ would return by 1988 because a prophecy relating to generational timing, had taken place after only forty years. Jesus, in that statement however, did not say that Jerusalem would fall at the conclusion of the generation—but before the generation had been completed (Lk. 21:20-32). Generational limits are outlined in Psalm 90, as 70-80 years (Ps. 90:10).

[73] Foxe, John. Foxe's Book of Martyrs. Ages Software. Albany, Oregon. USA. 1996, 1997. p. 75.

---

[74] See also Joel, chapter three.

[75] Revelation 13:1

Chapter 9: Is That a Fact?

[76] "Restoration and Controversy" Wikipedia.
<http://en.wikipedia.org/wiki/Sistine_Chapel> 31 October 2006.

[77] White, Bobby. "In San Francisco, Red-Light Denizens Fight to Stay Seedy" Wall Street Journal. Front page. 24 October 2006.

[78] Scofield, CI. "Scofield Reference Notes (1917 Edition), Book Introduction—Revelation." 6 Sept. 2006.<http://bible.crosswalk.com/Commentaries/ ScofieldReferenceNotes/srn.cgi?book=re&chapter=000>.

[79] Vine, W.E. Vine's Expository Dictionary of Biblical Words. New York. Thomas Nelson Publishers. 1985.

[80] I Thessalonians 5:23

[81] Both this quote, and the four points made directly above it, are taken from William Biederwolf's The Second Coming Bible Commentary. Baker House. Grand Rapids. p. 547. 1924, 1985.

Chapter 10: The Berean Call:

[82] Rainer, Thom S. The Unexpected Journey. Zondervan. Grand Rapids, Michigan. 2005. p166.

[83] Angels are now in a higher authority over the believer (Ps. 8:5), but will one day be subservient (I Cor. 6:3). They are now "ministering spirits" sent from God's throne to minister to our needs (Ps. 34:7, Heb. 1:13,14).

---

[84] Genesis 2:22, I Tim. 2:12, 13 –Notice, in particular, how Paul states this as something he does not personally allow. It would be well, however, to beware of how we react to such advice, when the apostle so speaks. He was certainly one of those with "flowing oil!"

[85] Subjection to authority in no way implies inferiority, but humility and meekness. The meek shall inherit the earth (Ps. 37:11, Matt. 5:5). Anarchy is nowhere supported within the Scriptures.

[86] "New Age" is a term referring to any one of varied religious experiences: from eastern mysticism, to outright Satanism. It is essentially a western way of being "spiritual" without engaging in Christian worship.

[87] James 4:5

[88] I Cor. 12:31

[89] Hurlbut, Jesse L. THE STORY OF THE CHRISTIAN CHURCH. Grand Rapids: Zondervan Publishing House. 1967, 1970. Original copyright 1918, 1933, 1954 by Holt, Rinehart, and Winston, Inc.

[90] Revelation 17:5, 18:2-4

[91] This is the conflict, continually waged within first century church, between what was then called "the circumcision" (representing those advocating adherence to Jewish ceremonial laws) and a simple life of faith wherein we simply walk in the Spirit and divine grace (Galatians 5, Ephesians 2).

> For if you live according to the flesh you will die; but if by the Spirit you put to death the deeds of the body, you will live.
>
> For as many as are led by the Spirit of God, these are sons of God.
>
> Romans 8:13,14

[92] Webster, Noah. AMERICAN DICTIONARY OF THE ENGLISH LANGUAGE. 1828. Foundation for American Christian Education. San Francisco, California. 1967.

316

---

[93] This is a translation technique sometimes utilized when much controversy surrounds a particular word. A similar tact is employed in the translation of "baptism" for example: transliterating "baptizo" from the Greek in Matt. 3:16, instead of simply saying that Jesus had been immersed. This is because of widespread use of sprinkling, in some segments of the church.

[94] This corresponds to Strong's numbering system: G 3532, G 3534, and G 2992 respectively.

[95] See Leviticus 25

[96] Strong's G1249. *diakonos* –similar to a waiter: someone who runs errands.

[97] This does not mean that lawful restraint, through the police, court system, etc. is invalid. Government, in such a case, acts as society's watchdog to maintain certain minimal codes of conduct. Government in this case is "God's minister to you for good" (Romans 13:3,4). Nor should the comments made here be taken as an incentive to *dis*respect ministers or church leadership. Such is not only wrong, but foolish—that's like sitting up to spit in a doctor's face, who is treating you for a sickness (Hebrews 13:17)!

[98] This is the ideal situation, of a church that is at peace within the society in which it finds itself—we first find this situation, after the chief persecutor of the saints, had himself been converted (Acts 9:31).

Chapter 11: —trumpeting from the heavens

[99] For there is no difference, for all have sinned, and come short of the glory of God. (Romans 3:23)

[100] Please note that this is not a small issue, at all. Marriage is "holy matrimony." In the sanctioning of homosexual unions by sealing their relationship with marriage, we make a statement to the society at large: that *God* approves of such unions!

[101] Revelation 8:13

[102] Malachi 2:10

[103] Believers are sealed by the Holy Spirit (Ephesians 1:13, 4:30). In the light of this particular judgment, with the locusts of the Apocalypse—no wonder the apostle Paul cautions against offending the Holy Spirit (Eph. 4:30)!!

[104] Albury Publishing, Tulsa Oklahoma. 1996, 1997.

[105] See also Daniel 11:32

Chapter 13: Behold, a Green Horse:

[106] Strong's number G5515. Note that elsewhere, within the New Testament, this same Greek word is translated "green" (Mark 6:39, Rev. 8:7, 9:4).

[107] http://en.wikipedia.org/wiki/Islamic_symbols. 5/28/2007.

[108] Gabriel, Mark. Islam and Terrorism (Front Line, Lake Mary, Florida, 2002) p. 84. Requote from *Lebanon and the heart of Islamic Revolution* , by Khalifa Nabil (Beirut, 1984), pp. 93, 120 –by

[109] Sharrosh, Anis. ISLAM REVEALED A Christian Aram's View of Islam. Nashville. Thomas Nelson Publishers. 1988. p 28.

[110] Ibid. p. 30

[111] These include, in addition to Isaac and Ishmael, six other brothers by his second wife (Genesis 25:2).

[112] Genesis 17:7, 21:5

[113] Ibid. p. 207

[114] Gabriel. p. 67

[115] A principle driving force within Islam is an incredibly violent hatred for Jews. See Mark Gabriel's book, *Islam and the Jews.*

---

[116] This is obviously a diversion from C.I. Scoffield's view of dispensations. We utilize this simpler approach, of three major dispensations, before Christ's returning, to address a broader issue, regarding Islam itself.

[117] II Cor. 5:1-4, Rev. 20:1-4, 21:1-4

[118] An example of this wide disparity in beliefs is the Islamic assertion that Jesus did not actually die on the Cross, but that He will do so, after His second coming. See < http://en.wikipedia.org/wiki/Mahdi>. For a more comprehensive study I recommend Islam Revealed by the excellent apologist Anis Shorrosh, or Mark Gabriel's books Islam & the Jews: The Unfinished Battle and Islam & Terrorism:What the Quran Really Teaches.

[119] **Asymmetric warfare** is a term referring to the "underdog" finding an Achilles heel in his opponent's armor: David's use of a sling to slay Goliath, is an example of this. This differs from terrorism, which utilizes random attacks upon the general populace to demoralize its culture, and bring it under submission to one's claims or demands.

[120] Reported studies have shown that upwards of 25% of documented Muslim conversions to Christianity involve persons who have had a dream or vision (of Jesus). See "Religion: It's not a loud revolution, but Christian media and the Bible are reaching Muslims" World Magazine. < http://www.worldmag.com/articles/12033> 15 July 2006. 9 August 2006. I know that many, particularly those in the church of "Sardis" teach that God has no hands but our hands. "Surprise!" God still has ways of getting His message out —directing sincere seekers of truth in extreme circumstances, even today, as He did within the biblical record (see Acts 10:1-6). The God of the Bible, is still *alive.* (This does not mean that every vision, or dream, is to be taken at face value any more than every person claiming to be a certified MD or surgeon should be allowed to cut you open, and operate on your vital organs. We live in a day of great deception (Matt. 24:4,11, II Thes. 2:9). Yet, the quacks do not invalidate bona fide professions.)

Chapter 14: Woman In The Sun:

[121] At the time of the 9/11 terrorist attack, the US was poised to officially meet with Yassar Arafat on September 23, 2001, to prop up his faltering organization, in an official move to sanction the land-for-peace provisions of the Oslo Accords. Colin Powell's official sanctioning of a Palestinian state was delayed by the 9/11 attacks until November 19th of that year. See, John McTernan & Bill Koenig's, *Israel The Blessing Or the Curse.* Heartstone Publishers, Nov. 2001, April 2002. 144-145.

[122] As explained earlier, in chapter 3, when comparing the writers of the four gospels.

[123] Ephesians 6:12

[124] Note of warning, to the reader: The use of the term "Dark Ages" is very politically incorrect!! Modern (post modern) man does not accept the concept of evil, much less the thought of the world being in darkness, during this period of time when leading up to the Protestant Reformation.

[125] True, spiritual, praying may only be accomplished in true submission to God, through the enabling of the Holy Spirit (Romans 8:26, Jude 20). Praying formula prayers by rote, ritual, rosary, or prayer beads, does not impress Heaven (Matt. 6:6-8). Effective prayer is based upon relationship (note opening emphasis of "Lord's prayer" –Matt.6:9, James 5:16).

[127] This term about saltiness, is a direct reference to Christ's warning to the church, of impending judgment, when we loose our distinctiveness (Matthew 5:13).

[127] In this instance, the prophet Daniel was party to a vision, but had to pray with modified fasting for twenty-one days to gain insight into what had been revealed

to him. The reason? The angel sent to give him understanding had been intercepted by a powerful demonic principality (Daniel 10:1-10).

[128] Note, also, that in Revelation 11, the first 3½ clock with its Gentile emphasis ("trodden down of the Gentiles") is not so intense as the 12th chapter's focus on Israel's diaspora, "in the wilderness" —where she is "led away captive into all nations" (Luke 21:24). In the first case the emphasis is on the Gentiles, in the second, on Israel's distress.

[129] This is an extremely important symbol, and will be more carefully presented next chapter. We will not belabor, or argue the point, however. For a further discussion of this, and other topics presented within this chapter, you may wish to visit the ministry web site at

< http://www.maranatha-min.net/TheUPLOOK/2005-4=Seed-1.htm>.

[130] The church, up until the Reformation, sought to become the go-between between the souls of men and God, saying that it was through the Church and/or Mary that we gain access to God. The Roman Catholic Church continues to affirm that it has the last word on truth (not the Bible, as true Protestants affirm). See

< http://www.fundamentalbiblechurch.org/Foundation/fbchasro.htm> 17 August 2006.

[131] See population statistics posted by "A Division of American-Israeli Cooperative Enterprise." <http://www.jewishvirtuallibrary.org/jsource/Judaism/jewpop.html> 2005. 18 March 2007.

[132] Because this book is intended as an composite and introductory overview of John's Revelation, we will not belabor the significance of the exact wording of this, and Daniel 9:26 & 27. For Bible prophecy students familiar with Daniel's seventieth week, this event marks the beginning of that week. A most important "detail" most often missed is the distinction made in prophecy between a

"prince" and "king." In brief, a prince bears indirect rule (as do demons, exercising influence over humans). "Kings" can only be human, for they must bear direct rule. Even Christ is called a prince, until He returns in glory (compare Isaiah 9:6 with Revelation 19:16). This small "detail" makes all the difference in the world when seeking to determine when the seventieth week begins. See the ministry posting, ". . . from Prince to King" < http://www.maranatha-min.net/TheUPLOOK/2005-7-prince-1.htm>

Chapter 15: Wings of an Eagle . . . Heart of a Man:

[133] "Calvinists" principally of Presbyterian and Reformed churches, follow the writings of the brilliant French/Swedish theologian, John Calvin. The principle distinction of his teaching, and major emphasis, is on predestination –God's knowing beforehand, and having predetermined, all of human history and events (Romans 8:29, Ephesians 1;4,5, 11). I believe God to be larger than this: for, although He knows all—He has so much overall power that He can allow us free will . . . and still bring about His purposes, in spite of our foolishness. You can not second guess God, but He can certainly do it to you, and I (Prov. 16:9, Ps. 19:12,13).—and to the Devil himself (Job 41:1-5).

[134] "Do They Know It's Christmas? -- David Aikman on Christianity in China." National ReviewOnline 22 Dec. 2003. 7 Aug. 2006. < http://www.nationalreview.com/interrogatory/aikman200312220001.asp>.

[135] At present, the Red Chinese economy has been growing at a rate of over 9% (the US, by contrast, is slowing its own growth to under 3% to avoid inflation) and remains healthy. When have we ever heard of a Communist state experiencing such prosperity?? Unless the Lord builds a house (or nation) the labors are in vain (Ps. 127:1). See also < http://www.chinadaily.com.cn/english/doc/2005-03/21/content_426718.htm>

---

[136] Marshall, Peter & David Manuel. The LIGHT and the GLORY. Fleming H. Revell Company. Old Tappan, New Jersey. Copyright 1997 by Peter Marshall Jr. & David Manuel, Jr.

[137]

<http://www.americanpresident.org/history/GeorgeWashington/biography/Impactlegacy.common.shtml> 8-6-06

[138] Matthew 6:9-14

[139] Revelation 11:15

[140] *Church of the Holy Trinity v. United States.* Argued and submitted January 7, 1892. Decided February 29, 1892. Justice Josiah Brewer delivered the opinion of the court.

[141] See also Zechariah 12, particularly verses 10-14.

[142] Isaiah 30:27 & 28 state that the Lord will send the nations and peoples of the earth through a sieve (or sifter) of vanity. In other words, there will be a fearsome delusion that will ensnare all but the wise virgins, prior to the Lord's returning. Compare with II Thessalonians 2:11,12. This is what the Midnight Cry is all about.

Chapter 16: 1984 *in* 2010:

[143] "Britain plans total electronic surveillance of roads." Christian Science Monitor 11 January 2006. 04 Oct. 2006.
<http://www.csmonitor.com/2006/0111/p01s01-woeu.html>.

[144] "A world of connections: A special report on telecoms." Center section of The Economist. 28 April 2007. (The Economist, dubbed "the periodical of Presidents & Kings" –is a transatlantic publication known for its globalist and free trade advocacy).

---

[145] This technology is already being deployed, through chip implantation, for medical monitoring within this country see < http://www.adsx.com/pressreleases/2006-09-20.html > 5 Oct. 2006.

[146] US government policy officially holds that this is *not* a "national ID"— however, it *is* government mandated personal identification, that will be issued nationally. So, what gives? It looks like a duck, walks like a duck . . .(!!)

[147] "FAQ: HOW THE REAL ID WILL AFFECT YOU." CNET 6 May 2005. < http://news.com.com/FAQ+How+Real+ID+will+affect+you/2100-1028_3-5697111.html > 5 Oct. 2006.

[148] US gets RFID passports. The Register. <http://www.theregister.co.uk/2006/08/15

/us_gets_rfid_passports/> 15 August, 2007. 31 Jan. 2007.

[149] SPYCHIPS

[150] To their credit, the word "fear" is actually utilized in Revelation 14:7 to add emphasis. In many other places, however (as in Acts 13:16, for example) it is supplanted with "softer" terminology. In Acts 13:16 –with the same word *phobeo* used in the original Greek, the NIV reads, "you who *worship* God" vice, those who *fear* God. It doesn't take too much to understand the significance of the change, in such an instance. Fear is much more intense, and demands more attention and immediate priority, than does simple "worship." You may say you worship, but what you fear tells me where your *real* priorities lie.

[151] It is beyond the scope of this study to detail the origins of Antichrist. However, he always descends from the north. Note the key text we have already quoted, from which Christ refers to the abomination of desolation—and its context (Daniel 11:29-31) then, of course, there is Gog and Magog in Ezekiel 38 . . .

[152] II Thes. 2:3-5

[153] John 7:48

[154] I Corinthians 1:19

[155] Revelation 10:10

[156] The development of the automobile is supported by Daniel's prophecy (12:4)

[157] "Sugar Daddy" –a "yes man:" one who flatters, in order to manipulate—never denying felt needs, even for our own good (Heb. 12:6, Daniel 11:32)...

Chapter 17: Living With Demons:

[158] Omestad, Thomas. "IRAN UNPLUGGED ITS RADICAL PRESIDENT TAUNTS THE WORLD . . . ." U.S. NEWS & WORLD REPORT. 02 October 2006: 30.

[159] Van Kampen. Robert. THE SIGN of Christ's coming and the End of the Age.Wheaton: Crossway Books,1992. p. 238.

[160] Herr, Normal PhD. "Television & Health." THE SOURCEBOOK FOR TEACHING SCIENCE.
<http://www.csun.edu/science/health/docs/tv&health.html > 26 September, 2006.

[161] Parents Television Counsel. "Facts and TV Statistics."
<http://www.parentstv.org/PTC/facts/mediafacts.asp> 27 September, 2006.

Chapter 18: Window of . . . Opportunity:

[162] An obvious oversimplification, stated to make a serious point. Gas prices go up-and-down for many reasons. Many factors come into play: the availability of refineries, as in Hurricane ravaged New Orleans, for example—or Saudi oil price manipulation, to undercut competition . . . and even in-fighting within OPEC, as with Shiite Iran, who now stands out as the big bully on the block, pouting with a big stick (nuclear weapons) in the face of the Sunni house of

Saud (in Saudi Arabia). Energy conservation is just one of many factors in the battle against allowing oil to be used as a weapon.

[163] Various sources report that a 100 mpg passenger vehicle will soon be available for purchase by metro commuters. See "A Plug for Hybrids: 100 mpg prototypes are on the road. Needed: safe, cheap, batteries." US News & World Report (online) < http://www.usnews.com/usnews/biztech/articles/061001/9hybrid.htm > 01 October 2006. 16 October 2006.

[164] See the government website at <http://www.eia.doe.gov/fuelrenewable.html >

[165] See Wall Street Journal article "*Reality Check* How California Failed in Efforts To Curb Its Addiction to Oil." 2, August 2006. p. 1.

[166] CESP, Stanford. "Much Talk, Mostly Low Key, About Energy Independence." <http://cesp.stanford.edu/news/brazil_is_best_in_class_in_production_of_ethanol_from_sugar_cane_says_victor_20060207/> 18, September 2006.

[167] D'Oro, Rachael. "Alaskans know it: Oil and Ecology *Do* Mix." AP article. Posted <http://www.amasci.com/~rarnold/oil_and_ecology_do_mix.htm>. Accessed 1-23-07.

[168] April 16, 1999. Viewable at <http://www.oralchelation.com/faq/wsj4.htm>. Accessed 1-19-07.

[169] Human standards change, but not God's - I Cor. 7:12-15, or Matt. 5:32.

[170] Is this not what evolution teaches? If the amoeba pulls itself up by its bootstraps from the primordial ooze, on its way up the chain, towards man: Have we not "made ourselves"???

[171] See Hebrews 12:6 and following

[172] Visit <http://maranatha-min.net/Book/Oil/Fr_countr.html>

326

Printed in the United States
81853LV00003B/22-84